D0876086

RELIGION AND CULTURE SERIES

Joseph Husslein, S.J., Ph.D., General Editor

THE CHRISTIAN CHURCHES OF THE EAST

VOLUME II

THE CHURCH OF THE HOLY WISDOM AT CONSTANTINOPLE
("St. Sophia": consecrated in 537; a mosque in 1453; a museum since 1934)

THE CHRISTIAN CHURCHES OF THE EAST

VOLUME II: CHURCHES NOT IN COMMUNION WITH ROME

By DONALD ATTWATER

People do not realize how much faith, goodness, and Christianity there is in these bodies now separated from the age-long Catholic truth. Pieces broken from gold-bearing rock themselves bear gold. The ancient Christian bodies of the East keep so venerable a holiness that they deserve not merely respect but complete sympathy. — POPE PIUS XI

THE BRUCE PUBLISHING COMPANY
MILWAUKEE

Nihil obstat: Joannes A. Schulien, S.T.D., Censor librorum
Imprimatur: ✠ Moyses E. Kiley, Archiepiscopus Milwaukiensis
Die 26 Septembris, 1947

(Revised Edition)

Printed in the United States of America

FOR THE PEACE

OF THE WHOLE WORLD,

FOR THE GOOD ESTATE

OF ALL THE HOLY CHURCHES OF GOD,

AND

FOR THE UNITY OF ALL

LET US PRAY TO THE LORD

KYRIE, ELEISON

(From the *eirenika* of the
Byzantine Liturgy)

INTRODUCTION TO VOLUME II

THIS second volume of The Christian Churches of the East was first published, as a separate book, in 1937. It is intended to be a handy guide to the organization and present state of those Eastern churches which are not in communion with the Holy See of Rome; it is, therefore, not primarily an historical or theological work, though there is a good deal of history in it and sufficient elementary theology to give some idea of where and how these churches differ from the teaching of the Catholic Church. The book is not meant to be polemical: I have tried to find the truth and to set it down objectively; I have done my best to be fair to the people about whom I have written, and nothing whatever has been said in malice. Inevitably I have had candidly to state some things that were discreditable to the Catholics concerned, and I have done so with the words of Pope Leo XIII in mind: "We have nothing to fear from the publication of documents; truth can do the Church no harm."

Obviously there is a great deal of matter in common between the non-Catholic and the Catholic Eastern churches. I have tried to avoid tiresome repetition by frequently referring the reader, expressly or by implication, to the pertinent part of Volume I. It has been impossible to get rid of repetition entirely; what little there is generally occurs in the historical opening of each section, and even then sometimes in an expanded form. Liturgical and disciplinary particulars have not been repeated, except when it was desirable to draw attention to differences between Catholic and dissident practice.

Like Volume I, this makes no claim to be anything more than a popular work, an *oeuvre de vulgarisation*. The writer has had some personal experience of the dissident Christians of the Near

East, but for the historical parts and accounts of more remote churches he has had to rely, as before, on the works and information of others. Some of the numerous books consulted are noted in the bibliographies, and it is hoped that the reader will make use of these bibliographies, particularly for learning more about the earlier history of these churches. The writer has had to dismiss centuries of time and events of the greatest importance in a few pages, or even paragraphs, because his principal concern is with recent times and contemporary conditions. But that earlier history must not be neglected; without some knowledge of it, subsequent events are often hardly intelligible. I would particularly direct attention to the expert pertinent articles in the various Letouzey dictionaries, edited by the late Abbot Cabrol, the late Dom Henri Leclercq and others, so far as they are published. Some of those articles are veritable small treatises of the greatest value. In the bibliographies herein the asterisk (*) indicates that the book is by a non-Catholic, the dagger (†) that it is by a member of the church concerned.

A special word of acknowledgement is due to the third edition of *Les Eglises orientales et les Rites orientaux*, by Father Raymond Janin, A.A. (Paris, 1935), in which I could nearly always find information about present conditions that I sought in vain elsewhere, and the plan of which book I have to a considerable extent followed. The schematic arrangement of Chapters III–VI and IX–XII was necessary for the clear and orderly treatment of a very complex subject; for the same reason I made no attempt to treat the various churches in strictly chronological order or according to ethnic or geographical affinities: to have done so would have resulted in the most complete confusion. I have instead taken them more or less in the order of their emergence as autonomous churches, the Orthodox being dealt with before the others because of their overwhelmingly greater importance.

Nobody can be more conscious than the writer of the inadequacy of this book, even as an introduction. In the words of a reviewer, "It is not the symptoms but the causes of Orthodoxy which can help us towards its understanding," and to be adequate an examination of the dissidents should include analysis of such things as Hesychasm and Sophiology and the Byzantine conception of the Godhead and the Incarnate Word. But there must be taken into consideration, not only the limitations of a given writer, but also what the general reader is prepared to read: and this writer will be content if he has been able to produce an outline, a framework, useful as an introduction to the subject, which can be expanded and filled in and made vital by further and more significant reading.

For so many of us our first difficulty *vis-à-vis* the Orthodox (and for that matter our Oriental fellow Catholics too) is lack of elementary knowledge: Who are they? "How did they get there?" We cannot love what we do not know. And unless we love them we cannot think in practical terms of the reconciliation of the separated Christians of the East with the traditional Christianity of the West. In our dealings with our dissident brethren we have to be both knowledgeable and affectionate. "A man is not believed," as St. Vincent de Paul says, "because he is clever but because he is well liked and known to be good. Satan is very clever – and we don't believe a word he says, because we don't like him. Nobody will believe us unless we are loving and forbearing with them." It has been my task to try to add in small measure to our knowledgeableness. Our lovingness is a matter for our own hearts.

DONALD ATTWATER

CONTENTS

LIST OF ILLUSTRATIONS

THE CHRISTIAN CHURCHES OF THE EAST

VOLUME II

CHAPTER I

THE DISSIDENT EASTERN CHURCHES IN GENERAL

THE Dissident Eastern Churches, sometimes most misleadingly called the Eastern Churches (or even Church) without qualification, are the representatives of those ancient Christian bodies that separated themselves definitively from Catholic unity and the communion of the Holy See during the thousand years following the middle of the fifth century.

An outline of these unhappy events has been given in the first volume of this work (pages 4–13). It is sufficient to recall here that the critical happenings were the Nestorian schism, after the Council of Ephesus in the year 431, the so-called monophysite schism, after the Council of Chalcedon in 451, and the gradual separation of the remaining Christians of the East, the great Eastern Orthodox Church, after the Crusades. So today there are the dissident churches of the East, namely:

The *Nestorian Church* (Irak and Syria).
The Monophysite
Syrian Jacobite Church,
Coptic Church (Egypt),
Ethiopic Church (Abyssinia),
Armenian Church, and
Malabar Jacobite Church.

and *The Orthodox Eastern Church,* consisting of the ancient patriarchates of Constantinople, Alexandria, Antioch, and Jerusalem and twelve other independent churches.

Though at various dates these Eastern churches became separated from the centre of unity at Rome, either by schism or heresy, they nevertheless all still profess the Catholic faith, in a greater or lesser degree, almost in its entirety; they have maintained the precepts of Christian morality more or less as held by Catholics; they are governed by canon law with which that of Eastern Catholics is at least nominally identical; they worship God with liturgies and rites which they share with Eastern Catholics and which the Church recognizes as of equal authenticity and dignity with those of Rome; with one or two local and doubtful exceptions, their orders and sacraments are valid. In considering these dissident Eastern Christians, therefore, it must be understood from the outset that, contrary to a common misunderstanding, they are not sorts of Protestants. As ecclesiastical bodies they have maintained organic continuity with churches that were in communion with Rome and they represent the authentic Catholic Christianity of the East of the first ten centuries, modified by the history of the subsequent ages during which they have been separated from, and in varying measures opposed to, the theological developments and religious life of the Catholic Church.

The attitude of Rome towards these churches is accordingly quite different from her attitude towards other bodies of non-Catholic Christians. There is only one true Church of Christ (to which we believe that Orthodox and other individuals belong invisibly, seeing that we may not without solid reason question their good faith); nevertheless, the Holy See does not regard the Eastern dissidents as being (like Protestants) simply human assemblies, objectively considered, but accords to them the title of "church" in some sense. For example, when Pope Pius IX in 1868 invited the dissident Orientals to send representatives to the Vatican Council, the invitation was addressed "To all the Bishops of the Churches of the Eastern Rite who are not in Communion with the Apostolic See."[1] Furthermore, their sacraments being objectively valid, the Church recognizes that validity

[1] The other invitation was addressed "To All Protestants and other Non-Catholics."

in practice.[2] An Oriental who is reconciled with the Church does not have to be baptized or confirmed nor need he make a general confession of his life (he can do so as an act of devotion if he wishes, of course).[3] Moreover, a Catholic is bound to ask to be absolved by and to receive viaticum from an available dissident Eastern priest if he is dying and no Catholic priest is at hand (and he may receive permission to do so in some other circumstances laid down by the Holy See).[4] There are historical examples of this happening, for instance among Japanese Catholic soldiers and Russian Orthodox chaplains in the Russo-Japanese war.

The dissident Orientals, in their turn, whatever some of their theologians may have speculated and in spite of contrary practice in certain historical circumstances, recognize as valid the orders and sacraments of the Catholic Church. The question of Orthodox teaching about sacraments administered outside their church has been complicated for Westerners by apparent inconsistency in practice. Orthodoxy does not deny to be a sacrament that which dogma affirms to be one, or *vice versa;* but in general prescribes the repetition of sacraments administered outside her communion because heresy, schism, and hostility to Orthodoxy of the Church concerned make deficient, or even completely void, sacraments that are otherwise dogmatically valid. But if the canonical requirements have been fulfilled and the degree of alleged heresy and hostility is not excessive, such sacraments may be recognized by an exercise of *economy* – the Church supplies whatever deficiency there may be. Thus it is found that converts

---

[2] Except in the case of the Copts and Ethiopians, among whom baptism is often administered so carelessly that there is a doubt of its validity. Those who come into Catholic communion from these are therefore baptized, confirmed, and, if clergy, ordained conditionally.

[3] For a brief note on the apparent lack of jurisdiction in the sacrament of penance, see *Clergy Review,* Vol. IV, No. 4, October, 1932, p. 336, and for a discussion of delegation to a priest for confirmation, see Deslandes in *Echos d'Orient,* No. 157, January–March, 1930, p. 5.

[4] E.g., converts from schismatic Eastern churches are sometimes authorized to assist at Mass and receive communion, with rigorous safeguards and for a time, in dissident churches when no Catholic priest is available for long periods.

to Orthodoxy from Catholicism are re-baptized, re-confirmed, re-ordained, or not, according to the circumstances of the person and the time.[5]

Non-Catholic Orientals believe that the Church has no visible single head on earth under Jesus Christ, but they all agree that the pope as Bishop of Rome and Patriarch of the West is first of the patriarchs and chief bishop. That is to say, they regard him as first among equals, having a primacy of honor, but deny his primacy of jurisdiction and his divinely guarded infallibility as religious teacher. Even such an one as the Russian archpriest Bulgakov, who whittles away episcopal authority, holds that a council to be oecumenical must be presided over by the pope.

The elements of the Christian faith which all dissident Eastern churches hold in common with the Catholic Church (though rarely formulated with the detailed precision of the west and sometimes understood with shades of difference in meaning) are: the unity of God in three divine Persons (the Holy Trinity); the fall of Adam and the resulting original sin of all mankind; that sanctifying grace was given to man at the beginning, lost by Adam, restored by Jesus Christ, the redeemer of mankind; the incarnation, passion, death, and resurrection of Christ, who is very God but in whom are united two natures, human and divine (except the monophysites); the sinlessness, divine maternity (except the Nestorians), and perpetual virginity of His mother Mary; a universal church, one, holy, catholic, and apostolic, founded by Jesus Christ as the depository of His revelation of religious faith and conduct, and the common ark of salvation for all mankind; the real presence of the body, blood, soul, and divinity of Christ in the Eucharist; His institution of seven special mysteries (sacraments) for our salvation; the absolute need of divine grace for salvation; the resurrection of the body and everlasting life in heaven or hell; the Eucharist a true and proper sacrifice; the lawfulness of the veneration of saints and their images and relics; the authority of Tradition and Scripture; the

[5] For a study of the principle of *economy*, see Douglas in *Theology*, Vol. XXIV, No. 139, p. 39.

necessity for salvation of membership in the Church, at least invisibly; the obligation of the moral law; the infallibility of the Church, which is normally expressed through oecumenical councils.

The principal divergences of the different dissident Eastern churches from Catholic teaching and practice are set out in their places hereafter. But in considering these divergences as so many obstacles to Christian reunion care must be used not to take too narrow a view. Doctrinal divisions, disputes about worship and order, are not the whole story. As Christopher Dawson has pointed out, behind every heresy there lies some kind of social conflict; and to the extent that these conflicts in the past were not resolved, neither was agreement reached or unity restored. "There can, I think, be no question," Mr. Dawson writes, "but that in the history of Christendom from the patristic period down to modern times, heresy and schism have derived their main impulse from sociological causes, so that a statesman who found a way to satisfy the national aspirations of the Czechs in the fifteenth century, or those of the Egyptians in the fifth, would have done more to reduce the centrifugal force of the Hussite or the monophysite movements than a theologian who made the most brilliant and convincing defence of communion in one kind or of the doctrine of the two natures of Christ. Whereas it is very doubtful if the converse is true, for even if the Egyptians had accepted the doctrine of Chalcedon they would have found some other ground of division so long as the sociological motive for division remained unaltered" (see his *Judgment of the Nations*, Part II, cap. 4, New York, 1943).

These few introductory remarks apply to all the separated Eastern churches; other matters of general application will appear in what follows, as well as much that is distinctive only of this or that church. It may be as well to emphasize that the three groups into which they fall, Orthodox, Monophysite, Nestorian, are quite separate and no more in communion with one another than they are with the Catholic Church; and that of these, the Orthodox are overwhelmingly the most important and numerous.

CHAPTER II

THE ORTHODOX CHURCH IN GENERAL

IT APPEARS that historically the epithet "Orthodox" distinguished those Christians who were faithful to the council of Chalcedon,[1] but for a long time the term has been confined as a title to those Eastern "Chalcedonians" who are no longer in communion with the Holy See of Rome. Catholics and Orthodox freely call each other by those names without thereby intending to beg any questions as to their respective orthodoxy or catholicity.

The Orthodox Church is a federation of nineteen separate Orthodox churches and the process of history has been such that these bodies have practically all developed into *national* units, each one self-governing and independent of the others. Their principle of unity (apart from oecumenical councils, which they have not attended or recognized or attempted to summon since the schism) is purely internal, they have no external or juridical bond corresponding to the Supreme Pontificate in the Catholic Church; it is therefore extremely remarkable that they have retained so much unity as in fact they display. This unity of faith, morals, and worship is undoubtedly due in some measure to lack of precision in definition and to a willingness to differ; in theory the unity is complete, in fact it is a substantial agreement which today shows some tendency to weaken (there are currents

[1] See P. de la Taille in *Orientalia Christiana*, Vol. V, No. 21, February, 1926, p. 281. Latterly, monophysite Copts, Jacobites, and others have taken to adding "Orthodox" to their names, which is confusing. Some Byzantines in communion with Rome call themselves "Catholic-Orthodox," quite reasonably. In the *berat* which the Sultan formerly gave to a newly elected Catholic Melkite patriarch, he was called head of the *Rum kathulik millet*, of which the English equivalent is "Catholic Orthodox nation."

of opinion trickling toward Rome, toward Protestantism, toward Modernism), and the weakening is due not a little to the close association of many of the churches with the civil power. On the other hand, the fundamental internal solidarity of Orthodoxy, underneath what often appear alarming quarrels and party differences, must not be underestimated. Moreover, what is frequently called the erastianism of the Orthodox churches must be looked at in its historical setting. Imperial Constantinople set the example: the Emperor was a sacramental being, regarded as the vicegerent of God on earth in a way that the Patriarch never was (the popes in the Middle Ages tried, and failed, to bring about an analogous position in the West, with the Holy Roman Emperor in subordination to the Church); in Russia an imperial despot, Peter the Great, riveted chains of civil control on the church; and in the Balkans during centuries of Turkish oppression the church was the only corporate expression of national life and aspiration, so that it is not surprising that when freedom came to Greece and Rumania and Serbia and Bulgaria there was a connection between church and state so close as to be bad for both.

Nor must the attitude of Orthodoxy toward nationalism be misunderstood. Historically it has developed into a number of independent churches on a national basis, and religio-national tension is often acute; but in principle the "Rumanian Church," for example, is simply the Orthodox Church in Rumania, just as the "French Church" is the Catholic Church in France. The principal Orthodox canonists agree that the ecclesiastical divisions established by the "apostolic" canon 34 was on a basis of territory and not of nationality or race, and that the Orthodox Church has never recognized a right of autocephaly in a nation as such: to do so would be an example of the heresy of phyletism condemned at Constantinople in 1872. That the branches of the church are today in the main national is a result of the process of secular history and politics, and the position is greatly aggravated by chauvinistic governments.

On the other hand, it cannot be disguised that the Orthodox

churches from time to time lend themselves to the use of the state for national and political ends;[2] "hellenization," "russification," "serbianizing" are constantly cropping up in their history and, especially among the Greeks, sometimes for the purposes of ecclesiastical aggrandizement. And nowadays there are the repeated efforts of chief hierarchs to exercise jurisdiction over people of their own national origin in foreign countries, e.g., the Bulgarian primate over Bulgars in Greece and Yugoslavia, the Serbian patriarch over Serbs in Albania. This is contrary to canonical tradition, as indicated above, and tends to make nonsense of Orthodoxy as a widely dispersed but unified church. It is in fact flat ecclesiastical nationalism, such as Constantinople condemned in 1872.

RELATIONS BETWEEN THE CHURCHES

The various Orthodox churches are the *Patriarchates of Constantinople, Alexandria, Antioch, Jerusalem, Moscow, the Serbs* (Yugoslavia), and *Rumania;* the *Katholikate of Georgia;* the *Exarchate of Bulgaria;* and the *Churches of Cyprus, Sinai, Greece, Albania, Finland, Poland,* and *Japan.*

Alexandria, Antioch, and Jerusalem are still often referred to as the *Melkite* churches.[3] The *Greek* churches are those of Constantinople, Greece, and Cyprus, and, in a measure, Alexandria, Jerusalem, and Sinai. The *Slav* group consists of Russia, Yugoslavia, Poland, and Bulgaria. These churches can also be divided theoretically into *autocephalous* and *autonomous:* an autocephalous church is one subject to no outside jurisdiction whatsoever,

---

[2] This is not unknown in "the West," but Catholics less easily lend themselves to the policies of the civil power. French missionaries are notorious for "frenchifying" — but then they sincerely believe that the best thing that can happen to the representative of some ancient non-European civilization is to bcome a pseudo-Frenchman. On this see the Archbishop of Westminster, "White Against Black in Africa" in *The Month* (London, October, 1935).

[3] The monophysites of these patriarchates dubbed those who accepted Chalcedon *melkites,* "emperor's men" (Syriac *malok,* king). The name is often confined to the Catholic Byzantines of those patriarchates, but the Orthodox are equally Melkites. The Melkites abandoned their Alexandrian and Antiochene liturgies, etc., for the Byzantine usages of Constantinople by the end of the thirteenth century.

while an autonomous church, though self-governing, is still under the limited authority of a patriarch or other hierarch outside itself. But these last are tending to disappear; for example, the dependence of Finland's church on Constantinople is very limited. The ordinary relations between the different churches are slight; whenever a new chief bishop is appointed he informs the heads of the other churches by means of a "letter of peace," and that is about all. But of recent years extraordinary relations have become more and more frequent and the chief churches are in increasingly close touch with one another.

It is a common idea in the West that the patriarch of Constantinople, who calls himself "The Oecumenical Patriarch," is as it were the pope of the Orthodox Church. This is quite erroneous. There have indeed been patriarchs since the schism who wanted to attain for their see an analogous position to that of the bishop of Rome, and there were moments when they nearly succeeded;[4] but in the past hundred years the territorial extent of the patriarchate has been reduced to a shadow and its more bizarre ambitions have disappeared with its powers. These powers have always fluctuated, and the theoretical and actual relationship of Constantinople with the other Orthodox churches is a long and extremely complex chapter in ecclesiastical history. But today the position is plain: the patriarch of Constantinople has a primacy of honor only, and enjoys a certain unique prestige among Orthodox Christians throughout the world.[5] That is all. It is true that the Oecumenical Patriarch loses no opportunity of asserting or trying to get recognized spheres of authority and jurisdiction outside his own patriarchate, but these are now only

---

[4] When the tsar Alexis in 1663 asked (*inter alia*) whether Constantinople was the final court of appeal for all the Orthodox churches, Dionysios III and the other three patriarchs made a significant admission: "Before the Universal Church was rent by papal pride and ill will," they said, "*this privilege belonged to the Pope of Rome*. Since then it belongs to the throne of Constantinople."

[5] Even Peter the Great, when he abolished the patriarchal throne of Moscow, wrote to the patriarch Jeremias III at Constantinople in 1721 asking him to recognize what was being done. But it would have been all the same had Jeremias refused to oblige.

incidents of ecclesiastical politics — they do not bear witness to any certain rights.[6] Even his authority over all Orthodox people of Greek nationality living in countries where there is no regular hierarchy has been challenged by the holy synod at Athens, though at present the objection is withdrawn. For the rest, no Orthodox church takes any important decision without informing the Oecumenical Patriarch of it, and some of them still apply to him for the holy chrism.[7] Nor must every excursion of that patriarch outside his own territory be set down as a tendencious interference; for there is no doubt that the protothrone of Orthodoxy has properly a general solicitude for all the churches and duty to watch over and help them when they are in difficulties.[8]

To that protothrone belongs the right to convene a general council of those churches, a gathering which many Orthodox have been demanding for a very long time, and in 1923 the patriarch Meletios IV Metaxakis took the step of holding a preliminary congress at Constantinople. It was an incomplete gathering, and nothing more was done then. In 1930 the patriarch Photios II Maniates called a further conference, which took place in the monastery of Vatopedi on Mount Athos, but without representatives of the Church of Russia. This conference drew up a programme of work to be done before and at a future preparatory council or pro-synod, and Photios in due course summoned this pro-synod to take place on Mount Athos at Pentecost, 1932. But everything was against it: the two chief divisions of the Russian Church could not agree on how their church should be repre-

---

[6] And they are generally unsuccessful. Nowadays they nearly always take the form of "friendly advice," sometimes of befriending a bishop in difficulties with his superiors (e.g., the Russian bishop Eulogius; see p. 84). The patriarch's action in Hungary (see p. 93) seems at the present to have been ineffective.

[7] E.g., Alexandria, Jerusalem, Greece, Cyprus. Formerly Constantinople had the sole right to bless chrism for the whole Orthodox church. The origin of this custom was doubtless economic, since there are over fifty ingredients of chrism, some of them rare and costly; but by the thirteenth century at least its consecration had come to be looked on as a token of high jurisdiction.

[8] Even recently it used to be said that the head of the Greek nation was not the king at Athens but the patriarch at Constantinople. But all idea of the Oecumenical Patriarch as "ethnarch" is now over.

sented, the throne of Jerusalem was vacant, the Bulgarian "schism" had not been settled, the Church of Greece was raising difficulties. At the last moment Photios called off the pro-synod "until better times" — and a council of the Orthodox churches seems as far away as ever.

In the course of its deliberations the Bertram-Luke commission at Jerusalem (see p. 43) found it necessary to examine whether the Orthodox Church provides a competent authority for the adjudication of disputes in particular churches. After a prolonged examination of extensive material, historical and actual, the commission came to the conclusion that the constitution of the church provides no such authority; that neither the Oecumenical Patriarch nor the four patriarchs of the ancient thrones together nor any other body had power to settle disputes arising in a particular autocephalous church, unless invited to do so by the church concerned (1921 report).

It is not surprising that the need for a limited central authority of some sort, or at least a clearinghouse for business affecting all the Orthodox churches, is keenly realized by some, and in 1935 the Rumanian patriarch, Miron, and the Serbian patriarch, Barnabas, suggested the establishment at Constantinople of a permanent synod of representatives of all the churches. The suggestion was well received in most places except Greece (where it was viewed as a covert advance against the Hellenism of the protothrone), but it was refused by Constantinople; there the Greek view was shared, and it was feared that such a permanent synod would mean the final extinction of what little remains of the authority of the Oecumenical Patriarch.

THE HIERARCHY

All Orthodox patriarchs and other primates govern their churches by means of an assembly of bishops called the Holy Synod, and the primate now tends more and more to be merely the president of this synod, without room for personal initiative; moreover, the civil power is often represented at meetings of the synod and so hampers and seeks to control its free activities.

Church property, whether national, diocesan, or parochial, is usually administered by mixed or entirely lay councils or even by government officials.

In the Byzantine hierarchy an archbishop was at the head of a series of metropolitan provinces, whose hierarchs were called metropolitans and were equivalent to Western archbishops. But "archbishop" has long been an almost purely honorary title; and though metropolitans are numerous, metropolitan provinces are disappearing in some churches and all eparchies (dioceses) are being reduced to one level, their bishops subject immediately to the chief hierarch and his synod. (In Russia archbishops rank below metropolitans.) The bishop is normally assisted by two councils, a clerical one for spirituals and a mixed one for temporals; chapters of canons are a purely Western institution, unknown to the East (except in some Catholic Byzantine churches), but the bishop has an auxiliary or a vicar general (*protosynkellos*) and a *curia* to help him.

Parishes also are administered by one or more councils (*ephory, epitrophy*) for temporal affairs, of which the parish priest is not necessarily a member. The priest is chosen sometimes by the ephory, sometimes by the parishioners at large, but he has to be approved and appointed by the bishop.

Episcopal visitations are rare events in most countries (the priest is the minister of Confirmation), as are diocesan and provincial synods, but occasionally the bishops of a country meet in council apart from the regular holy synod.

Among the dignitaries of the Orthodox Church there are archdeacons, archpriests, archimandrites, exarchs, and chorepiskopoi.

The *archdeacon* is what his name signifies, the chief of the deacons, and is not a priest.

The *archpriest* or *protopope* or *protopresbyter* is the highest rank conferrable on a married priest; it is often honorary; otherwise he is equivalent to the Western "rural dean." In some churches there is a distinction between an archpriest and a protopresbyter.

An *archimandrite* is properly the abbot of a large monastery, but the title is freely bestowed as a titular dignity upon non-monastic clergy; e.g., the chief priest at the Greek church in London is "The Great Archimandrite."

An *exarch* may be the head of an independent church, as in Bulgaria, but ordinarily is a priest or bishop with a special charge, such as a patriarchal delegate.

Chorepiskopos is now only a title of honor, sometimes with duties attached; the church of Constantinople alone still sometimes confers episcopal consecration on a chorepiskopos.

The pastoral clergy are free to be married, and in practice nearly all are married. But they do not enjoy the same freedom in this respect as the layman. The age-long discipline of the East is that a married man may be ordained to the diaconate and priesthood and retain his wife. He may not be married after receiving the diaconate or, if his wife dies, marry again. Bishops must be single or widowers, and for that reason are chosen from among the monks or must receive the monastic habit before being ordained to the episcopate. Many deacons remain in that order for life, and a priest may not discharge diaconal duties in a solemn liturgy.

Although all Orthodox bishops are technically monks, few of them have ever led the monastic life: the requirement means in practice that the bishop must be single or a widower and have been invested with the monastic habit before his consecration. Moreover, a good many so-called monasteries have no specifically monastic life but are bishop's residences or other establishments having an administrative staff of monks attached.

THE ORTHODOX TODAY

It is difficult to do more than generalize roughly about the spiritual state of so large and widely spread a body as the Orthodox. A majority of the clergy, miserably underpaid, still get only a minimum education and training and, at least in rural districts, are rarely called on to preach or give religious instruction (that is the schoolmaster's job, when there is one).[9] The authorities (which include men of wide learning and deep spirituality) deplore and seek to remedy this state of affairs. In Greece the sacerdotal standard is steadily rising, and this improvement is yet more marked in Rumania. Nevertheless there is still very much ground to be made up in these matters. On the other hand, as an Anglican scholar, Dr. Kidd, observes, "the religious life of the people never requires . . . to be kept alive by the energy of the clergy." But the spiritually weak get little help and the vicious are not sufficiently restrained, so that in individuals religion can easily die completely. To the observer from outside it appears that the religion to which the majority are so greatly attached is a matter of exterior observances, and that these do not include frequent reception of the sacraments. But this is to lose sight of the undoubted interior spirituality of which these observances are both a cause and an effect, and of the fact that the people identify themselves with the celebration of the Liturgy in a way that is unknown in the West.[10] The lack of proper instruction inevitably encourages superstition and, while great importance is attached to church-going and most rigorous fasting, immorality in general may, often from ignorance, too easily prevail beneath an aspect of piety. But this is only to say that people are human beings; to fail one's religious principles is not a peculiarity confined to the Orthodox. In most Orthodox churches the higher clergy are handicapped by their too close dependence on the government; the church becomes a political instrument and their election to offices is decided by party interests. But there is never wanting at the very least a leaven of noble spirits, conscious of abuses and failings and urgent to remedy them for the glory of God and the salvation of the children of Jesus Christ.

---

[9] The high standard of education of many of the Catholic Eastern clergy, gained during a training in which they are quite cut off from the laity, sometimes weakens their bond with their unlettered country flocks. This was an element in the Podcarpathian schism (see p. 82).

[10] To the Catholic objection that preaching is so little used in Orthodox churches, the retort is often made that "Westerners need more preaching, because they take no active part in their Mass."

It is sometimes made a matter of reproach to the Orthodox that in modern times they have done no missionary work among the heathen (except the Russians, heavily subsidized by the imperial government for political ends). The reason is easily found in the fact that up to one hundred years ago most of the Orthodox churches were being tyrannized over by the Ottoman Turks, and were themselves continually subject to Mohammedan propaganda and pressure; since then it has been as much as they could do to reorganize themselves and maintain their Christianity in a world that is increasingly materialistic and secularized. Moreover, the Orthodox countries have no colonies – the first and easiest field for missionary enterprise in modern terms; and to venture into the "spheres of influence" of other powers is to court political and international complications and sometimes religious disasters.

A matter of great concern to some of the Orthodox churches is the spread of Freemasonry, especially in the Near East. In the so-called Anglo-Saxon countries Freemasonry is known principally as a secret society with social, philanthropic, and convivial activities – in fact, a respectable, middle-class amusement; but on the continent of Europe its ultimate aim is, in the words of Pope Leo XIII, "the overthrow of the whole religious, political, and social order based on Christian institutions and the establishment of a regime founded on principles of complete Naturalism."[11]

In 1936 the Orthodox patriarch of Antioch, Alexander Tahhan, and eight of his metropolitans were known to be freemasons; in the patriarchate of Alexandria there were in 1926 ten lodges, with several bishops among their 5000 members; in Yugoslavia, Rumania, and Bulgaria the society has made considerable headway even among the clergy; and in all these countries the influence and pressure of Freemasonry has made itself felt in social,

[11] Among some continental Catholics opposition to and fear of Freemasonry is almost a mania; this exaggeration is usually allied with a crazy antisemitism. Even in its English form Freemasonry is opposed to the common good insofar as men may be preferred to positions of responsibility on account not of their fitness but of friendship and patronage, and because of the potentiality for mischief of such an uncontrolled secret society.

political, and ecclesiastical affairs to the extent that the common people — who are not eligible to be freemasons — are aware of it and are correspondingly indignant.

The Orthodox congress at Mount Athos in 1930 characterized Freemasonry as a "wicked and un-Christian organization," and in 1932 the position in Greece was such that the holy synod took action. After long consideration and discussion of the matter it issued a formal condemnation of Freemasonry as not simply a philanthropic association but a system of naturalistic religion which sought to combine all men, Christians, Jews, Mohammedans, Buddhists, etc., into a "higher unity," regardless of revealed truth; all members of the clergy of the Church of Greece were therefore forbidden to belong to it. This proceeding was approved by the Oecumenical Patriarch (Photios II), but he did not feel called on to take any immediate action himself, nor have his successors done so up to the present. In 1932 the Russian bishops at Karlovtsy approved the condemnation pronounced at Mount Athos.

The political liberation of the Balkan states during the nineteenth century led to an inflow of Western political ideas, especially those of the anticlerical, masonic, and liberal French republicans. Until World War I, the Orthodox churches were rigidly controlled and even oppressed by politicians, brought up in this French anticlerical school, who believed that every form of organized Christianity must be reactionary and a danger to the sovereignty of the State. It was fashionable, too, among the educated to despise the Church, which was regarded as belonging more to the Byzantine past than to the European future of their national history. But the bulk of the population was faithful to Orthodoxy. After the war, however, Western industrial civilization penetrated more and more into the Balkans, its inevitable accompaniments of Communism and godlessness spread among town workers and peasants, and old-fashioned continental liberalism lost its hold. The various churches show an earnest, if puzzled, determination to master the new situation. World War II has had a further disintegrating effect by more deeply underlining national and political differences; politics and rival cultures and social conflicts continue to be the factors aggravating the disunity of Christians, as they have been throughout history, as Christopher Dawson has emphasized. And the divisions are going deeper not only within the Orthodox Church, e.g., Greeks against Bulgars, Karlovtsy Russians against U.S.S.R. Russians, but between Orthodox and Catholics too. The ecclesiastical loyalties of Serb and Croat are used as weapons in their secular rivalry; in the Italian invasion of his country the Orthodox Greek once more sees blatant aggression from the Catholic "Franks."

Dr. Kidd sums up the characteristics of Orthodoxy thus: ". . . in doctrine its system is traditional, with little room for development; in government, it holds together by a loose administrative system and so contrasts with the more centralized organization of the Roman Catholic Church; and in worship, it gives little scope for preaching, and so ignores what is all in all to the Protestant sects. In one word, the Orthodox Church, in its general aspect, is more than anything else a society for worship." That is not to say, as is so commonly supposed in the West, that Orthodoxy is "stiff with gold and gorgeous with ceremonial," and no more: one more example of alleged oriental formalism, stagnation, and unchangingness. It has a living hold on large numbers of people, and of late years it has begun to exercise considerable influence outside the ranks of its own faithful.

RELATIONS WITH THE WEST

The attitude of the Orthodox to the Catholic Church and the reunion of Christendom is referred to incidentally in several places in this book, but an historical note may be given here of the reception accorded to Pope Pius IX's invitation to the Orthodox bishops to participate in the Vatican Council (*cf.*, p. 2). By an unfortunate error the text of the invitation was printed in the *Journal de Rome* before it was delivered to the bishops, and the comments on it both of the Catholic and Orthodox press were of such a nature as to give a fair pretext for refusal on the part of those to whom it was addressed.

The patriarch of Constantinople, Anthimos VI, handed back the letter to Dom (afterwards cardinal) John Pitra, O.S.B., without even reading it, declaring that attendance at the council would be useless in the circumstances. The patriarch of Alexandria was ill and Mgr. Ciurcia tendered the invitation to the archimandrite Neilos, who refused to receive it. "If," he said, "his Holiness had written personally to the patriarch, and not published his letter first in the press, his Blessedness would have been happy to consider it." The patriarch of Antioch, Jekotheos, received the letter with signs of deepest respect from Father Zacharias, O.S.F.C. Later in the day he returned it by the hand of a bishop, with the message that the patriarch must first consult his other bishops: nothing more was heard of it. The invitation was also returned by the patriarch of Jerusalem to the two canons who brought it; he could not accept it, he said, because his fellows had not done so; but, he added, "I pray always for union; may the Holy Spirit be with the council. May God bless you."

All the other Orthodox bishops who are recorded to have replied to the invitation refused it, mostly on the ground that they could not act differently from the patriarchs; and all complained that the Holy See had arranged the council without consulting the Orthodox East. At the same time there were among the bishops of the patriarchate of Antioch and the church of Cyprus strong expressions of desire for reunion and of regret that the patriarchs had acted as they had. If the Pope's invitation ever reached the Russian bishops, the imperial government saw to it that they did not reply.

Pope Pius IX's letter "*In suprema Petri*" (1848), addressed primarily to Eastern Catholics, had given great offence to the Orthodox. Then in 1894, on the occasion of his episcopal jubilee, Leo XIII in the encyclical "*Praeclara gratulationis*" issued an appeal to them direct to return to Catholic communion; it was expressed in the most courteous and gentle terms, free from all harsh words and controversial allusions, kind, fatherly, and loving. It drew from Anthimos VII, patriarch of Constantinople, and

Courtesy, *Christian East*

THE OECUMENICAL PATRIARCH BASIL III (d. 1929)

Courtesy, *Catholic Herald*

SHRINE OF OUR LADY AT KYKKO, CYPRUS

twelve of his bishops, an incredibly offensive reply, openly rude and abusive. This was answered unofficially and well by Father Maximos Malatakis, a Greek Catholic of the Byzantine rite.

In our own day we see much better things and a greatly improved spirit on both sides: Orthodox clergy and laymen attend reunion congresses, such as those at Velehrad in Czechoslovakia,[12] their clerical students are found in Catholic universities, and more, both Orthodox and Catholics, realize the need to study each other's beliefs and point of view and not to be misled by prejudice or unhistorical fables.

On the other hand, it is well known that of late years official relations between some of the Orthodox churches and the Church of England have been exceedingly amiable. The first overtures of Lutheran Protestants to the Orthodox go back to 1574; Anglican relations began somewhat later, at the time of Cyril Lukaris, in 1616 (see p. 25). About 1677 the bishop of London, Henry Compton, built a church for the Greeks in Soho, where there are still a "Greek Street" and a "Compton Street." The first Westerner to "turn Orthodox" in later times that I have come across was the Hon. Frederick North, an Anglican who was received into the Orthodox Church in Corfu in 1791. North was son of that Lord North who was the English prime minister who helped to provoke the American Revolutionary War. The first authoritative book in English on the Orthodox Church was Philip Lodvill's *Orthodox Confession of the . . . Eastern Church,* published in 1762. In 1920 and 1930 an Orthodox delegation was sent to the Lambeth Conference, and a joint doctrinal commission was set up. In 1922 the Oecumenical Patriarch (Meletios IV) recognized Anglican orders, and Jerusalem and Cyprus concurred in the decision; five years later the same prelate recognized them on behalf of the Church of Alexandria, and in 1936 the holy synod of Rumania accepted them. The whole question of Anglican-Orthodox relations is a most complex and difficult one, and need

---

[12] Official representatives of the Oecumenical Patriarch, of the Bulgarian Church, and of the Armenian Church took part in a reunion conference at Constantinople in 1930.

not be discussed here. But it may be noted that the recognition of Anglican orders by some churches means no more in practice at present than that members of those churches may receive Anglican sacraments in special cases of emergency or isolation: "inter-communion" and ecclesiastical unity between the Orthodox Church and the Church of England as such are still a long way off, not least because the Orthodox authorities are increasingly aware that Anglicanism is not homogeneous, either in faith, conduct, or worship.[13] This was strongly marked in 1939, when the holy synod of the Church of Greece considered the question of Anglican orders. The synod emphasized that only the whole Orthodox Church, and not any local church, is competent to pronounce on this matter; but so far as the Church of Greece was concerned, she was willing, if an Anglican clergyman "turned Orthodox," to receive him without reordination, by economy (see p. 3).

The archpriest Bulgakov, too, says on the subject of Anglican orders that their validity or invalidity is "a canonical and not a dogmatic question, which can be decided for the Orthodox Church [i.e., the whole church] only by a competent ecclesiastical authority." He sums up in a sentence the much misunderstood attitude of the Orthodox toward the inter-confessional, "pan-Christian" movement (Lausanne, Stockholm, Edinburgh): "The participation of Orthodoxy in this movement does not at all signify that it can renounce any part whatever of its tradition, that it can accept a compromise or reconsideration. . . . *Orthodoxy is present at such conferences to testify to the truth*"[14] (italics ours).

---

[13] It is sometimes said that the Orthodox want a *rapprochement* with the Church of England solely on grounds of temporal and political expediency. There may be a measure of truth in this at times and places (e.g., in Palestine under the British mandate), but in general it is untrue and slanderous. The Orthodox gladly accept the good offices of Protestant or "undenominational" philanthropic bodies but sometimes find they are accompanied by proselytism: then we get, for example, the condemnation of the Y.M.C.A. by the holy synod of the Church of Bulgaria in 1926 and 1928.

[14] Not as characteristic but as indicative of the misunderstanding of Orthodox opinion in some sections I may quote the comment of the Bukarest *Glasul Monahilor* on the official visit of Anglican clergy to Roumania: "We are delighted that these Protestants wish to return to Orthodoxy." In an

It is evidence of the current interest in Orthodoxy that in 1946 a benefaction was made to the University of Oxford for the establishment, for an experimental period of three years, of a lectureship in Eastern Orthodox, especially Russian, culture and religion.

The Orthodox in North America are dealt with elsewhere in this book (pp. 148–155). In England the Greeks have churches in London, Liverpool, Manchester, and Cardiff, and the Russians in London; there are also chapels for Russians in Oxford and for Serbs and Rumanians in London. Moreover it is in the last-named city that the Oecumenical Patriarch's exarch for Western Europe resides.

BIBLIOGRAPHY

†Constantinides, *The Orthodox Church* (London, 1931).

Fortescue, *The Orthodox Eastern Church* (London, 1911).

*Kattenbusch, *Die orthodoxe anatolische Kirche* (Freiburg, i.B., 1892).

*Langford-James, *A Dictionary of the Eastern Orthodox Church* (London, 1923).

†Papadopoulos, *et al.*, *Die Orthodoxe Kirche auf dem Balkan und in Vorderasien* (Leipzig, 1939).

Pierre, *Notes d'Ecclésiologie Orthodoxe* in *Irénikon,* tome X, Nos. 2, 3 et seq. (Amay, 1933–34).

*Hardy, *Orthodox Statements on Anglican Orders* (Milwaukee, 1947).

---

issue of *Pantainos* in 1921 the archimandrite Chrysostom Papadopoulos (later archbishop of Athens) wrote an article on the history of the Catholic Church in England that was simply grotesque; unhappily, equally grotesque things have been written by Catholics about the Orthodox Church.

CHAPTER III

THE ANCIENT PATRIARCHATES

1. THE PATRIARCHATE OF CONSTANTINOPLE

THROUGHOUT most of the later Middle Ages the patriarchate of Constantinople embraced all that we now call the Balkans, Russia from the White Sea to the Caucasus, and Asia Minor. Not for nothing did the ecclesiastical head of this vast territory call himself the Oecumenical Patriarch,[1] and it is not surprising that Constantinople should officially call itself The Great Church, though that expression seems originally to have referred specifically to the cathedral of the Holy Wisdom.[2] At the height of its prosperity over six hundred metropolitan and episcopal sees looked to the throne of Constantinople for patriarchal authority. Yet with all that the first place among Eastern sees, above Alexandria and Antioch, conceded to New Rome by the disputed 28th canon of Chalcedon in 451, was not formally recognized by Old Rome till centuries later.

As has been related in volume I, the Emperor John VII hoped that the reunion concluded at the Council of Florence in 1439 would guarantee help for him against the Turks. As the danger came nearer and nearer Pope Nicholas V did all he could to per-

---

[1] John IV the Faster adopted this title at the end of the sixth century. Pope St. Gregory the Great in protest called himself "Servant of the Servants of God," and forbade John to use so pompous a designation; but it has been used ever since (though not when writing to the popes). The title was always meaningless and is now harmless.

[2] "St. Sophia." Built under Justinian from 532 to 537, and architecturally the most important single church that was ever built. It was a mosque from 1453 to 1934 and is now a museum.

suade Western monarchs to go to the rescue; to their shame not one of them would budge. And on May 29, 1453, the only Western "powers" helping the Greeks at the last defence of Constantinople, the city that had conserved European culture through the barbarian dark ages, were a handful of men sent by the pope and five ships and seven hundred men from the republic of Genoa. On that day the troops of Mohammed II took New Rome by assault (and massacred its citizens – just like Fourth-Crusaders). The last Liturgy had been sung in the Church of the Holy Wisdom; Constantine XII had made what Gibbon calls the funeral oration of the Roman empire – and when night fell the last Roman emperor, Constantine Caesar Augustus Palailogos, the one hundred and twelfth since Caesar Octavian, lay dead at the gate of St. Romanos, killed at the head of his soldiers.

Curiously enough the taking of Constantinople by the Turks did not mean a diminution of patriarchal authority, but the contrary, for the sultan Mohammed made the holder of the office civil head of all the Orthodox under Turkish rule – with investiture at the hands of his Mohammedan overlord. The see was vacant at the time, and Mohammed naturally filled it with a prelate who would not maintain the union with the West. Only the previous year the union had been formally proclaimed in the Holy Wisdom church by Cardinal Isidore of Kiev (who had had to flee from Russia), and Constantine XII died in communion with the Holy See; but the union was unpopular,[3] and the patriarchal throne was given to its chief opponent, George Skholarios (Gennadios II). Communion with the Holy See was formally severed in 1472.

The sufferings for centuries of Orthodox and other Christians under the Turks is a theme of general history; but it may be noted that during the 490 years that have elapsed since the fall of the city there have been 107 patriarchs of Constantinople of whom only 33 have died in office (and eight of these came to a violent

[3] Its great upholder, the learned, generous and good Bessarion, metropolitan of Nicaea, had retired to Rome in despair. He, too, was made a cardinal, and on the death of Paul II in 1471 was very nearly elected pope.

end).[4] Moreover, such have been the choppings and changings, generally under pressure from the Turkish government, that these 107 different patriarchs represent 165 terms of office (e.g., Cyril Lukaris was patriarch seven times in all). The average total tenure of a patriarch has been under four years. Sir Charles Eliot in his *Turkey in Europe* gives a terrible picture of the rapacity of the Phanariote clergy and the depths to which they sank at times under the Sultan: often the patriarchal office was sold to the highest bidder, and sometimes was bought as an investment by a shameless ecclesiastic who was then turned out because someone else had offered a better price. Nevertheless, during the sixteenth to the eighteenth centuries Greek ecclesiastical influence reached its height: Alexandria, Antioch, and Jerusalem became almost totally dependent on Constantinople, and Serbs, Bulgars, Rumanians, Melkites, and others were governed by Greek bishops.[5] On the other hand, the loss of the Church of Russia was a terrible blow; in 1589 Jeremias II of Constantinople had to acknowledge the new patriarchate of Moscow (see p. 52).

After the loss of the church of the Holy Wisdom the patriarch had to find another cathedral, and eventually in 1603 fixed on the church of St. George, in the Greek quarter at Constantinople called the Phanar. Thenceforth the patriarch with his court and synod are called collectively "The Phanar," just as we speak of "The Vatican" in the West; and till our own day the patriarchal establishment, with the wealthy lay people living in the adjoining quarter, formed a mighty centre of Greek influence.

[4] Some may be fairly regarded as having lost their lives in defence of Christian religion and life, as martyrs in fact. Nevertheless, it must not be supposed that Turks were all black or Christian subjects of the Ottoman empire all white, or that Turks had all the advantages. A British consul at Aleppo reported in 1866 that, "if a Turk has an advantage over a Greek adversary in the religious sympathy of his judges, the Greek has generally more money to bribe them with; and if a Greek has not the advantage of supporting his case by Christian evidence he has an equal facility of suppoenaing Musulman witnesses ready to swear to anything for a couple of dollars." Quoted by Luke in his *Making of Modern Turkey*, cap. III.

[5] It is this sort of thing that makes one a little incredulous when dissident Greeks talk about the "imperialism" of ecclesiastical Rome — these were not "missionary countries."

Several theologians, from the patriarch Maximos III (d. 1482) on, had written with the object of strengthening the breach with Rome, but at the end of the sixteenth century a bishop of Kythera, Maximos Margunios, worked for reunion – but rather wasted his time by trying to persuade Pope Clement VIII that the Holy Ghost proceeds from the Father alone. Then an even more surprising thing occurred: an oecumenical patriarch wanted to reform his church on Protestant lines. This was Cyril I Lukaris, who had correspondence with King Charles I and Archbishops Abbot and Laud in England as well as with the Lutherans.[6] He published a Calvinistic confession of faith in 1629, and in the next nine years he was on and off the patriarchal throne accordingly as the influence of the protestantizing party ebbed and flowed. Lukaris was at last strangled by order of the sultan Murad IV,[7] and he was succeeded by his chief opponent, Cyril II Kontaris, who had been patriarch for very brief periods twice before during these troubles. Kontaris was not only an energetic and successful leader for true faith, but returned to Catholic communion in 1638. The sultan deposed him almost at once, deported him to Tunis, and there had him murdered in 1640.[8]

In consequence of these happenings Dositheos, patriarch of Jerusalem, held a synod in that city in 1672, at which the churches of Constantinople and Russia were represented, whereat Protestantism was formally condemned (an attempt was made to whitewash Lukaris). There was appended to the acts of this Synod of Jerusalem a confession of faith, bearing the name of Dositheos, and these documents form one of the standard official pronouncements on Orthodox beliefs.

---

[6] He sent the *Codex Alexandrinus*, the third oldest bible known, to Charles. It is now in the British Museum.

[7] A rumour was put about that certain Jesuits had encouraged the plot to bring about his death. There is no evidence for this. But the French ambassador at Constantinople, Comte de Césy, and the Imperial ambassador, Rudolph Schmidt, were not certainly innocent. They, and the representatives of another religious order, played an active and important part in the anti-Lukaris opposition.

[8] The cause of his beatification as a martyr was begun by order of the Holy See, but was never finished.

Sixty-odd years before the beginning of the crash of the nineteenth century the patriarch of Constantinople made his last big effort in centralization. In 1766 the Phanar obtained from the sultan Mustafa III[9] an order for the suppression of the Serbian independent church, and it was brought directly under Constantinople; in the following year exactly the same was done with the Bulgarian church of Okhrida. But this imposing edifice soon began to show signs of cracking, and in 1810 the free Serbs under Karageorge put themselves under the independent archbishop of Karlovitz in Hungary (see p. 96). Then came the Greek war of independence. Many of the Constantinopolitan clergy openly supported the revolt and the patriarch Gregory V, though he had obediently denounced the rebels, was hung at his own door in his vestments after the Liturgy on Easter day in 1822. (The Greeks, on the other hand, murdered the Shaykh ul-Islam). In 1833 independent Greece proclaimed that it had an independent church, and twenty years later the oecumenical patriarch had to recognize it. Then came the landslide. The Church of Bulgaria declared herself autocephalous in 1870, Serbia in 1879, Rumania in 1885; Bosnia and Herzegovina were autonomous in fact, if not in theory, after 1880. All these withdrawals from his jurisdiction the patriarch of Constantinople was forced unwillingly to recognize sooner or later – all except Bulgaria, and her independence Constantinople did not recognize for seventy-five years. A synod held at the Phanar against the Bulgarian schism in 1872 denounced phyletism (nationalism in ecclesiastical matters) as a most poisonous heresy – but nobody took any notice. At the time of the Balkan War of 1912 the mighty patriarchate of Constantinople had been reduced to the territories of the then Turkey in Europe and in Asia Minor, with 94 eparchies and under 4½ million faithful all told. Since then many eparchies have been lost to Greece, ten to Serbia, seven to Bulgaria; Anatolia and Eastern Thrace have been emptied of their Christian populations; Albania has seized her autonomy; and Italy wanted independence for her

[9] This sultan fixed the patriarchal tax (*backsheesh*) payable on taking up office at 120,000 francs.

Orthodox subjects in the Aegean. The Great Church has almost disappeared.

Moreover, the position of the Phanar in relation to the Turkish government at Ankara has been extremely unsatisfactory in spite of the stipulations of the Treaty of Lausanne (1923) in its favour, and the Turks did not scruple to support an attempt to set up a tiny Turkish Orthodox church. The patriarch Meletios IV, a leader of Hellenism, had to flee to Athos in 1923. There he resigned (he became Meletios II of Alexandria), and was succeeded by Gregory VII (d. 1924) and then Constantine VI; the last named was brutally expelled from Turkey at once on the ground that he was a Greek liable to repatriation. His successors were Basil III (d. 1929) and Photios II (d. 1935).[10]

ORGANIZATION AND PRESENT STATE

Patriarch. His title is "His All-Holiness the Archbishop of Constantinople, the New Rome, and Oecumenical Patriarch." Some account of his position and prerogatives have been given in the previous chapter. He must be a Turkish subject, of mature years, and at least seven years a bishop, but the regulations for his qualifications and election have become somewhat obsolete since 1923; at present he is elected by the bishops resident in Turkey. He is president of the permanent holy synod, which is the effective authority of the church. The present patriarch is the Lord Maximos V, elected in 1946.

Bishops. The eparchies immediately subject to the patriarch are now in fact reduced to four, Derkos, Chalcedon, Prinkipo, and Imbros, whose bishops are all called metropolitans. They are elected by the holy synod.

Four eparchies of the Dodekanese, viz., Rhodes, Leros, Kos,

---

[10] One of the annoyances devised by the Turks is the law of 1934 which forbids all ministers of religion to wear any distinctive costume outside their churches (this includes nuns). The oecumenical patriarch is one of the three or four religious leaders exempted from this regulation (the Catholic Byzantine bishop is another). This fatuous standardization had already been applied to lay people's clothes, and the Turks are now as badly and as uniformly dressed as the English or the Americans.

and Karpathos, are (or were) subject to Italy, which after 1924 was in negotiation with the Phanar for their recognition as an autocephalous church. An agreement was reached with the patriarch Basil III but he died before its publication. Photios II would not ratify it without a plebiscite of the people, which Italy refused, and in 1934 the four metropolitans withdrew themselves from the patriarch's jurisdiction; but so far the Phanar has not legalized their action.[11]

Holy Synod. Since the synod must consist of twelve bishops (excluding the patriarch) and there are only four eparchies in Turkey, titular metropolitans or bishops are created, somewhat in excess of exact requirement. The six senior members of the synod retire every year and are replaced by six others. The patriarchal *curia* is very large and most impressively titled (e.g., the Great Ekklesiarch, who is a master of ceremonies, the Great Khartophylax, or archivist, the Protosynkellos, chief secretary), but as most of the officials now have few or no duties doubtless they will be reduced in time.

Clergy. The late patriarch Photios II worked hard to raise the spiritual and intellectual standard of his clergy, and sent promising students to the best Orthodox centres in foreign countries. The theological college at Halki, founded in 1844, has done much good work, but too small a proportion of the parochial clergy have studied there. The monasteries of Mount Athos are under the jurisdiction of Constantinople (see p. 179); all its other proper monasteries have been lost to the patriarchate.[12]

The faithful. The number of Orthodox Christians left in Turkey does not exceed 80,000 (excluding the Dodekanese); they are mostly in the neighbourhood of Constantinople and include many wealthy Greek merchants, precariously protected by the Treaty of Lausanne.

---

[11] Italy acted in a high-handed way in relation to the Orthodox of the Dodekanese, and the pressure she brought to bear was not legitimate. As these islands are now transferred to Greece, no doubt their dioceses will be incorporated in the national church.

[12] An attempt at the beginning of the century to form an organization of nursing nuns was a failure.

Greek colonies abroad. After fifty years of disputes the Church of Greece in 1908 was recognized to have immediate jurisdiction over all those Greeks who lived in a country which had no regular Orthodox hierarchy, except for the two very old established colonies at Venice and Vienna. But in 1922 this jurisdiction returned to Constantinople,[13] and the Patriarch Meletios IV appointed a titular archbishop to be exarch for the Orthodox Greeks of *Western Europe;* his residence is in London.[14] Gregory VII in 1924 did the same for *Central Europe,* with residence at Vienna, and appointed a metropolitan for *Australia* at Sydney. The Greek church organized by Meletios IV in U.S.A. is referred to on page 153. In 1936 the Central European exarchate was united to that of Western Europe whose exarch has the title of the metropolitan see of Thyateira.

BIBLIOGRAPHY

*Cobham, *The Patriarchs of Constantinople* (Cambridge, 1911).

*Rausch, *Geschichte der orientalischen Kirchen von 1453–1898* (Leipzig, 1902).

Hofmann in *Orientalia Christiana,* nos. 47, 52, and 64 (Rome, 1928–1930).

*Every, *The Byzantine Patriarchate 451–1204* (London, 1947).

[13] This does not apply to Africa, which comes under Alexandria, and the other churches recognize the position as *de facto* rather than *de iure.*

[14] Doubtless London was chosen in preference to Paris in order to have facilities for contacts with the Church of England. There are four Greek Orthodox churches in England, but ten in France.

2. THE PATRIARCHATE OF ALEXANDRIA

The patriarchate of Alexandria, in early times the first see after Rome, never recovered from the defection of practically all the Egyptians to Monophysism, and when in the year 567 a Catholic patriarchal line was again established it was to govern only a small minority, mostly Greeks in lower Egypt. At the Arab invasion, where once had been a hundred Catholic dioceses, only a handful of faithful was left; the patriarch from time to time even resided at Constantinople, and by the end of the thirteenth century the Alexandrian liturgy and usages had been supplanted by the Byzantine.

Alexandria drifted into schism sometime after 1200, but during the later Middle Ages several of its patriarchs had very friendly relations with Rome, e.g., Nicholas I (d. *c.* 1225) and Niphon (d. *c.* 1367). Philotheos I, after shilly-shallying, adhered to the Union of Florence, and the union subsisted perhaps even until the Turks overran Egypt in 1517: Philotheos II (d. *c.* 1523) seems to have been a Catholic. After this time the Orthodox patriarchate in Egypt was at its lowest ebb; the patriarchs were simply ornaments at the Phanariote court, nominees of the Oecumenical Patriarch, and their tiny flock, which was said to have only half a dozen churches, was ruled by a minor prelate. Among the patriarchs was Meletios Pegas (d. 1603), a notable anti-papal controversialist. The work of Franciscans and Jesuits in the seventeenth century was not without fruit and the patriarch Samuel Kabasilas or Kapasoulis (d. *c.* 1724) sent a definite profession of Catholic faith to Pope Clement XI in 1713. He withdrew it for a time under pressure at Constantinople, but died in communion with the Holy See.

Alexandria recovered somewhat during the nineteenth century, Mohammed Ali insisting that the patriarch should reside at Alexandria and himself choosing Hierotheos II, in 1846. After his death Constantinople was again able to exercise its usurped power of appointment, until in 1899 it failed to get rid of Mgr. Photios, who had been translated from Palestine at the request of the Alexandrian clergy and people. This vigorous but easy-going prelate, who was a determined opponent of Russian influence in the Levant,[15] made a strong but not completely successful effort to reorganize the patriarchate, whose faithful were increasing by both Greek and Syrian immigration. He established a holy synod, and schools, hospitals, and other charitable works were begun, but suffered through inefficient administration. Photios died in 1925 and was succeeded by Meletios Metaxakis, ex-patriarch of Constantinople.

Meletios II at once proceeded to act with the determination that the political situation had prevented him from fully exercising at the Phanar; monks serving parishes were sent back to their monasteries, order was restored in public worship, a college for clergy and school teachers was established at Alexandria, two new dioceses were organized, the Gregorian kalendar imposed for fixed feasts. Meletios was a strong enough man to impose his will on his holy synod, but by many his reforming zeal was looked on with suspicion: he had actually proposed to modify the traditional dress of the clergy, he was in favour of married bishops, and his theological views were said to have a Protestant and "modernist" flavour, while his recognition of Anglican orders when at Constantinople had scandalized many.[16]

But the greatest difficulty he had to contend with was that which had handicapped his predecessor; namely, the objection of the growing Syrian Orthodox element in Egypt against the local church being a predominantly Greek institution. Most of

---

[15] Russia engineered his removal from Jerusalem.

[16] The "liberalism" of Meletios has been exaggerated: he advocated no change in the Orthodox faith and insisted that there could be no union, with Anglicans or anybody else, not based on a common belief in the same Christian doctrines. For many years he was one of the leading and most widely experienced hierarchs among the Greeks.

the Greeks not being naturalized Egyptians, whereas most of the Syrians were, the government supported the Syrian claims, and in 1932 Meletios put forward a new constitution for the church: this provided *inter alia* that the laity should be excluded from patriarchal elections and that there should be one bishop of Syrian nationality. These arrangements pleased neither side, the Syrians demanding two bishops, and Meletios died in 1935 without the matter having been settled. After disputes lasting seven months a successor was elected by the holy synod choosing from among three candidates submitted by a number of delegates, over half of whom were laymen. The patriarch appointed was Nicholas Evanghelides, at that time metropolitan of Hermopolis.

He was at length successful in negotiating an accord with the government whereby future patriarchs should be chosen by an assembly of which two thirds should be laymen, and wherein the element of Syrian origin should be properly represented; it was also agreed that all clergy coming in from outside should become Egyptian subjects, and that the committee for administering church property should be reorganized.

ORGANIZATION AND PRESENT STATE

Patriarch. His title is "His All-Holiness the Pope and Patriarch of the Great City of Alexandria and of All Egypt," and he resides ordinarily in the monastery of St. Sabas at Alexandria. The patriarch does not consecrate the holy chrism but gets it from the Oecumenical Patriarch. The present patriarch is the Lord Christopher II.

Bishops. All are of equal rank and called metropolitans. In 1927 the eparchies were fixed as follows: Leontopolis, living at Zagazig, Pelusium (at Port Said), Hermopolis (at Tantah), and Ptolemaïs (at Cairo); for the faithful living in Africa outside of Egypt there are Nubia (at Khartum), Carthage (at Tunis), Tripoli (at Alexandria), Aksum (at Addis Ababa) and Johannesburg.[17]

---

[17] At the time of writing the sole Syrian bishop has been given one of the *distant* sees, viz., Aksum.

Holy synod. This consists of the metropolitans with the patriarch, and in theory rules the church. But normally it meets only once every six months.

Lower clergy. They are mostly Greeks. Until 1926 there was no seminary or training organization for them at all in Egypt; the College of St. Athanasius founded by Meletios II, reorganized by Nicholas V, now has about fifty students, a quarter of whom are Syrians: the most promising students are sent to be trained abroad. The parish priest is chosen by the parish concerned, and is sometimes a monk. The establishment of a joint seminary at Alexandria for the patriarchates of Alexandria, Antioch, and Jerusalem has recently been projected.

Monasticism. There are five small monasteries (really patriarchal establishments), of which the more important are St. Sabas at Alexandria, St. Nicholas at Cairo, and St. George at Old Cairo.

The faithful. These total some 125,000, of whom three-quarters are Greeks and the rest Syrians. A number of the Syrians have adopted Egyptian nationality; nearly all the Greeks are not Egyptian subjects but merchants and traders resident in the great towns. The number living elsewhere than in Egypt is not large. The Orthodox have a considerable prestige in Egypt, partly on account of the rank of the throne of Alexandria but more because of the wealth and influence of many of its members. On the other hand, they have no influence at all among the Egyptian people: their institutions, hospitals, schools, etc., are wholly Greek and, unlike the Catholic and Protestant establishments, do nothing for the Copts and Mohammedans. Greeks and Syrians attend different churches so far as possible; when there is only one church for both, the antiphonal singing is sometimes Greek on one side and Arabic on the other — but this does not prevent brawling. (The 20,000 Catholic Byzantines in Egypt are mostly Syrians.)

BIBLIOGRAPHY

Macaire, *Histoire de l'Eglise d'Alexandrie* (Cairo, 1894).
Maspero, *Histoire des Patriarches d'Alexandrie* (Paris, 1923).

3. THE PATRIARCHATE OF ANTIOCH

At the time of the trouble at Constantinople in 1054, the Melkite patriarch of Antioch, Peter III, implored Cerularius not to separate himself and his church from Rome and the West, and from that day to this, though grievously reduced by the monophysite schism and by apostasy to Islam, the patriarchate of Antioch has been of great historical interest and ecclesiastical importance because of the large number of its patriarchs, bishops, and faithful who were in communion with Rome. Finally in 1721 there was a definite emergence of two hierarchies, Catholic and dissident Orthodox. It has even been claimed that throughout that period the Antiochene patriarchs considered themselves subject to the pope as supreme pontiff, but this is certainly an exaggeration.

Peter III's successor, Theodosius III, seems to have been in schism, but when the Crusaders captured Antioch in 1098 they acknowledged the Catholicity and jurisdiction of its then patriarch, John IV; after the death of the papal legate Adhemar du Puy their attitude altered and they treated John so badly that he fled to Constantinople. This began the series of patriarchs of Antioch who lived in the imperial city, and were mostly Greeks.[18] But Theodosius V signed the act of union at Lyons in 1274 and resigned rather than repudiate it.[19] The patriarch Dorotheos I accepted the Union of Florence, and there is reason to think that the three Melkite patriarchs did not lapse into schism

[18] One of them was Theodore IV Balsamon (d. 1203), the greatest of Orthodox canonists. It was largely due to him that the three Melkite patriarchates adopted the Byzantine liturgy in place of their own ancient rites.

[19] Saracen writers of the fourteenth and fifteenth centuries make a clear distinction between the Melkites, who submit to the pope of Rome, and the other Christians (Jacobites, etc.), who do not.

again until the Turks cut off Syria from the West in 1516 and the Greeks seized the patriarchal throne of Jerusalem from the Syrians in 1543.

Probably in the latter part of the fourteenth century the patriarchs of Antioch established themselves at Damascus and for two centuries they were mostly Syrians, Constantinople from time to time improperly nominating a Greek whose business it always was to work against the Romeward tendency of the native Syrians. For in 1560 Joachim V had been a Catholic, and in 1585 the ex-patriarch Michael VII, and with the seventeenth century there began a strong movement toward definitive reunion. The patriarchs Athanasius II (d. 1619), Ignatius III, Euthymios II Karmi (who welcomed the Jesuits into his territory; d. 1634), Eutychius (d. 1643), Makarios III Zaim (d. 1672), and Cyril V Zaim (d. 1720), and the bishops Euthymios Saifi of Tyre, Gregory of Aleppo, Gerasimos of Saidnaia, Pathenios of Diarbekr, and others, all made formal profession of allegiance to the Holy See between 1600 and 1720.[20]

When Athanasius III Dabbas died, a schismatic, in 1724, a Catholic, Seraphim Tanas, was elected in his place; he took the name of Cyril VI. Thereupon those who were not in favour of communion with Rome (and some who were) selected one Sylvester and sent him off to Constantinople, where he was consecrated and put forward as the true patriarch of Antioch. From this time on there are two lines of Byzantine patriarchs of Antioch, one for Catholics, one for dissidents.[21] After this the Phanar

[20] The Franciscans, Jesuits, and other Western clergy seem at this time to have recognized all Melkite bishops in Syria as the legitimate ordinaries of their rite. It must be understood that such reconciliations as the above and others like them are of very unequal value. From at least the seventeenth century down to our own day in the dissident East, reunion with Rome (or threat of it) is a common weapon in ecclesiastical politics. Prelates would "turn Catholic" when it served their interests to do so, and revert to schism when circumstances changed. Athanasius Dabbas, mentioned in the next paragraph, was a case in point.

[21] The Catholic patriarch is the historical as well as the spiritual successor of St. Evodius, St. Ignatius the Godbearer, and the Flavians. The Orthodox have contested the validity of the election of Cyril VI, but the synod of Constantinople itself admitted it by claiming to depose him. Sylvester had the support of only five bishops out of fifteen.

would not take any more risks, and saw to it that, canon law or no, only its own Greek nominees should rule the Orthodox of Syria.[22] But the Antiochene church was almost solidly Syro-Arab and became more and more impatient of the Greek hegemony. At last, on the retirement of the patriach Spiridion, in 1898, the bishops nominated in his place Meletios Dumani, a Syrian. The Phanar protested and asked the sultan to withhold the *berat* of appointment, but Russian political interest was at work and the *berat* was given Meletios. For eight years the Greek patriarchs at Constantinople, Alexandria, and Jerusalem would not recognize him, but he did not mind and even got rid of the three Greeks who were among his bishops. On his death in 1906 he was succeeded by another Syrian, Gregory IV Haddad, who was almost entirely self-educated, having been only to a primary school.

On the death of Gregory IV, in 1928, the patriarchate of Antioch was torn by a dispute that lasted five years. Most of the bishops, determined to get rid of lay participation in patriarchal elections, nominated Arsenios Haddad, whereupon the lay notables and some of the clergy, including three bishops, called "the Damascus party," elected the metropolitan of Tripoli, Alexander Tahhan. Neither side would give in and there were in effect two patriarchs, each ruling a separate party;[23] the Oecumenical Patriarch, the other Orthodox patriarchs, the civil authorities, all tried in vain to bring about peace; a reconciliation appeared to be reached at the end of 1932, but it was not till a few weeks later that the trouble really came to an end – with the death of Arsenios. All parties then recognized Alexander Tahhan as legitimate patriarch. But peace does not come easily to this church, and in 1935 there were further troubles, arising out of the threat

[22] They also saw to it that the Turks ill-treated the Catholics: there was bad persecution from 1817 to 1832.

[23] This quarrel, with its intriguing, pride, and violent controversy, was a matter of great scandal in Syria; and it is not surprising that when in June, 1929, Mar Gabriel Tappuni was elected Catholic Syrian Patriarch of Antioch at Sharfeh, by acclamation, in five minutes, and within two months of the death of his predecessor, religious Orthodox asked in print, "Is it possible that the Holy Spirit, who moved so plainly at Sharfeh, is wanting to our bishops?"

of the faithful of the dioceses of Emesa and Laodicea to turn Catholic if they were not given more acceptable bishops.[24] Their wishes were complied with. But the deposed metropolitan of Emesa, Epiphanios, formed an "Independent Orthodox Church of Antioch," with several bishops, which was excommunicated by the patriarch. The rivalries of freemasons played a part in these schisms.

During World War I many Orthodox, in common with other Christians, were massacred by the Turks in Syria, and the cessation of imperial Russian interests there meant that the support and money of Russia were lost to the Orthodox at one blow. These misfortunes, followed by the dissensions just described, have brought the state of the patriarchate very low, and the patriarch Alexander Tahhan hardly has the ability to reorganize and restore his church. The simpler among the faithful are anxious to help in this work, but their zeal is not mixed with discretion, while the more educated are becoming less and less concerned about religion.

ORGANIZATION AND PRESENT STATE

Patriarch. His title is "His Holiness the Patriarch of the God-beloved City of Antioch and of All the East."[25] He lives at Damascus. According to regulations drawn up in 1929 he is appointed by the bishops from among three names submitted by the electoral assembly, which consists of all the ruling bishops, the patriarchal vicar of Antioch,[26] a priest from Damascus, and twenty-four lay people.

---

[24] Naturally a number of the Orthodox, disgusted by these dissensions, have joined the Catholic Melkites. A few of them have changed their rite as well as their hierarchical allegiance and become Maronites. Fundamentally Catholic and Orthodox Melkites, Jacobites, Catholic Syrians, and Maronites are all of one race, and are all sprung ecclesiastically from the original undivided patriarchate of Antioch.

[25] "The East" is the Roman prefecture *Oriens*.

[26] None of the five governing patriarchs (Catholic Melkite, Syrian and Maronite, Orthodox Melkite, Jacobite) who have the title of Antioch live there. "Antakiyeh" is now a two thirds Mohammedan town with about 30,000 inhabitants.

Bishops. All the existing eparchies of the patriarchate are situated in Syria west of the river Euphrates between Turkey-in-Asia and Palestine. They are Bairut,[27] the Lebanon, Tripoli, Epiphania (now Hama), Aleppo, the Hauran, Seleucia (at Zahleh), Tyre and Sidon, Arkadia (at Shaikh Tabba), Emesa (now Homs), and Laodicea (now Lattakieh). The bishops all have the title of metropolitan. There are also two bishops for Melkite emigrants in *North America* (see p. 154), one for *Brazil,* and one for the *Argentine,* subject to the patriarch of Antioch.

Three candidates for a vacant see are put forward by the eparchy concerned, from whom the other bishops make a final choice.

Holy synod. This consists of the patriarch, his episcopal vicars at Antioch and Damascus, and two other bishops in turn. Although in theory this synod governs the church, it practically ceased to function under Gregory IV. Recently the whole bench of bishops has been dealing with important matters.

Lower clergy. There was no seminary till one was organized at the monastery of Balamand in 1904; it was closed in 1912 and not reopened till 1929; it is still not prosperous. The pastoral clergy, therefore, are ignorant and untrained, and most of them in rural parts have to ply a trade to support themselves and their families. There is a certain number of clerics at the College of the Three Moons (i.e., the Three Holy Hierarchs) at Bairut.

Monasticism. There are a dozen small monasteries, of which the most important are St. George's, at Homeira, that at Balamand, and St. Thekla's at Malula. There are not more than about one hundred monks all together.

The faithful. There are at least 220,000 dissident Melkites in Syria,[28] practically all of them Syro-Arabs, numbers having emigrated to the Americas in consequence of Turkish persecution and of the difficulty of making a living in Syria. The common

---

[27] On the occasion of the reception given to Cardinal Tappuni, Catholic Syrian Patriarch of Antioch, in January, 1936, the Orthodox Bishop of Bairut was, at his own request, represented by his protosynkellos (vicar general).

[28] There are 160,000 Catholic Melkites in Syria, to say nothing of Maronites, Syrians, Armenians, and some Latins and Chaldeans.

people are on the whole well disposed toward reunion with Rome and, especially around Tripoli, several thousands became Catholic Melkites in consequence of the divisions among the Orthodox. The patriarch himself received Cardinal Tisserant with great respect when he visited Bairut in 1939; but such courtesies are common in the East. Since Russian political activities came to an end in Syria and with it their schools, the dissident Melkites have been extremely badly off for educational facilities.

BIBLIOGRAPHY

Lammens, *La Syrie*, 2 vols. (Bairut, 1921).
Lorch, *Die römische und griechische Kirche in Syrien und Palästina* (Stuttgart, 1911).
*Every, *The Byzantine Patriarchate* (London, 1947).
*Treppner, *Das Patriarchat von Antiochien* (Freiburg, 1891).

4. THE PATRIARCHATE OF JERUSALEM

The small patriarchate of Jerusalem, carved out of Antioch, was recognized by the Council of Chalcedon in 451 in order that the bishop of the Holy City might have a position more worthy of the dignity and sacredness of his see; before then, since the expulsion of the Jews (including Christian Jews) in the year 135, he had been merely a suffragan (as we should say now) of the metropolitan of Caesarea, where the Roman governor of Palestine lived.[29] The new patriarchate suffered somewhat from monophysite defections, but it was a centre of religious life to which pilgrims came from all parts until, in 637, it was reduced to servitude under the Arabs ("Saracens").[30] From the establishment of the Latin kingdom of Jerusalem by the Crusaders in 1099 until some time after the recapture of the city by Saladin in 1187 the patriarch lived at Constantinople. During this time many of his rights fell into abeyance and he became dependent in a varying degree on the Oecumenical Patriarch, a state of affairs that lasted for 700 years. A state of separation from Rome emerged after the Crusades.

The legate of the patriarch of Jerusalem signed the Union of Florence, and it seems to have subsisted tenuously until, with the Turkish conquest in 1517, control by Constantinople became practically absolute: since 1543 the patriarchs have all been Greeks. There is, however, evidence that in the sixteenth century two successive partriarchs, Sophronios V (d. 1608) and Theo-

---

[29] At that time Jerusalem was called Aelia Capitolina, and was a place of no civil importance at all. The Council of Nicaea in 325 accorded a "succession of honour" to the see.

[30] It is said that we owe the church of the Holy Sepulchre being still a church to the fact that the conquering Omar refused to pray in it lest his followers should therefore turn it into a mosque.

phanes IV (d. 1646), were in communion with the Holy See, and three following nominees of Constantinople, Nektarios (d. 1669), Dositheos (d. 1707), and Chrysanthos (d. 1730), were three of the best hierarchs that ever occupied the throne of Jerusalem. It was the second of these who, in 1672, held a synod to oppose the protestantizing of Cyril Lukaris (see p. 25). Other patriarchs lived in Constantinople, for greater convenience in dealing with the civil power, the last of these being Athanasius V (d. 1845).

In 1872 the patriarch Cyril II refused to join his fellow patriarchs in their condemnation of the Bulgarian schism – Russia was supporting the Bulgars, and Russia was the protector and benefactor of the Orthodox Church in Palestine. The Jerusalem holy synod professed to depose Cyril, setting up Prokopios in his stead, and a violent and complicated quarrel ensued which lasted for many years, involving the Phanar, the Turkish Porte, and the Russian government. In 1875 the sultan imposed on the patriarchs of Constantinople and Jerusalem new regulations for the election of a patriarch of Jerusalem, but the disputes and intriguing still went on, patriarchs being elected and deposed in the most scandalous and confusing way.[31] Eventually Gerasimos was translated from Antioch in 1891, but on his death in 1897 there was another disedifying struggle between Greek and Russian influences,[32] in which the Greeks triumphed, Damianos Kassiotis being elected.[33]

Damianos had a long and troubled pontificate, his troubles be-

[31] Photios, later of Alexandria, was patriarch for a few months, but Russia did not want him and got him removed. He was only 29 years old.

[32] The Russian candidate was the archimandrite Euthymios who was responsible for the attack on the Franciscans outside the Holy Sepulchre church on November 4, 1901, when fifteen friars were injured.

[33] I have before me a copy of the *berat* of "Sultan Abdul Hamid al-Ghazi, son of Abdul Mejid, appointing Damianos Effendi as patriarch of Jerusalem." It is an interesting and reasonable document. Throughout the Orthodox are referred to as "the Romans" (Constantinople was New Rome). A curious provision is that "The monks who live in the monasteries of the Georgians, the Abyssinians, the Syrians and the Copts and all the remainder of the Roman sects, great and small, shall acknowledge the said Damianos as their patriarch." It would be nice to hear what the monophysite Abyssinians, Syrians, and Copts said — but the wording goes back to the days of the khalif Omar ibn-Khattab in the seventh century.

ginning after the "Young Turk" revolution of 1908. The position in the patriarchate of Jerusalem was (and is) that a practically solid body of Palestinian (Syro-Arab) lay people and lower clergy were governed and controlled by a caucus of Greek monks (the Brotherhood of the Holy Sepulchre: see below, p. 46), with various Greek prelates and a Greek patriarch at their head, since the sixteenth century. With their civil liberties newly acquired in 1908 the Orthodox Palestinians demanded that they should take part in the administration of their church by means of a mixed council, that there should be more resident bishops, and better educational facilities.[34] Damianos inclined to uphold these demands, but his synod straightway deposed him. Thereupon the Palestinians appealed to the Sublime Porte, and that Mohammedan authority pronounced that a Christian synod can elect but cannot depose. The Greek monks averted bloodshed by (it is said) sprinkling vitriol on the mob, and closed all the native churches. When the Turks sent a commission to investigate, both sides accused their patriarch of "trimming," and worse, and so things went on. But Damianos refused to be deposed, and at the end of 1911 the mixed council was granted, together with an allocation of one third of the yearly income for schools, hospitals, etc. But it hardly began to be operative before World War I began.[35]

In 1918 the synod again tried to depose its patriarch, on the allegation of his being an accomplice of the Turks (in spite—perhaps because?—of the fact that they had carried him away prisoner when the British took Jerusalem from them in 1917); but Damianos bowed his head to the storm and clung on—it was only an incident in a situation that threatened to bring ruin to the whole patriarchate. Before the war Russia had poured money into Palestine, to say nothing of the alms of fifteen thou-

[34] One result of the financial troubles in 1908 was the closing of the only seminary in the patriarchate, at the monastery of the Holy Cross near Jerusalem. But even there they did not encourage native aspirants.

[35] The leaders of the opposition to Damianos were two men several times mentioned elsewhere in this book, Meletios Metaxakis and Chrysostom Papadopoulos, both titular archimandrites of the Brotherhood of the Holy Sepulchre at this time.

sand pilgrims annually (most of them from the same country): now all that was gone, and in 1922 the debts of the patriarchate were estimated at $3,000,000 (£600,000). Moreover, the Palestinian Orthodox, not content with the mixed council that the British high commissioner (as representative of the mandatory power) wished to make effective, were clamouring for further concessions. Great Britain appointed two commissions, the "Bertram-Luke" and "Bertram-Young" commissions,[36] and intervened to prevent a financial crash; much landed property was compulsorily sold (mostly to Zionist organizations), help to tide over the crisis was got from U.S.A., and a moratorium for the debts was proclaimed.[37] Then on August 14, 1931, affable and peace-loving Damianos, a master of tact and tactics in incredibly difficult times, died at his summer residence on the Mount of Olives.

Now that there was question of electing a new patriarch, the struggle between the Greek prelates and monks and the Arabic-speaking Palestinian faithful broke out in an aggravated form. In the days of full Turkish domination these diverse elements had formed a unity: they were all "Romans," i.e., Christians of the orthodoxy of Constantinople, New Rome. But this unity had been undermined and falsified; the diverse elements no longer thought of themselves as all "Romans"; the natives were now Palestinians or "Arabs," the Greeks were now Hellenes. Moreover, they had become rather bitterly Hellene. For centuries the brotherhood had had to resist continually what it regarded as the encroachments of the Catholic Church (represented by the Latins), the exactions of the Ottoman Turks, and, more recently, the growing power of Slav Orthodoxy; then, from 1908, there had been the further struggle with the insurgent Palestinian Orthodox clamouring for their "place in the sun" – that was the issue to be

---

[36] They published two extremely valuable reports. See bibliography.

[37] The Brotherhood of the Holy Sepulchre wanted to accept an offer from the National Bank of Greece which would have made the patriarchate simply an Hellenic dependence: the King of the Hellenes was to be official "Protector of the Holy Places." The Palestinians naturally stood out against this, so did the patriarch, and Great Britain forbade it.

fought out. And this issue, as the Bertram-Luke commission made clear, was made more difficult by the mentality of the Brotherhood of the Holy Sepulchre, which had produced two serious misconceptions among them. The members had come to look upon themselves as an Hellenic garrison, and had lost sight of the fact that their privileged position in Jerusalem carried with it very great obligations both to local Orthodox Christians and to the Orthodox Church at large, without racial or any other distinction. This arrogant attitude had bred the extraordinary and entirely uncanonical notion that the brotherhood was the governing body of the Orthodox Church of Jerusalem, indeed, that it was practically synonymous with that church. This was certainly the position in fact, and the circumstance that the hierarchs of the church were all members of the brotherhood gave an entirely misleading and illusory appearance of right to the contention. The Church of Jerusalem is, or ought to be, governed by bishops-in-ordinary, like any other church. Furthermore, the brotherhood had come to regard itself as custodian of the Holy Places, not in trust for all the Orthodox churches, but as agent or mandatory of the Hellenic nation, which was assumed to have special interests and rights in those sacred shrines. The archimandrite Kallistos semi-officially expressed these "rights" as including actual ownership.

Naturally enough, the native Orthodox tended to exaggerate their own side: in their more heated moments they represented the Greek monks to be a gang of foreigners who had robbed the people of their birthright; they claimed that all the patriarchal endowments should be in the communal ownership of themselves, and that the Holy Places were a private property of the local church of Jerusalem. Such statements are absurd, but they must not be allowed to obscure the reality of the Palestinians' grievances and the reasonableness of their protest against the Greeks' highhandedness. Their just complaints boiled down to such matters as the appointment of a metropolitan for Nazareth who could not speak Arabic and was an unworthy bishop, the neglect to provide schools, whether clerical or secular, and the "freezing out" of Palestinian monks from the brotherhood or the keeping of them in subordinate positions.

It is impossible to give here any account of the confused events of the four years following the death of Damianos. The "fundamental law" of 1875 was taken as the basis of the election,[38] and the Palestinians declared that their clergy would not take their part in it. They continued these obstructionist tactics, basing themselves on the Bertram-Young report, in the hope that the incoming patriarch would be obliged to accept their demands as a condition of his election; the Greek authorities, having admitted the need of reform, took the line, which was approved by the British administration, that the patriarchate could only be reformed when there was a patriarch in office. At length, in June–July, 1935, an election was carried out on an *ad hoc* system, devised in London on the basis of the 1875 law; the Palestinians still refused to participate; and Timothy Themelis, titular archbishop of the Jordan, was duly elected patriarch of Jerusalem.[39]

The aggrieved Palestinians refused to recognize Mgr. Timothy, and in an effort to conciliate them he promised a number of reforms in their favour that at once raised a cry from the Greeks that "Hellenic privileges in Palestine were in danger." After long negotiations, in which a representative of the British government took part, an arrangement was come to in 1938 providing for patriarchal and episcopal elections, the administration of church property by a committee of clergy and laity, and other matters, in all of which the native Palestinians were given a voice.

---

[38] I must quote an amusing passage from an account of the position given in *America:* "The 'fundamental law' assigned certain functions to those extinct officials the sultan of Turkey, the grand vizir of the Ottoman empire, and the mutaserif, or local governor, of Palestine and Jerusalem. British authority has laid it down that King George V is sultan of Turkey *ad hoc* (the close resemblance which his Majesty bears to the late Abdul Hamid will naturally leap to the eye at once), the British Secretary of State for the Colonial Department becomes the grand vizir of an empire that has ceased to be, and the High Commissioner for Palestine is set to fulfil the functions of the mutaserif."

[39] Years ago, when he was a deacon, Mgr. Timothy spent some years at Oxford. The first recorded Orthodox to study at that university was Metrophanes Kritopoulos, about 1618. He was afterwards patriarch of Alexandria.

ORGANIZATION AND PRESENT STATE

Patriarch. His title is "His Holiness the Patriarch of the Holy City of Jerusalem and of All Palestine," with the addition of several districts that are purely titular. Actually his jurisdiction extends only over Palestine and most of Transjordania. He applies to Constantinople for the holy chrism.

Bishops. There are only two eparchies besides that of the patriarch; namely, Ptolemaïs (Akka) and Nazareth. But there are up to ten titular archbishops who discharge various offices, and bear the titles of The Jordan, Mount Tabor, Kerak, Gaza, Lydda, Madaba, Pella, Petra, Philadelphia, and Sebaste. They are mostly in charge of one or other of the important shrines. All these hierarchs are elected by the holy synod and they and the patriarch can now be chosen only from among those who have become Palestinian citizens; the appointment of each must be approved by the British high commissioner.

Holy synod. This is composed of the patriarch, the resident metropolitans, the titular archbishops, nine titular archimandrites, and the archdeacon. All must be members of the Brotherhood of the Holy Sepulchre. In theory they govern the church, but the extent to which they actually do so depends, as elsewhere, on the personality of the patriarch, and also on their relations with the whole body of Holy Sepulchre monks.

The Brotherhood of the Holy Sepulchre consists of some 160 monks called *hagiotaphites* ("Holy-Sepulchrites"), and was originally formed to look after the various Holy Places[40] and defend them against aggression. Its controlling function with regard to the whole patriarchate has grown up since the sixteenth century, and it has been practically entirely Greek in composition (though not so in theory) for a very long time. The patriarch is head of the brotherhood *ex officio.*

The chief monasteries are those of St. Constantine and of St. Helen. They are close to the Holy Sepulchre church and together

---

[40] The Orthodox have the principal rights in the church of the Holy Sepulchre at Jerusalem and the church of the Nativity at Bethlehem, and are represented at all the chief shrines.

form the centre of patriarchal and synodical activities, with the patriarch's residence, five churches, the liberary, printing press, and so on. The communities total some hundred monks. Fifteen monks form the community of the Holy Sepulchre itself and serve the church, and twelve serve the church of the Nativity at Bethlehem. Their numerous other houses at Jerusalem and elsewhere have no regular communities. The administrative duties of the monks are so extensive that the discipline of their monastic rule is necessarily considerably relaxed, but the brotherhood has given some very worthy hierarchs and good scholars to the Orthodox Church from time to time. Its charities, too, are extensive. Up to 1920, at least, it distributed £3,000 annually in paying rents for the needy alone; in 1935 about a third of its income, £9,000, was spent on Arab house rents, schools, etc.

Other monks. The only monastery in the patriarchate not directly concerned in the duties of the Brotherhood of the Holy Sepulchre (though it belongs to the brotherhood) is that of Mar Saba, in the desert between Jerusalem and the Dead Sea. With the probable exception of St. Catherine's at Mount Sinai it is the oldest Orthodox monastic community, having continuity with the foundation of St. Sabas in 491. The present community numbers some twenty-five monks who provide a very good example of traditional Eastern monasticism. There are four very small convents of Orthodox nuns in Jerusalem.

Parochial clergy. These are exclusively Palestinians, who receive no regular training and are consequently for the most part ignorant and inefficient. This is no reflection on them, but on the Greek authorities who have seemed quite indifferent to the welfare of the common people, at any rate when compared with the conservation of their "privileges." There are about 60 parishes and less than 100 clergy.

The faithful. The Orthodox faithful of the patriarchate number about 45,000 souls, all of them Palestinian Syro-Arabs except a couple of hundred Greek lay people. Like their fellow Melkites in the patriarchate of Antioch, they have suffered from the closing of schools formerly subsidized by Russia. More and more do they want to get rid of their Greek ecclesiastical masters, but many of them on the other side of the Jordan and in Galilee find a quicker way: they see there are Catholic Melkite bishops at Amman and Haifa who are of their own race, rite, and language, so they do the obvious thing and become Catholics.[41] But there seems to be less real religion among the indigenous Orthodox in Palestine than there is among their fellows in Syria: they have been in closer touch with European materialism and secularism.

BIBLIOGRAPHY

**Report of the Commission . . . to Inquire into the Affairs of the Orthodox Patriarchate of Jerusalem* (Oxford, 1921).

**The Orthodox Patriarchate of Jerusalem. Report of the Commission* (Oxford, 1926).

*Graham, *With the Russian Pilgrims to Jerusalem* (London, 1913).

Lorch, *Die römische und griechische Kirche in Syrien und Palästina* (Stuttgart, 1911).

*Every, articles in *Eastern Churches Quarterly,* Vol. VI, No. 7 (1946) and Vol. VII, No. 2 (1947).

---

[41] Unfortunately in the rest of Palestine the Catholics are nearly all Latins and the clergy mostly foreigners. If Leo XIII had been pope in 1847 he would perhaps have sent a Byzantine and not a Latin Patriarch to Jerusalem.

CHAPTER IV

THE NEWER PATRIARCHATES

1. THE PATRIARCHATE OF MOSCOW

THE Russians date their conversion to Christ from about the year 988, when St. Vladimir, grand-prince of Kiev, gave the new religion to his people.[1] The earliest agents of Christianity seem to have been Germans, other Northmen (Vladimir himself was a Varangian), and Bulgars; but Vladimir married a Byzantine princess, Anna, and the influence of Constantinople soon became preponderant. Bishops were sent to the Russians from there, who not only brought with them their Byzantine rites but also perhaps anti-Latin and separatist ideas, for this was the period of Cerularius (Vol. I, p. 8). Russia was in touch and had normal relations with Western Europe until the Mongol invasions in the thirteenth century; but in the circumstances of the times it is impossible that the fact and significance of communion with the Holy See of Rome can have had much importance in their religious consciousness. Greek influence was predominant in their church (it continued to be part of the patriarchate of Constantinople till 1589) and, in the words of Father Pierling, S.J., "One looks in vain for an exact date or outstanding event that can be registered as the point of departure for the separation between Russia and Rome. It came about by implication, without shock or apparent reason, simply because of Russia's hierarchical submission to the patriarch of Constantinople."

There were, for example, diplomatic relations between the

[1] There were Christians in Russia before Vladimir, e.g., his grandmother, St. Olga.

Russian princes and the popes during the Middle Ages and a certain amount of intermittent activity on the part of preachers from the West, as well as such incidents as the request of Prince Basil (Vasilko) of Vladimir in Volhynia and his brother Daniel of Galich (Galicia), who was subsequently crowned king of that principality, to be admitted to communion with Pope Innocent IV in 1247. Moreover, bishops of the southwestern eparchies on occasion went to the nearest Latin archbishop to be consecrated, and from the thirteenth to the fifteenth century Latin monks and others in the Novgorod province seem to have regarded themselves as in communion with their Orthodox neighbours. But with the coming of the Tartars there began the era of the more isolated development of the Russian Church. It became, partly of necessity, self-sufficient and suspicious of external influence; and to the peoples of the West, Russia was an unknown land whose people were thought of not simply as schismatic but even as heathen. And Russia's western neighbours, especially the Teutonic Knights, took such aggressive advantage of her troubles with the Mongols, and later, that it was difficult for the ordinary Russian to believe that Catholics were Christians either.

St. Vladimir was a Northman and his capital Kiev, "the God-protected mother of Russian cities," was in the heart of what is known now as "The Ukraine." For two hundred and fifty years it was the political and ecclesiastical centre of Russia, and the chief hierarchs continued to call themselves metropolitans of Kiev for two hundred years after they had resided at Moscow. After the fall of Kiev in 1240 to the Mongols the centre of state power gradually shifted to Moscow, and eventually the Muscovites, who were less purely Slav than the people of the West and Southwest, reserved for themselves the name of Great Russians and called the others Little Russians and White Russians. Each of these three elements has its own language, descended from a common tongue that was spoken by them all before the twelfth century. At the Council of Florence Russia was represented by a Greek, Isidore, metropolitan of Kiev (Moscow), who was in favour of reunion. Pope Eugenius IV created him cardinal

Courtesy, *Soviet News*

THE PATRIARCHS ALEXANDER III OF ANTIOCH, CHRISTOPHER II OF ALEXANDRIA, ALEXIS OF MOSCOW, AND THE KATHOLIKOS KALLISTRATOS OF GEORGIA (left to right)

MONASTERY OF MAR SABA, PALESTINE

Courtesy, Fr. Eugene Hoade

CHURCH OF MAR SABA

AT KARLOVTSY IN 1935
Front row left to right: Mgr. Theophilus, Mgr. Antony, Patriarch Barnabas of Serbia, Mgr. Eulogius, Mgr. Anastassy

Courtesy, Fr. F. Wilcock

RUSSIAN BISHOPS IN EXILE
Group taken at the hostel for Russian refugees founded at Louvain by Cardinal Mercier. In the center: Mgr. Eulogius

RUSSIAN CRUCIFIX

Courtesy, *Soviet News*

ALEXIS, PATRIARCH OF MOSCOW

Courtesy, Burns & Oates

VLADIMIR SOLOVYEV

Courtesy, Fr. F. Wilcock

BRINGING THE SACRAMENTS TO THE SICK IN A RUSSIAN HOUSEHOLD

OPEN-AIR BAPTISM IN SERBIA

and sent him home as legate to confirm the union, but the grand prince of Muscovy, Basil II, and his other bishops would have none of it and Isidore had to escape to Rome. Nevertheless the Council of Florence was not entirely fruitless, for it was the remote cause of the reunion of the southwestern Russian dioceses in 1595. A definite movement toward reunion had been started there, and in 1458 Pope Pius II nominated a monk called Gregory to be metropolitan of Kiev;[2] by arrangement with Casimir IV of Poland he was allowed to exercise jurisdiction over the eight dioceses of the Kiev ecclesiastical province that were then under the control of Poland and Lithuania.[3] This lasted only till the beginning of the sixteenth century, when they slipped back into schism. During the second half of that century the Jesuits came to Vilna, Yaroslav, Polotsk, and elsewhere, and at once set themselves to work for the definitive reunion of the Kievan bishops and their flocks. At length in 1595 Michael Ragoza, Metropolitan of Kiev, and the bishops of Vladimir, Lutsk, Polotsk, Pinsk, and Kholm met at Brest-Litovsk in Lithuania and petitioned the Holy See to admit them to its communion, and on December 23 the reunion was solemnly proclaimed in the hall of Constantine at the Vatican. These Byzantine Catholics are represented today by the Ruthenians (or Ukrainians)[4] in Galicia and elsewhere (Vol. I, page 67).[5]

THE PATRIARCHATE

But six years before the Union of Brest-Litovsk an event of the greatest importance and significance had taken place in Great Russia. Ever since the fall of Constantinople to the Turks and

---

[2] The definitive separation of the see of Moscow from that of Kiev took place in 1461.

[3] All White Russia and the Ukraine west of Kiev was under the political suzerainty of Poland and Lithuania from the middle of the fourteenth century till 1772–1795.

[4] Historically this is the far less significant name of the two: *Ukraine* only means "the borderland" or "marches." In the West the Russians were first called Ruthenes and then Muscovites.

[5] Kiev itself fell away from unity in 1632, when the great Orthodox theologian Peter Mogila became its metropolitan.

the checking of the Tartars on the river Ugra in 1480, the grand princes of Moscow had more and more looked on themselves as *tsars,* Caesars, heirs of the Byzantine *basileis.* The imperial power of Old Rome had gone and her church was "in schism"; the imperial power of New Rome had gone and the direct influence of her church was circumscribed by the infidels; Moscow, then, was the Third Rome, civilly and ecclesiastically. This idea was confirmed by the marriage (encouraged by Pope Paul II and Cardinal Bessarion) of Ivan III with Sophia Palailogos, a niece of the last Roman emperor, in 1473; he was now the Ruler of All the Russias, the bearer of the two-headed eagle, the secular arm of the Orthodox Church.

Accordingly during the reign of Feodor, son of the first tsar, Ivan IV the Terrible and Anastasia Romanova, the independent patriarchate of Russia was established. The Greeks had, of course, strongly opposed any such innovation, but in 1589 the patriarch of Constantinople, Jeremias II, was in Moscow and he was persuaded (not without trickery) to consent and to invest the metropolitan Job as first patriarch of Moscow. Two years later the other Orthodox patriarchs in synod concurred in what had been done, giving Moscow the fifth place, after Jerusalem (instead of the second that she claimed).

The new patriarchate functioned for only one hundred and ten years, and among its eleven patriarchs two names stand out. One is Philaret Romanov (d. 1633), who was co-ruler with his son the tsar Michael, and the other is Nikon, the son of a peasant, who came to the patriarchal throne in 1652.[6] He was a learned and righteous man and a reformer, and his zeal against imperial control of the church eventually led to his fall. But before this happened in 1666, Nikon's liturgical reforms, sanctioned by a synod in 1654, had set Russia by the ears: from a Western point of view they were matters of trifling importance – the number of alleluias to be sung, the pronunciation of the Holy Name, the manner of crossing oneself, and so on – but they helped to break

[6] He was not a Russian but a Volga Finn of the Mordvinian tribe.

up the solid Russian structure of church, state, and nation by contributing to bring about appalling schisms that have lasted from that day to this.

The ecclesiastical reforms of Nikon were not, as is usually said, the chief cause of this great *raskol* (schism): what lay behind it was the rationalist, "Protestant," and pseudo-mystical elements in Russian religion faced with a crisis at the moment when the state was reconstructing herself to come into line with the states of Western Europe – the West, which represented that thing which the mass of Russians had learned through ignorance to fear, and because of fear to hate, the Latin Church. "*Raskol* was a judgement pronounced against the Church of Russia as a whole, against her national exclusiveness, against the particular mentality she had imparted to the people to the exclusion of Christian Catholicity" (Danzas).[7] It became, as it were, a struggle between the state church and the national religion.

The government (which also deposed Nikon) proceeded against the schismatics with ferocity: the monastery of Solovky was besieged (for ten years!) and its monks massacred, the holy archpriest Avvakum was put to death – with the usual result of persecution: the schism spread, it was followed by hundreds of thousands of people, including monks and priests, and eventually obtained a hierarchy of bishops.[8] And soon, of course, it split up into sects. By the nineteenth century the *raskolniky* could be divided broadly into the *Starovery,* Old Believers (or Old Ritualists), "more Orthodox than the Orthodox," with their hierarchy, dioceses, and monasteries, on the one hand, and the split-off sects on the other. These sects, again, could be roughly divided into the so-called rationalist bodies and the messianic pseudo-mystics,

[7] But Miss Danzas' book on *The Russian Church* (New York, 1936) must be read with reservation and controlled by some such similar short account as Dr. Zernov's *Moscow the Third Rome* (New York, 1937).

[8] Actually, not for two hundred years. With the Catholics of Japan in the seventeenth and eighteenth centuries, the Old Believers are an example of a church run for centuries by the laity, who never attempted to assume the functions of clergy because they believed in the necessity of an apostolical priestly succession.

covering the whole gamut of religious fanaticism:[9] *Molokany*, who drank milk in Lent, *Subbotniky*, Sabbatarians, *Dirkovtsy*, who prayed before a hole in a wall (representing spirit surrounded by matter), *Priguny*, jumpers, *Stranniky*, wanderers, *Moltshalniky*, who never spoke, *Dukhobory*, spirit-wrestlers, and, most-important of all, *Skoptsy*, self-castrated, and *Khlysty*, flagellants. These last draw attention to the extremely strong manichaean element in these sects and to the hysteria which led to mass suicide by fire or burying alive: but the element of licentiousness, though not absent, has been much overemphasized. Halfway between the Old Believers and the sects proper were the *Bezpopovtsy*, priestless ones, who acknowledged hierarchy and sacraments in principle, but were historically deprived of both.[10] Nor were these sects confined to the common people: in the eighteenth and early nineteenth century the semi-secret organization of the Khlysty penetrated into the army, into the princely families, and into the imperial palace itself.

Generally speaking the *raskolniky* proper were distinguished by a more austere morality than the Orthodox, enjoyed considerable material prosperity, were generous to their less fortunate brethren, and were at the same time zealous for education but very uncritical in their culture. Points of resemblance to the characteristics and position of Protestant dissenters from the state Church of England at the best period of Nonconformity are at once evident.

THE CONSTITUTION OF PETER THE GREAT

The Church of Russia was more and more incapable of neutralizing the tendencies that were depriving her of all rights against the state, she was becoming secularized, and the last links

---

[9] This was nothing new in Russian religion. For example, from early times those who had deliberately taken up the role of "fools for Christ's sake" (*yurodivy*, Gk. *saloi*) had been distinguished by wild exaggerations and popular veneration.

[10] The Baptists (*Stunda*), who have so many adherents in later times, appeared only in the middle of the nineteenth century and did not strictly form part of the *raskol*.

of her chains were forged by the tsar, Peter the Great. When the patriarch Adrian died in 1700, Peter forbade the election of a successor, and after a delay of twenty-one years produced a new constitution for the church – one which has had a strong and injurious effect on the organization of other Orthodox churches as well.

The centre of this constitution was the *Holy Governing Synod,* which was to have complete control over the church under the "Autocratic Sovereign." It was composed of the metropolitans of Petersburg, Moscow, and Kiev, half a dozen prelates appointed by the tsar and removable at his will, the imperial and military chaplains, and the procurator; these twelve members were later reduced to six. It was in fact a civil-service committee of state officials; to wit, bishops, whose president was the tsar himself. As he was never present the metropolitan of Petersburg deputized, but the real controller of the synod was the lay *procurator,* who was a minister of the crown. The other bishops were equally state officials, and the parish clergy besides their own work were compelled to act as local representatives of various state departments. The *raskolniky* were rebels, not against the divine authority of the church, but against the state. The church was a government department, like the treasury or the armed forces.

Peter's immediate object was the complete submission of the ecclesiastical to the civil power, and it was attained so far as government and administration were concerned. His ultimate object was a completely secularized nation: here he had a degree of success among the governing class and the growing middle class, but with the people at large he failed. He failed partly because of the violence of his persecuting methods (his wife Eudokia Lopukhina and his son Alexis were among its victims), but more because of the monasteries, which kept religion alive among the folk and reacted to persecution with a powerful spiritual revival: that from the days of St. Sergius of Radonezh the common people had looked on the monks as their real fathers in God and defenders of Orthodoxy gave added weight to the movement. Its great leader was Paisy Velichkovsky (d. 1794), a monk first of Mount Athos and then of Neamtu in Moldavia, who spread throughout the monasteries the institution of the *starets,*[11] already traditional in Russian religious life, and encouraged studies, especially of mystical theology and of the Greek fathers. Another outstanding monk at this time was Tikhon of Zadonsk (d. 1783); he had a more exact knowledge of the Catholic Church, and was therefore more well-disposed thereto, than was usual in Russia.

The living currents of reform and renewed spiritual life in Russia during the nineteenth century had no effect either on the state church or the masses of the people, whether Orthodox or *raskolniky:* they were intellectual, even aristocratic, movements, whose significance was not realized till after the decree of liberty of worship in 1905 and, still more, after the revolution of 1917. The most important were the Slavophils, whose leader, A. S. Khomyiakov (d. 1860), found in the "Russian soul" the potentiality of an earthly counterpart of the kingdom which is not of this world; his work was carried on by Kireevsky, Aksakov, Samarin, and other laymen. Khomyiakov's religious ideas were revived in our own time in a modified form by Father Paul Florensky, the archpriest Sergius Bulgakov, and a group of theologians of the Paris theological college. On the other side were the "Westernizers," with their Vissarion Bielinsky (d. 1848) on the extreme left, but their westernizing did not include reunion with the Western Church in its programme (which was, indeed, antireligious). Of all the great religious men whose names did honour to Russia in the nineteenth century, names which include Gogol, Dostoievsky, and Tolstoy, only one clearly saw the significance of Rome for the church of his country, and he was one of the greatest of them: the philosopher and theologian Vladimir Solovyev (d. 1900).[12] There were, of course, other distinguished people who came into communion with Rome — Princess Eliza-

[11] Literally, "old man" (cf., the colloquial Greek for a monk, *kalogeros*). The nearest Western equivalent is a spiritual director, but the *starets* is not necessarily a priest.

[12] "All the exponents of modern Russian theology and Christian philosophy have been brought up on Solovyev," writes Professor Fedotov.

beth Volkonsky, M. D. Zherebtsov, Mrs. N. S. Ushakova, Mrs. Narishkin, Princess Bariatinsky, Prince Gagarin, Count Shuvalov – but they had no influence outside their own noble circle.

During the last years of the nineteenth century in Russia "religious particularism and universal messianism, national pride and anarchist trends, mysticism and rationalism, Europe and Asia, and many more apparently irreconcilable ideas clashed in a way that is best reflected in the writings of Dostoievsky" (Danzas).

Meanwhile the official imperial policy of "Orthodoxy, autocracy and nation" had been carried on, with varying degrees of zeal, secularism gaining all the time, for only lip service was given to Christianity. Of the sovereigns that followed Peter the Great, Catherine II (d. 1796), Nicholas I (d. 1855), and Alexander III (d. 1894) stand out specially as carrying on the work of binding the church to the state,[13] particularly at the expense of the Ukrainian Catholics, who after the partition of Poland were aggregated by force to the state church: since their rite was Byzantine they must belong to the Orthodox state church, otherwise they were traitors – such was the argument. Until the Poles revolted in 1863 Latin Catholics were left alone. After the assassination in 1881 of Alexander II, the "Tsar Liberator," so called because he emancipated the serfs and inaugurated other reforms, a stranglehold was put on political life and extended to ecclesiastical life by the famous Constantine Pobiedonostsev, procurator of the holy synod. No one has ever questioned the good faith of this baffling and apparently self-contradictory man, who translated *The Imitation of Christ* into Russian and pursued a cynical and unyielding political policy within the church, which he "carried out with a fearfully complete knowledge of private lives," but he was one of the most hated men not only in Russia but in Europe.[14]

[13] P. J. Tshaadaev (d. 1856), in many ways a forerunner of Solovyev, was declared insane by imperial decree (!) in 1836 and forbidden to publish his writings on account of their Catholic tendency.

[14] Norman Douglas, the novelist, W. J. Birkbeck, the ecclesiological writer, and Mandell Creighton, Anglican bishop of London, all met Pobiedonostsev

His power came to an end in 1905, when the tsar, Nicholas II, granted a constitution to the state and freedom for the practice of any religion. This decree profoundly stirred religious minds, projects for reforms of the church again began to ferment, and there was soon a strong movement for the convening of a national ecclesiastical council — but that was only to come in the day of terror and darkness. Rozanov, Merezhkovsky, and Berdyaev revived the ideas of Khomiakov and Solovyev, but they were still estranged from the common people, and the societies that opposed the civil constitution granted in 1905 were not infrequently led by bishops and priests. The reactionary exploits of such representatives of the clergy as Bishops Germogen and Antony Khrapovitsky (whom we shall meet again later) compromised the church in the eyes of the progressive middle classes as much as anything in the past and had a grave bearing on the revolution. A minority, but an influential minority, of the Russian clergy kept the banner of "Orthodoxy, autocracy, and nation" flying till the last — and when the end came all Russia knew that the metropolitans of Petersburg and Moscow were the nominees of Gregory Rasputin.[15]

At the time of the revolution the Russian Church was divided into 65 dioceses. They were all directly subject to the holy synod, but three of them, Petersburg, Moscow, and Kiev, had precedence, their hierarchs being called metropolitans; fourteen others were called archiepiscopal. There were also a number of auxiliary bishops, called "vicars." There were, all supported by the state, some 180 ecclesiastical schools preparatory to the 59 seminaries proper, of which most were not at all in a flourishing state and in the early years of the twentieth century tended to be centres of discontent and revolutionary activity. The theological academies of Petersburg, Moscow, Kiev, and Kazan, on the other hand, had some extremely brilliant professors and were

at the coronation of Nicholas II. The first called him "a silent, bloodless, all-powerful creature, a Torquemada"; the second admired and liked him; the bishop and the procurator "discovered a real mutual respect."

[15] It is necessary to point out that this man was never a priest or a monk but a married layman.

equipped with excellent libraries: in 1914 they had over 800 students between them.

Ever since the days of St. Sergius of Radonezh (d. 1392) the "white" or secular clergy had been sharply differentiated not only canonically but in popular estimation from the "black clergy" or monks (from among whom all bishops and other responsible dignitaries were taken). In general, especially away from the towns, the "white clergy" were handicapped in properly fulfilling their calling by poverty and family cares (they were all married), insufficient general education, complete dependence upon ecclesiastical and secular authorities, sometimes by lack of real vocation. Constituting a separate class, they were socially isolated both from the mass of people and from the cultured classes.

The monks, on the other hand, in spite of the strong measures at their expense of Peter the Great and others, continued to be looked on as really representing the church, as examples of true Christian virtue, and as the only spiritual counsellors and directors – it goes without saying that not always were they worthy of their reputation. In 1910 there were 452 monasteries of men, of which 298 were subsidized by the state; they had 17,583 monks and "novices." There were as well 400 monasteries of women, with 52,927 nuns and "novices."

The three greatest monasteries were those of the Caves of Kiev (Pecherskoy), founded by St. Antony and St. Theodosius, both called "Pechersky," between 1013 and 1062, the Troitsky (Trinity) near Moscow, founded by St. Sergius of Radonezh, and the Alexander-Nevsky, established at Petersburg in 1724, formerly the residence of the metropolitan. Others scarcely less famous were the Donskoy at Moscow, Simonov, Novospassky (where the Tartars were beaten off from Moscow), St. George's at Novgorod, Novodievichy (saved from Napoleon by a brave nun), the Ascension at Tver, Solovky in the White Sea, Sarov, Rostov, Yaroslav, Uglich, Valaam in Finland, and the Pochaevskaya Laura in Volhynia.

The pre-revolution Orthodox population of Russia was some

80 to 90 millions, with from 15 to 20 millions more adhering to the dissenting sects: of those the Old Believers at least may not improperly be counted as Orthodox. The total population of the empire was about 150 millions.

AFTER THE REVOLUTION

The fall of the imperial power in 1917 set the Russian Church free to hold the long-demanded national council (*sobor*), the first since 1666, which opened in Moscow on August 15 and continued till the autumn of 1918 when the civil war made its adjournment necessary. Its chief work was unquestionably the restoration of the patriarchate, and in November, 1917, while the bolshevists were bombarding the Kremlin, Tikhon Belavin, the metropolitan of Moscow, a modest and unassuming man whose simple goodness made him greatly revered, was elected the first patriarch of the new line. In the following month the bolshevist government began the issue of those decrees which were to implement its policy of militant atheism: on December 4 all ecclesiastical and private landed properties were confiscated, on the eleventh, all schools, including seminaries, were withdrawn from ecclesiastical control; on the eighteenth, civil marriage was instituted; in January all state subsidies were withdrawn from the church and its institutions; and on the twenty-third, church and state were definitely separated. Among the provisions of this last decree were that the church could not own even church buildings and that no religious instruction of any sort should be allowed in schools.

This is not the place to examine the atheistic "ideology" of Marxian Communism or to trace the history of the persecution in Russia, the biggest, most remorseless, and most thorough persecution in the whole history of Christianity.[16] It must suffice to

---

[16] It is directed against other religions, but Russia was overwhelmingly Christian, and against others besides the Orthodox, but Russia was overwhelmingly Orthodox; most of the Catholics are of foreign extraction and live in the western and southwestern provinces. The best known of the Catholic victims who were deliberately put to death was Mgr. Budkiewicz, shot in 1923.

say that genuine Communism is a religion, a "religion of godlessness," and that both in theory and practice it aims at the extirpation of all spiritual religions and the destruction in people's minds of all supernatural truths, motives, and values.[17] The decree of January 23, 1918, and subsequent legislation had a veneer of tolerance and equity ("Every citizen may profess any religion or no religion; every loss of legal rights involved in the confession of any faith or of no faith is abolished," said article 3, and so on), for the Russians were a religious people and the new regime could not afford to go too far at first; but the professions of "religious tolerance" were offset from the start by a campaign of open and direct atheist and materialist propaganda which is begun in the schools and carried into every department of life, and by equating religious activity with counter-revolutionary activity: this at once opened the way to direct and violent proceedings against individual Christians as "plotting against the people."

This, of course, is a very old dodge; but such a charge has not always in history been dishonest and malicious. In the penal times in England, for example, there were some Catholics who fomented armed rebellion and conspired against the life of the sovereign and the ministers of state. Just so in Russia there were some people who used religion as a political weapon against the revolution, and others who used un-Christian methods to defend their religion or their property or both. But the soviet power went far beyond restraint of these, and there was bitter oppression of the innocent. As Lenin himself said, Marxist objection to religion is not primarily on account of the iniquities and shortcomings of professing Christians (and others), but that the premises on which the whole edifice of religion is built are no more than images and reflections of human ideas.

---

[17] This is essential to Communism and is not, as some hold, a temporary policy or passing phase: Communism is a great deal more than a perverse economic and social scheme carried to its logical conclusion. Its advance can be successfully met neither by the anti-propaganda of those whose material interests it threatens, nor by the denunciations of outraged traditionalists, nor by a Christianity adapted to *bourgeois* requirements and prejudices.

At least 28 bishops and 1400 priests were put to death between 1917 and 1923,[18] many of them in circumstances of the most revolting barbarity; so late as 1932 the bishop of Archangel, Antony, died in prison of harsh treatment and neglected dysentery. Thousands of clergy and lay people who distinguished themselves by religious activity were put in prison and the labour camps of the islands of Solovky, the Urals, and Siberia, or to forced labour in various industrial undertakings, wherein a third of the prisoners died every year from ill usage, privation, and disease. All private and many public churches were closed and turned into clubs, anti-religious museums, cinemas, and dance halls, or else destroyed, the holy images and sacred vessels and vestments being profaned and burnt or sold; in the cities, especially, shrines were closed and demolished, and eikons and relics that had been venerated for centuries were thrown onto public bonfires.

Special measures were taken against the monasteries, those ancient strongholds of the people's religion. Even before the decree of January 23, 1918, the great Alexander-Nevsky Laura in Petrograd had been forcibly secularized and the deeply venerated chapel of the Saviour desecrated, but that decree made no specific reference to monastic houses. However, it was explained that they were in the hands of the local soviets, with the result that by 1922 practically all the monasteries of men and women, over 650 of them, had been closed and their communities scattered. Some of the buildings, such as the Troitsky-Sergievskaya Laura, were turned into museums, others into prisons, sanatoriums, asylums, schools, technical institutes, others were pulled down. And the campaign was carried on with great skill. In 1922, for example, churchmen were maneuvered into appearing to make a stand, not on some high spiritual issue, but on the confiscation of ecclesiastical *property*. And boundless

---

[18] Accurate figures are impossible to obtain. A refugee bishop in 1926 gave 2691 secular priests, 1962 monks, 3447 lower clergy and nuns. Official soviet statistics for 29 (out of 87) provinces up to 1926 record the sequestration of 1030 Orthodox churches, 29 others and 29 mosques. Practically all of them were turned over to secular uses.

harm was done by the cleverly equivocal use of the term The Church: making it designate ecclesiastical authorities only, or some group or section, or even a single individual, cleric or layman, whom it might be convenient to represent as typifying the certain mind of the whole church as such.

Though anti-religious propaganda of the most ingenious and effective kind never relaxed and the various organizations of militant atheists continued to increase their membership and activity, the work going on on a huge scale, there was a considerable slackening of direct persecution from the years 1924 to 1928.

With the inauguration of the first Five-Year Plan, whose anti-religious side was in the hands of the League of Militant Atheists, a fresh campaign was begun to commandeer bells, shut churches, and drive out their priests: religious people were now identified with the *kulaks,* prosperous peasants who resisted the collectivising of their farms. By the end of 1929 public opinion from all parts of the world abroad was making itself heard in the U.S.S.R., and on February 2, 1930, Pope Pius XI published a vigorous protest against the persecution in the form of a letter to the vicar-general of Rome, Cardinal Pompili.[19] This world-wide indignation coming on top of the critical economic state of the country and the general discontent, the Soviet government thought it prudent to relax pressure somewhat and to discountenance "the collectivizing of farms by means of the seizure of church bells." But the attempt to exterminate religion by education, propaganda, and civil disabilities continued, and the Council of People's Commissars announced a Godless Five-Year Plan whose professed object was "not to leave a single house of prayer in the territory of the U.S.S.R., and to root the very idea of God out of the minds of the people." The biggest propaganda effort of all was undertaken, but a report on the progress of the plan in 1932, while its statistics were imposing, showed

---

[19] For an account of the activities of the Holy See on behalf of the persecuted Russians up to 1926 see *"Silence" de Rome,* by the Abbé Charles Quénet (Paris, 1926); see also d'Herbigny, *L'Aide Pontificale aux enfants affamés de Russie* (Rome, 1925).

that its sponsors had expected even bigger results. Then came the new constitution in 1936, which re-affirmed "freedom for the conduct of religious worship" but left untouched the law of 1929 which specifically forbade any other religious activity, charitable, recreational, cultural, or, especially, educational. Ministers of religion as such were no longer to be subject to civil disabilities, so long as they were, in Stalin's words, "not hostile to the soviet power."

But with the electoral campaign of 1937 persecution again became intense. Over twenty prelates were arrested on charges of espionage, sabotage, terrorism and "fascism" generally. Clergy in Moscow were forbidden to visit the sick in hospitals; numerous churches were closed for non-payment of taxes; there was a "purge" of the antireligious propagandist organizations. The Metropolitan Stephen in Bulgaria protested publicly against the indifference of western Europe and America to what was going on.

The *sobor* of 1917 did not give complete control of the church to the patriarch but vested it in a holy synod of twelve bishops and an assembly of fifteen clerics and laymen; however, the circumstances of the persecution prevented these from functioning properly, and put a terrible weight of responsibility onto the patriarch Tikhon. He showed himself a fearless and firm opponent of the bolshevists and had great influence among the people, and on May 5, 1922, he was imprisoned in a monastery[20] This was the signal for the great post-revolution schism in the Russian Church, which was occasioned by the confiscation of chalices, eikon covers, etc. (under the pretext of relief for the victims of the famine of 1921–22),[21] but which had been prepared and staged by the government, relying on a number of

[20] Pius XI had just been elected pope and was very active on behalf of the persecuted Russians at the conference of Genoa (where England, represented by Mr. Lloyd George, successfully opposed any "interference" in the religious affairs of Russia); the pope officially asked the Russian delegation to release Tikhon, and was informed that he was not imprisoned.

[21] Pope Pius XI offered to ransom the vessels required for the Liturgy in favor of the famine sufferers; the Soviet government ignored the offer.

capable "Christian communist" members of the clergy. Two of these priests, Vvedensky and Bielkov, visited Tikhon in prison and obtained a commission from him to Agathangel, metropolitan of Yaroslavl, to administer the church during the patriarch's imprisonment. They then falsely announced that Tikhon had resigned his see, and formed a "Higher Church Administration" which they put forward as the supreme authority of the Russian Church; when Agathangel refused to recognize and join it he was exiled to Siberia. The metropolitan of Petrograd, Benjamin, then excommunicated Vvedensky: whereupon the Higher Church Administration deposed all bishops and priests who refused to recognize its authority and they were then at once arrested by the Guepeu.[22] Benjamin and three others were shot, and practically all the bishops faithful to the patriarch were exiled. Terrorized and deprived of their pastors, very large numbers of the clergy and laity recognized the Higher Church Administration, which undertook a programme both of healthy reforms and of liturgical and canonical innovations, all of which had a revolutionary rather than an ecclesiastical motive. But the movement was not unified: the leaders of the H.C.A. had each his own group, Krasnitsky the "Living Church," Granovsky the "Union of Church Rebirth," Vvedensky the "Union of the Old Apostolic Church," etc., all together generally being known as the *Living Church.* In May, 1923, this movement held a council at which it declared itself to be a proletarian revolutionary body, and a governing synod was appointed. It professed to abolish the patriarchate and gave to itself the name of the *Church of the Renewal,* declaring all subsidiary groups to be dissolved.[23]

---

[22] The "State Political Department," the name given in 1922 to the Tche-ka, the commission for the suppression of counter-revolution, now the NKVD.

[23] The "Reborn Church" of Bishop Antonin Granovsky (d. 1927) was already in schism from schism. It has now disappeared. There was also for some years the Autocephalous Ukrainian Church, led by the archpriest Basil Lipkovsky. It was known as the "self-consecrated," because it had no bishops. This body dissolved itself in 1930, a measure probably forced by the Guepeu, for its members were more than suspect of counter-revolutionary sentiments and alliance with "Polish fascism."

But in the following month the Renewed Church received an unexpected check. The patriarch Tikhon, under we know not what pressure, admitted offences against the Soviet government at the revolution and promised loyalty to the new regime, especially in relation to monarchist movements inside and outside Russia (this was aimed particularly at the Synod of Karlovtsy; see p. 83).[24] He was set at liberty (under surveillance) to live in the Donskoy monastery at Moscow and to discharge his office so far as he was able. Less than two years later he died, and at his funeral there was a tremendous popular demonstration of love and veneration; his tomb is regarded as a holy shrine. In that same year the Renewed Church began to decline in favour of the Patriarchal Church, whose faithful had been more than ever "in the catacombs" since the imprisonment of Tikhon. From his prison he had condemned the proceedings of the Renewed council in 1923, and his own release and holy death brought many clergy and lay folk back to his jurisdiction. The leader of the Renewed Church, Vvedensky, now a bishop (and married), had asked for the recognition of the other Orthodox churches but had been ignored except (as is commonly said) by Constantinople; but this alleged recognition is difficult to support from the available evidence,[25] which only points to a certain good will on the part of the Phanar toward Vvedensky and his followers.

The Renewed Church came to be called the *Synodal Church*, a name which gave a false impression that it represented the synodal church of before the restoration of the patriarchate. It soon gave up or discouraged some of its own innovations; and sporadic efforts were made to reunite with the Patriarchal Church on the basis of a recognition of the Renewed hierarchy: but the

---

[24] Tikhon's first duty was to his flock, and he was perfectly entitled to promise passive loyalty to the bolshevist government if this would enable him the better to discharge his religious duty to his church.

[25] The Phanar refused to recognize or be represented at the Renewed Church council in May, 1923, and recommended the Russian bishops not to attend it. Certain reports of the Contantinopolitan representatives at Moscow, however, were very complaisant with regard to the Vvedensky faction.

Patriarchalists had not forgotten the treachery and bloodshed in which the schism was born.[26]

On the death of Tikhon the Soviet government would not allow the assembly of a *sobor* to elect a successor, so the metropolitan of Krutitsy, Peter, was appointed "guardian of the patriarchal throne" to administer the church. He was imprisoned within a few months, and named as deputy patriarchal *locum tenens* the metropolitan of Nizhni-Novgorod, Sergius Starogrodsky. After a brief term of imprisonment Sergius in 1927, also no doubt under pressure, came to terms with the soviet power; he declared that there was no religious persecution in Russia, called on the faithful, whether at home or abroad, to cease working against the bolshevist regime, and threatened with deprivation those bishops who would not formally recognize the Moscow government. This action naturally aroused violent opposition against him both at home and in the emigration, but so far as the U.S.S.R. was concerned this died down, and for ten years Sergius was to a considerable extent free to devote himself to the reorganization of his church. To assist him he established a new patriarchal synod of bishops, which was duly "recognized" by the Soviet government.

After the release from imprisonment of the patriarch Tikhon the attitude of the "official" Russian Church toward the communist government was one of passive loyalty in political and social matters and an uncompromising opposition toward the materialistic spirit of Marxism: the loyalty of Tikhon and Sergius was quite different from the servility of the leaders of the Renewed church. But the church continued in the catacombs; many of its bishops, priests, and leading lay people remained in detention, and even the recognized synod was dissolved. A German journalist who was received by Metropolitan Sergius in October,

---

[26] When Mgr. d'Herbigny, S.J., was in Russia in 1925 he was unfortunately not able to interview any representatives of the Patriarchal Church; his account of the disagreement between the two parties given in *L'Aspect religieux de Moscou en Octobre, 1925* (Rome, 1925), is therefore somewhat onesided.

1934, reported that he was a stricken man, incoherent in his speech, pathetically anxious to affirm the benevolence of the Soviet government.

From 1933 on that government had to lessen its severity, both to appease the peasants who were restless under collectivization and to discourage the spreading religious influence of the sects: in particular, violent and public anti-religious methods were discouraged and discarded. But the more pestilent and dangerous corruption of minds, especially of children, still went on, together with relentless social and economic pressure: the church was tolerated, in the hope that it would "die a natural death."

On September 4, 1943, Metropolitan Sergius informed the chairman of the Council of People's Commissars, Joseph Stalin, that it was the wish of the Russian bishops once more to elect a patriarch and form a holy synod. Stalin replied that the government had no objection. And shortly after Sergius himself was duly elected patriarch of Moscow.

At the time a somewhat disproportionate importance was given to this event. It was from one point of view little more than the confirmation of a situation already recognized in 1927. But it had real importance in marking a stage in a new state of affairs that had arisen with the invasion of Russia by the Germans in 1941. Involved in a life-and-death struggle, the Soviet government had necessarily to put its anti-religious activities into "cold storage" – it could not afford a gratuitous cause of disaffection to a large body of its subjects. On the other hand, the leaders of the Russian Church have a tradition of patriotic activity in national defence; Sergius and his fellow bishops were not unmindful of Sergius of Radonezh, Alexander Nevsky, the patriarch Germogen, and the rest, and once again they rallied their people to their country's cause. Not for a moment must it be supposed that this attitude was not genuine and sincere. But some of the episcopal expressions of patriotism and loyalty were nauseating in their stridency and their flattery of the government, and expressed a hatred of the enemy but little fitting in the mouths and hearts of Christians. And the government in its turn became very polite to the church, and gave full recognition and publicity to the part it was playing in the "war effort."

But only six months after his election to the patriarchal office, on May 15, 1944, Sergius Starogrodsky died, after guiding his church through seventeen terrible years. The bishops unanimously elected to succeed him Alexis Simansky, who had been metropolitan of Leningrad since 1933.

The election of the patriarch Sergius and his successor were accepted by most of the Orthodox churches and groups that were free to do so. But some alleged the elections were simply political "moves," and invalid at canon law. Outstanding among these were the members of the Synod of Karlovtsy (see p. 83); they were at the time in German-occupied territory, but certainly would have refused to recognize the new patriarch in any case.

This development has been widely used as an argument for the view that the existing soviet regime is not inconsistent with Christianity; and many people, Christians and others, have accepted it as good evidence that the godless element in Marxism is definitely and permanently on the way out. It must therefore again be emphasized that atheism and a materialist philosophy are not accidental and temporary in Marxism: they are fundamental and essential. Unless and until the leaders of Communism go back on their origins and recast entirely the philosophy that underlies their policies, atheism will continue to be, as it were, the established religion of the U.S.S.R., implicitly if not explicitly.

In going so far as it has done in recent years, the Soviet government may be taking the risk of an undesirable (from its point of view) revival of Christianity. Or it may be that, in the tsarist manner, it is trusting in a subservient higher clergy. Or it is possible that it reckons there is no risk – that the Christians of Russia are incapable of seriously challenging the soviet setup at the points where Christianity and Communism disagree.

In any case, open persecution and discrimination are not the only, or the most subtle, ways in which Caesar tries to lay hands on or control the things of God. Christians can be lulled by flattery, fine words and favours from governments, not merely into a false sense of security and well-being, but actually into selling-out to Caesar, unconsciously and bit by bit.

That this view of the Russian situation is not unduly pessimistic is suggested by the following passage from an address given by Father William Fries, S.J., over the Vatican radio early in 1945: "There has been a change in the attitude of the Russian Church towards the bolshevik government. The negative passivity emphasized during the patriarch Tikhon's time has been replaced by collaboration. There had been hope that instead there would have evolved a relationship of peaceful separation based on complete religious freedom, such as we find in the United States of America. The history of the tsarist period shows what dangers lie in too close an association between church and state."[27]

There is no good reason for believing that the attitude of the Soviet government to religion is altering fundamentally; there is every reason to believe that, finding religion more difficult to eradicate than was supposed, that government is pursuing a present policy of secularizing the church and making it harmless by means of an apparent benevolence. That the present external tolerance may be succeeded by a renewal of official hostility to religion, more pronounced, clear, and actively violent, is the opinion of so well-informed and steady an observer as Paul B. Anderson, whose *People, Church and State in Modern Russia* discusses the whole problem most ably. That book clears up many difficulties and contradictions, such as the statements of Russian bishops that their church is not persecuted by the bolsheviks.[28]

---

[27] Another observer, Arthur Koestler, has remarked that the enthronement of a new patriarch "was a confession of the soviet regime's failure to create a new human creed, new ethical values, a new faith for which to live and die." That failure is certain. But whether the soviet leaders recognize it, even to themselves, is open to question.

[28] Speaking in Canada in 1943 the Metropolitan Benjamin, representative of the Russian patriarch in America, did not deny that the Russian government's policies constituted persecution; but he said, "Did not the Master tell us to take up the cross and that we are to be persecuted for His name's sake? If we are persecuted in Russia, don't feel sorry for us, for persecution

The fundamental relevant passage in the U.S.S.R. constitution is article 124: "In order to ensure to citizens freedom of conscience, the church in the U.S.S.R. is separated from the state, and the school from the church. Freedom of religious worship and freedom of anti-religious propaganda is recognized for all citizens." And what this means in practice can be summed up thus: there is in Russia legally freedom of religious profession and of worship; baptisms, church weddings, and religious burials are permitted; parents may give their children religious instruction at home; there is freedom to live with Christ in one's heart; but, as Mr. Anderson puts it, there is "no freedom for the evangelical commission to preach the gospel to all nations, not even to the Russian people"; or, it may be added, without contrary coercion to obey God rather than man when there is a conflict of duties. But one of the weaknesses of materialism is its failure to understand Christianity. In permitting freedom to meet together for the Eucharist, the soviet authorities made (from their point of view) a huge mistake. By taking away church property and by forcing the Christians of Russia to give up certain normal activities they made them concentrate on the most fundamental thing of all – the corporate assembly for worship and sacrifice wherein the faithful meet their Lord face to face.[29]

ORGANIZATION AND PRESENT STATE IN THE U.S.S.R.

The Patriarchal Church. As has been related, the Russian Church now again has at its head His Blessedness the Patriarch of Moscow and All the Russias. His cathedral is the church of the Baptism of Christ at Moscow. Nominally he is elected by the votes of the national church assembly, which consists of all

is a Christian privilege. . . . Don't pity us or be surprised when we suffer for Christ — rather rejoice with us. . . . The experience of the Russian Church has served to deepen religion in the Soviet Union."

[29] For the text of the new Statute of the Administration of the Russian Orthodox Church, see *Eastern Churches Quarterly*, Vol. VI, No. 6, p. 320. And for particulars of further modifications of the regulations in U.S.S.R., see *Irenikon*, Vol. XIX, No. 1, pages 73–87, especially page 78.

the bishops and numerous representatives of the lower clergy, but that this body has complete freedom of election is more than doubtful.

The *Holy Synod* was re-established at the same time as Stalin gave permission for the election of a patriarch in 1943. It consists of a council of some forty-five bishops, represented in permanent session by the patriarch and the metropolitans of Kiev, Leningrad, and Krutitsy in Moscow and three associate bishops elsewhere. The assent of the civil power must be obtained before convoking a general synod or a regional council.

The proceedings of the synod come under the supervision of the lay Commission on Religions, set up by the government some time ago, one division of which is concerned with the Orthodox Church and the other with non-Orthodox bodies.

It appears that all *bishops* are now appointed by the patriarch personally, in consultation with the pertinent government officials – all part of the process of giving the church material help in return for its support of and dependence on the soviet regime.

In 1928 and 1934 the Patriarchal Church was reorganized in conformity with the new civil districts of the U.S.S.R. According to this there is a bishop in the capital city of each province who, as well as ruling his own diocese, has a certain surveillance over the other dioceses within the province – he is, in effect, a metropolitan with suffragans. The twenty-two provinces are (capital cities in parentheses): Moscow, Leningrad, White Russia (Minsk), The West (Smolensk), Central (Voronezh), Azov (Rostov), North Caucasus (Piatigorsk), The North (Archangel), Ivanovo, Gorky, Tartar Republic (Kazan), Middle Volga (Kuybyshev), Saratov, Stalingrad, Sverdlovsk, Cheliabinsk, Western Siberia (Novosibirsk), Eastern Siberia (Irkutsk), Far East (Khabarovsk), Kiev, Kharkov, and Odessa: sixty-five dioceses in all, about the same number as before 1917; but another twenty-five are said to be projected. (See also *New Territories*, p. 78.)

The Living or Synodal Church. This party, governed by a synod of bishops, priests, and laymen, had an imposing organization far beyond its needs, for after 1927 it definitely declined, especially among the Great Russians. The innovations of married bishops, remarried widower priests, the Gregorian kalendar, the use of Russian for parts of the Liturgy, etc., were less emphasized, and revolutionary politics and dislike for the memory of the patriarch Tikhon came principally to distinguish the Living Church from the Patriarchal. Its remaining adherents have now been reabsorbed into the Moscow patriarchate.

The Patriarchal Church was extremely intransigent toward the synodalists, treating them rather as the *raskolniky* were treated in tsarist days, while the government was contemptuous but tolerant in their regard after Mgr. Sergius's recognition of the soviet regime made them superfluous to communist policy: nevertheless it is a serious exaggeration to suppose the Living clergy in general to have been bolshevist agents and potential apostates, in spite of the number of renunciations of holy orders that took place among them.

Clergy. Christian ministers were at first treated simply as enemies of society. Till 1936 they belonged to the class of *lishentsy;* that is, in effect, outlaws with no civil rights – neither the right to work nor to shelter nor to medical services, for factories and houses and hospitals are all state services. And their children were in a like position until they repudiated their father. They could be seen wandering half-clothed about the streets of the cities, begging for alms at the cemeteries and the doors of churches: "Brother, help me, in the name of Christ!" Words fail to express the spirit of these men, mostly simple and unlettered, who refused to purchase some degree of material security at the price of a denial of their sacred calling.

The new "Stalin" constitution of 1936 restored to the clergy the civil rights they were deprived of, including the electoral right. As Yaroslavsky, head of the Union of Militant Atheists, explained, this was done because the government considered ministers of religion a negligible group. Since then, an outstanding thing about many of the clergy has been their quiet social activity. Many of them have to earn their livings in ordinary trades and occupations, which gives them excellent opportunities unobtrusively to take an active part in social and economic life, and to win the confidence and trust of their fellows. And ever since the revolution there has been the phenomenon of the wandering priest, going from place to place with a pack on his back, christening, confirming, marrying, absolving, celebrating the mysteries where and when required.

There was, of course, no such thing as a seminary or ecclesiastical college; any training for the priesthood had to be given privately by individual priests, though it is said that the government allowed modest pastoral courses to be organized here and there. But after the patriarchal election in 1943 license was issued to re-establish the theological academy of Moscow. Here a thorough course of studies is being laid down, to extend over three years. Furthermore it is planned to establish a number of pastoral schools, on a metropolitan or diocesan basis, with two-year courses. No students will be accepted under eighteen years of age, and as many as possible will take both courses.

Monasticism. As has been said already, practically all the monasteries and convents in U.S.S.R. were "liquidated" by 1923, and the veritable Russian monasticism survived only at such places as Valaam in Finland and Pochaev in Poland. For a time certain pilgrimage centres were kept on to be exploited by the local soviet (the Sarov monastery, for example, was not closed till April, 1927), and religious were occasionally heard of that still tried to keep up some sort of community life as "labour groups," e.g., eighteen monks of the former monastery at Kitaevo, a number of nuns near Koselschina, thirty-five monks at the monastery of Makarjevsky, not far from Gorky, some aged monks in the Pecherskoy at Kiev, and a good many "active" nuns in that city.

But the scattering of thousands of monks and nuns throughout the land has meant that monasticism energizes and is an influence in the parishes – many of the religious in effect became missioners, and it is noticeable in how many police reports ex-monks and nuns were accused of religious "agitation." Moreover, many of them are now necessarily engaged in secular callings, and Mr. Artemiev and others declare that hidden monasticism exists, especially among the *intelligentsia,* that doctors in hospitals, for example, are secretly professed. *Vozrozhdenie* for April 12, 1931, reported a hospital in central Asia whose chief medical officer was a bishop and a meteorologist who was a hieromonk and conducted classes for religious studies.

But over and above such illegal survivals, regular monasteries have now been legalized again, and among those reopened are those of the Caves at Kiev, St. Alexander Nevsky's at Leningrad, and the Holy Trinity near Moscow. The last named is the seat of the revived theological academy.

The sects. Since the revolution there has been an intensification of the activities of the dissenters from the official Russian Church, less among the Old Believers and their associates than among the pseudo-mystical and Protestant sects (see p. 54). This is partly due to the fact that the government, ready to do anything that tended to break up Orthodoxy, treated dissenters with less severity than they experienced in the days of the tsars, and also because an epoch of terror and confusion always produces an insurgence of individualistic and uncontrolled fervour among people of a mystical and messianic temperament.

Not only has the religious madness of the Khlysty and others, which had been little in evidence since the days of the stern rule of Nicholas I (1825–1855), had a revival, but such Protestant bodies as the Baptists have become of more significance in Russia (especially among the poor in the towns) than they ever were before; and there are numerous more or less secret groups of people, often young people, at work on behalf of some or other religious idea, often an obscure or wild idea and at variance with traditional Orthodoxy. The head of the episcopal Old Believers had his seat outside Russia, at Belaya-Krinica in the Bukovina. This is now within the U.S.S.R., and efforts are being made to reconcile these Old Believers (who are said still to number nearly three million) with the patriarchate. Their Rogoshsky monastery in Moscow has been reopened.

General Observations. What is really the condition of the

Orthodox Church in Russia today? It is almost impossible to say for lack of sufficient evidence. The U.S.S.R. is a huge territory, and even were its religious state adequately surveyed the bias, either way, of the observers might make the results misleading. Official reports of the Soviet government itself tend to cancel themselves out: according as their object is to show the feebleness of religion or to stir up the godless propagandists to further efforts so they can be quoted against or in favour of religious vitality. Thus, the atheist paper *Bezbozhnik* (August 25, 1931) gives as an average case the town and district of Kremenchug in the Ukraine: here in one year the number of professing Orthodox of various obediences fell from 15,781 to 9410, of Old Believers from 3139 to 73, of other dissenters from 361 to 109, of Jews from 1690 to 831; Catholics and Lutherans had ceased to exist as organized bodies.[30] Of the professing Christians 41 per cent were over 50 years of age, 38 per cent between 30 and 50, 21 per cent under 30. On the other hand, Yaroslavsky, leader of the League of Militant Atheists, complained in 1934 of how the circulation of *Bezbozhnik* was sabotaged in the Ukraine and of how enthusiastically the Ivanov industrial district of Moscow celebrated Christmas with religious rites, and declared that "Whenever we stop fighting religion the church raises its head again." The new city of Magnitogorsk in the Urals had no church, but a voluntary collection raised 150,000 rubles to build one (the authorities confiscated the money). Four years later Yaroslavsky wrote that one third of the town dwellers were believers, and two thirds of the country folk, which would make about half the whole population professing Christians. But such statistics (even if reliable) do not get us far. What is the quality of their Christianity?

By the law of 1929, to keep a church in use twenty of the faithful must form an "ecclesiastical soviet"; they are responsible to the state for the building and its contents, for the heavy taxes and insurance premiums on it, and for any special expenses

[30] The Orthodox clergy put their church premises at the disposal of the few remaining Catholics.

(e.g., for repairs), all payable to the local soviet; they are, moreover, marked men, specially liable to arrest and deportation.[31] Therefore the existence of a parish, it has been pointed out, proves that there are twenty heroes living in it, "twenty who are ready for slow martyrdom and to lose all for their faith. Thirty-three thousand 'parishes' [the figure given in 1937] means thirty-three thousand groups of twenty; that is, 660,000 men and women who are risking everything for Christ." That little flock is sufficient to save the city – but in fact there are many more sincere, wholehearted and heroic Christians than that. That they are all old, and mostly women, is not true: they are of all ages, the biggest deficiency being of younger men. Outstanding in their religion is its material poverty – nothing could be more different from the gorgeously vested priest or the symbolic pot-bellied layman, represented by antireligious cartoonists with guns and bags of coins holding out their hands to the exploiting capitalist or the tsarist regime. And with this goes spiritual richness, the wealth that is derived from being driven back to the fundamentals of the Christian religion, without "frills" and without adventitious aids from the state or society or anywhere else; wealth that is the more valued for its costliness in suffering and suspicion endured and self-reliance and self-restraint exercised.

Obviously the Orthodoxy that still lives under such conditions as I have outlined is a firm and living faith, in nothing more clearly demonstrated than in its divine worship. "The Liturgy now has a new and severe beauty; never before has it been celebrated in so solemn and spiritual a way. The secret of this new revelation of religious beauty is first of all in the celebrating priest, but it takes hold of the worshippers, giving depth and meaning to every word of the reader, to every exclamation of the deacon. Even in the smallest churches the singing is lovely. The people are loath to leave the temple. . . . For many the

[31] The ecclesiastical soviet (many of the members are women) appoints the parish priest, and can rarely be controlled by the bishop or priest, who depend for their authority almost entirely on their personal character. In any case, perhaps as few as one "parish" in six has got a priest or a church.

Eucharist has again become a true mystery: the Chalice is seldom offered in vain — many receive communion, and all share in their joy" (G. P. Fedotov).

But from any human point of view the situation is desperate; even after allowing for official exaggeration and nominal membership the numbers enrolled in the various atheist organizations are terrifying and there is growing up a generation that has been taught from its earliest years that there is no God, that those who affirm Him are enemies of the people, that religion is dope to keep them down.[32]

NEW TERRITORIES

After 1939 the U.S.S.R. annexed or reoccupied a number of territories which include Orthodox populations. Such were as follows, going from north to south.

Estonia. When Estonia became an independent republic after World War I it had a population of about 1¼ million, predominantly Lutheran. The Orthodox minority numbered 300,000, of whom two thirds were Estonian and the rest Russian, including 10,000 Old Believers. After Estonia separated from Russia in 1918 fruitless application was made to the patriarch of Moscow to recognize the autonomy of these Orthodox. Recourse was then had to Constantinople, and the Oecumenical Patriarch granted a *tomos* of autonomy at the same time and in the same terms as to the Orthodox of Finland (1923). Estonian was to be the liturgical language of all who spoke that tongue, and the Gregorian kalendar was adopted even for the date of Easter.

The primate was the Metropolitan of Tallinn and All Estonia, who lived at Tallinn (Reval) and had all the Estonian Orthodox in his charge; the suffragan bishop of Narva was responsible for all the Russians. The University of Tartu (Dorpat) had a faculty of Orthodox theology; and there was a seminary at Petseri, an important Russian monastery with about thirty monks, under

[32] The importation of Bibles into U.S.S.R. in the Russian, Polish, Ukrainian, and Yiddish languages is forbidden. In any other language a tax of 6 rubles (nominally 5 shillings) must be paid on *each copy;* the tax is the same for all other religious books.

an abbot in episcopal orders. There was also a large Russian nunnery at Kuremäe (Piuhtitsy), with small daughter houses at Tallinn and Narva.

As elsewhere, there were considerable difficulties between the Russian and national elements, which are temperamentally very diverse; and some Estonian clergy put forward reunion with the Holy See as the solution of their troubles and repeatedly expressed an inclination to it. Unfortunately the Catholic Church was little known in the country, and its few representatives were nearly all foreigners. In the minds of many, too, Catholicity was identified with historical memories of gross religious persecution and aggression suffered at the hands of the Teutonic Knights.

When Russian troops occupied Estonia in 1940 and the country was annexed to the U.S.S.R., the aged Metropolitan Alexander renounced the autonomy of his church, and brought the faithful once more into the jurisdiction of Moscow.

Latvia, or *Lettonia.* The prewar population of Latvia was two million, of whom something over a half were Protestants and something under a quarter Catholics of the Latin rite. The majority of the 150,000 Orthodox were Russians; 50,000 or more of them were Letts and 13,000 of other nationalities, including some Germans. There were said to be another 90,000 Russians who were Old Believers and other sectaries. The Russians lived mostly in the province of Lettgallen.

After the country had finally gained its independence there was the usual (in the Baltic states) conflict between the Russians and the local Orthodox. The troubles went on for fifteen years, and saw the murder of Archbishop John Pommers, in circumstances which have not been made fully clear. This left the faithful without a bishop, and the Letts turned for help to the Oecumenical Patriarch. His representative reported that among the seventy-five priests of Latvia there was only one who was qualified by not having a wife to receive episcopal ordination: this was a widower, Father Augustine Peterson. The holy synod of Constantinople agreed to take the Latvian church under its wing and approved the election of Father Augustine, who was accordingly consecrated in 1936 by three Greek hierarchs as Archbishop of Riga and All Latvia. Later there were suffragan bishops at Iersek and Elgav (Mitau). The resolution of these difficulties by Contantinople was displeasing to the Russian patriarchate, but other Orthodox opinion seemed to be that it was a welcome (because harmless) reinforcement of the prestige of the Oecumenical Patriarch.

When Russia reoccupied Latvia in 1940 the short independent life of this small church came to an end; it is now a part of the patriarchate of Moscow.

Lithuania. Three quarters of the 2½ million people in Lithuania are Catholics of the Latin rite. Among the minorities are 55,000 officially registered as Orthodox, half of them Old Believers; they are nearly all Russians or of Russian descent.

After the Phanar had taken the new autocephalous church of Poland under its protection in 1924, a number of Russian clergy left that country in protest, and among them Eleutherius Bogojavlensky, formerly archbishop of Vilna. He retired to Lithuania, part of which had been in his diocese; and he was appointed by the deputy *locum tenens* of the Russian patriarchal throne, Sergius, to be "Metropolitan of All Lithuania and Vilna" as an autonomous eparchy, with his residence at Kaunas (Kovno).

Eleutherius was a zealous supporter of the canonical jurisdiction of the Patriarchal church in Russia; and so, when in 1930 the Metropolitan Sergius endeavoured to remove Bishop Eulogius in Paris from control of the Russian emigrants of the patriarchal obedience, he made Eleutherius his administrator for the churches of western Europe. When, therefore, Lithuania was incorporated in the U.S.S.R. in 1940, there was no difficulty about the local Orthodox being restored to the direct Moscow jurisdiction.

Between the wars of 1914 and 1939 these three independent Baltic states were pleasant and prosperous little countries, showing great promise for a happy future. Now, though having the status of separate soviet socialist republics, they have been swallowed up in the vast organization of the U.S.S.R.; and to that extent at the very least the people have lost their independence and freedom. The fate of their Orthodox churches is analogous. Those of Estonia and Latvia had troubles and difficulties as independent organizations; but they were in close touch with one another, working together, planning with the Church of Finland a common Baltic seminary: their future was promising. Now they have again become part of the vast Russian Church, not in the traditional way of locally independent churches under a common patriarchal jurisdiction, but as it were as suffragan sees of a colossal unified metropolitan province tightly in the grip of the soviet civil power.

The Western Lands. This name is given in Russian history to that territory from Vilna to the Carpathian mountains that, after World War I, became the eastern part of restored Poland. Its population was made up, roughly, of 3½ million Catholics of the Slav-Byzantine rite, 3 million of the Latin rite, and 3¾ million Orthodox. The last-named lived mostly in the central and northern parts of the area (Volhynia, Polesia, etc.), and were made up of 1½ million Ukrainians, 1½ million Byelorussians (White Russians), half a million Poles, and 125,000 Great Russians (44,000 of whom were Old Believers).

In 1924–1925 these Orthodox became an autocephalous church, with its chief see at Warsaw (see pages 142–145). But after World War II all of them, except a small minority, came under Russian rule, and so are now again part of the patriarchate of Moscow. For what is happening to the Eastern Catholics in this area, see Volume I of this work, page 75 *et seq.*

Bessarabia. Bessarabia has three million inhabitants and the northern Bukovina about half a million. Those of Bessarabia are very mixed, including many Rumanians and Ukrainians and some Russians; those of Bukovina are mostly Ukrainians; and in both territories the prevailing religion is Orthodoxy. From 1925 to 1940 the faithful formed part of the new Rumanian patriarchate, and included such important ecclesiastical centres as the metropolitan sees of Chisinau (Kishinev) and Cernauti (Czernovitz).

In 1940 these territories were annexed by the U.S.S.R., and accordingly are now regarded as within the jurisdiction of the patriarch of Moscow.

Podkarpatska Rus. This territory (sometimes called Ruthenia or the Carpathian Ukraine) is situated at the eastern end of Slovakia, and is inhabited by a people of Ukrainian and Byelorussian origin who are Catholics of the Byzantine rite. There used to be only a small minority of dissident Orthodox among them, but in 1920–1923 they were considerably reinforced by a serious schism from the Catholics (see Vol. I, pp. 88, 89).

After the troops of the U.S.S.R. occupied this area, the bishop of the Orthodox in 1944 petitioned Moscow for his diocese to be taken into the jurisdiction of the Russian Church (it had hitherto been dependent on the Serbian patriarch). This action was undoubtedly part of the complicated process which led to the declaration that, at the request of the alleged leaders of its people, the Podkarpatska Rus had been admitted to membership in the U.S.S.R. The territory was formally ceded by the Czechoslovak government to the U.S.S.R. in 1945.

In consequence, the Podcarpathian Orthodox are now part of the Russian Church. For the policy of the soviet authorities in respect to the Catholics of Slav-Byzantine rite in the Western Lands, and the Podkarpatska Rus, *vis-à-vis* the Orthodox Church of Russia, reference may be made to Volume I, page 89.

THE EMIGRANTS

At the end of World War I a very large number of Russians found themselves outside the new political frontiers of their country, notably the hundreds of thousands of refugees who had left Russia after the defeat of the "white" armies of Denikin, Wrangel, and Koltchak. These included a considerable body of clergy, and in 1920 over twenty prelates met at Constantinople and decided to form an autonomous church of these refugees, with the intention of establishing canonical relations with the patriarch Tikhon when that should be possible. A holy synod was constituted, under the presidency of Antony Khrapovitsky,

SERBIAN MONASTERY OF KRUSHEDOL

CHURCH AT GRACHANITSA, SERBIA

MIRON CRISTEA, FIRST PATRIARCH

RUMANIAN COUNTRY CHURCH

Courtesy, Edward Bowron

ST. JOHN'S CATHEDRAL, NIKOSIA, CYPRUS

Courtesy, C. S. Cosby Oakes

GREEK MONASTERY OF DAPHNE

Courtesy, C. S. Cosby Oakes

CHURCH OF PAROS, GREECE

MONASTERY OF PENTELIS,
NEAR ATHENS

the exiled metropolitan of Kiev, and at the initiative of Serbia its headquarters was fixed at Sremsky Karlovtsy (Karlovitz).

By no means all the emigrants were prepared to accept the jurisdiction of this synod, and it was soon involved in trouble with the patriarch Tikhon. In 1921 the synod passed a resolution in favour of the restoration of the Romanov dynasty in Russia (which it declared to be an ecclesiastical and moral question), and for this reason Tikhon, who had appointed Bishop Eulogius Georgievsky to be his representative for western Europe at Paris and Bishop Platon Rojdestvensky for North America, formally condemned the Synod of Karlovtsy. The synod tried in vain to bring and keep Eulogius and Platon within its obedience, and the refugees were soon split into opposing parties, the "Antonians" and the "Eulogians"[33] (after 1922 they were also split into those who recognized the Patriarchal church and the few who recognized the Living or Renewed church as the legitimate church in Russia). The position was aggravated when, in 1927, he Synod of Karlovtsy professed to depose and excommunicate Eulogius and Platon and when, in 1928, the synod flatly refused o obey the order of Sergius, deputy patriarchal *locum tenens*, calling on all Russian bishops, whether at home or in exile, to give up political activity and formally to recognize the bolshevist government. In June of that year Sergius declared the Synod of Karlovtsy and its followers to be excluded from Orthodox communion. He confirmed the powers given by the late patriarch Tikhon to Eulogius, who had declared himself innocent of all political activity, but in 1930 Eulogius took part in an Anglican ervice of intercession for persecuted Russians held in London. ergius looked on this as a "political gesture," a criticism of the oviet's regime; he refused Eulogius's explanation, and relieved im of his office. This caused a great to-do, but Sergius conrmed the sentence against Eulogius, and directed Archbishop

[33] Most of the Russians in France, Belgium, England, Germany, Italy, zechoslovakia, Switzerland, Holland, Scandinavia, Denmark, and Rumania lhered to Eulogius. He was further opposed to Karlovtsy because in 1926 e synod had formed the Russians in Germany, part of his territory, into a parate diocese.

Eleutherius of Lithuania to take over his duties provisionally. Thereupon Eulogius, who had the support of a number of refugee bishops in his refusal to obey a command which they alleged to have been given under bolshevist pressure, invoked the help of the patriarch of Constantinople,[34] and in 1931 Photios II declared Eulogius and his followers to be under his protection and in the jurisdiction of the Oecumenical Patriarchate. This raised an even greater to-do, many Russians of all parties strongly objecting to this dragging of Constantinople into their affairs: both Sergius and the Synod of Karlovtsy solemnly protested to the Phanar. There were, then, at this time three ecclesiastical obediences among the refugees in Europe: (1) that of Eleutherius of Lithuania, who represented the Patriarchal Church and was in his turn represented at Paris by Benjamin; (2) that of Eulogius, now an exarch of the patriarch of Constantinople; and (3) the Synod of Karlovtsy, which represented no one but itself and was in 1934 again excommunicated by Sergius after he had addressed a long communication to the Yugoslav patriarch Barnabas, setting forth the uncanonical status of that assembly.

Early in 1934 Eulogius and Antony met in Germany where a private reconciliation took place between them; this did not lead to much, but it encouraged Mgr. Barnabas of Serbia to try his hand at peacemaking and putting an end to these quarrels and cross schisms. He succeeded in bringing about a meeting of Antony, Eulogius, and other bishops at Karlovtsy in October, 1935, at which it was agreed to recognize the fact that Russian emigrants were divided into four organizations, Western Europe, the Balkans, America, and the Far East; these should from time to time send representatives to a common council, and each should be represented on the Synod of Karlovtsy, which was recognized as their supreme authority. This arrangement, o

[34] The attitude of the Oecumenical Patriarch was equivocal throughout. The Phanar never recognized a supreme authority over emigrants in the Synod of Karlovtsy and never formally repudiated the Living or Renewed church within the U.S.S.R. The churches of Antioch, Jerusalem, Yugoslavia, Cyprus, Sinai, and apparently Rumania recognized the jurisdiction of Karlovtsy over Russian emigrants; Alexandria and Greece did not.

course, did not affect those emigrants who recognized the jurisdiction only of Sergius and the Patriarchal church in Russia; and it was further weakened by the refusal of Eulogius to renounce his dependence on the patriarch of Constantinople. A fresh complication was introduced when the Synod of Karlovtsy condemned as heretical the theological teaching of the late Father Sergius Bulgakov at the Paris institute, who was widely supported by the Eulogians.[35]

Antony Khrapovitsky, the distinguished leader of the Karlovtsy synod, died in 1936. He was succeeded by Anastassy, former metropolitan of Kishinev and then in charge of his countrymen at Jerusalem, where he was very greatly respected.

When during World War II Germany occupied central and western Europe, the Nazis made every effort — not without success — to exploit Russian and other Orthodox differences for political ends; and no opportunity was missed for extending the authority of Archbishop Serafim Lade, a prelate who was "in Hitler's pocket." The adherents of the Karlovtsy synod, being so strongly anti-bolshevik, were encouraged and favoured, and some of them openly supported the Nazis; those who recognized the authority of Sergius and his successor in Moscow were suspect, and accordingly were treated very harshly; while the Eulogian leaders, taking a middle way, were courted both by the Nazis and by their opponents. The events of those years inevitably brought still further confusion, dispersion, and suffering to the Russian emigrants in Europe; their present state and their ecclesiastical future are still very obscure and uncertain.

Eulogius Georgievsky died in 1946, whereupon his followers divided into those who wish to remain under the Oecumenical Patriarch of Constantinople (led by Archbishop Vladimir of Nice) and those who recognize the Russian patriarch (led by Archbishop Serafim, sent from Moscow).

The Synod of Karlovtsy and its adherents consistently hold to

---

[35] Lest we be tempted to complacency, we Catholics may remind ourselves that we too have had our Great Schism of the West in 1378–1417 — and other lesser ones.

their own line and are trying to live down the fact that many of them were politically compromised during the war. The headquarters of the synod is of course no longer in Serbia, but at Munich; here in 1946 twenty-six of its bishops met and officially refused to recognize Alexis as patriarch of Moscow, "because of his unnatural alliance with the powers of godlessness and because of the servitude of the Church in Russia."

In 1939 there were estimated to be over a million Russian refugees dispersed among twenty-seven countries, of whom the bigger bodies were in France, Germany, the Balkans, North America, and the Far East. At that time their distribution and institutions were somewhat as follows.

Western Europe. There were 400,000 Russians in France, who had twenty-five parishes in and around Paris alone, with the fine cathedral of St. Alexander Nevsky in the rue Daru and a dozen other churches. The other chief centres were Nice, Lyons, Cannes, and Marseilles. In the disputes between Metropolitan Eulogius and the Synod of Karlovtsy a majority of the French parishes adhered to Eulogius; Eleutherius of Lithuania, who was represented by a bishop in Paris, had but a very small following.

Paris was the principal intellectual centre of Russian Orthodoxy: there was an important theological college there, directed by a bishop and numbering among its professors the archpriest Bulgakov and G. P. Fedotov, and an institute of religious philosophy under N. A. Berdyaev. There was a monastery of Our Lady of the Unhoped-for Joy, at Saint-Germer-en-Fly, with an orphanage, and a *skete* ("priory") at Mourmelon-le-Grand, near Reims.[36] Several Orthodox journals of the first importance were published by the Russians in France.

All the other countries of western Europe had their Russian colonies and places of worship in small numbers; their principal centre in England is the church of St. Philip (lent by the Angli-

---

[36] A Russian nun who worked among the poor of Paris was Mother Mar[y] Skobtsova; she died in a Nazi concentration camp after substituting hersel[f] for a condemned Jewess.

cans) in London. The seat of the exarch Eulogius was in Paris, and he had episcopal vicars in Nice, Prague, and Brussels, until the last became a regular see in 1937.

The formation of the numerous Russians of Germany into a separate diocese by the Synod of Karlovtsy was one of the grievances of Metropolitan Eulogius against that body. The first bishop, who had an auxiliary at Vienna, was recognized by the Nazi government, which presented a piece of land on which to build a new cathedral. During the war, Serafim Lade became archbishop of Berlin, and claimed some sort of jurisdiction over Russian Orthodox in whatever country the Nazis overran.

In Germany, France, and other countries there were several *podvorie* (hostels), where women lived in community without vows and devoted themselves to the care of orphans and other charitable works.

The Balkans. The biggest Balkan colony of Russians was in Rumania, numbering 70,000 souls, but those of Bulgaria were more prominent, owing to the work of Damian Govorov, former archbishop of Tsaritsin. This remarkable and holy old man (he was born in 1855 and died in 1936) founded in 1920 the Brotherhood of St. Vladimir for the restoration of religion among young Russians. Two years later, with the help of this brotherhood and of the church and government of Bulgaria, he founded at Staminaka, near Plovdiv, the small monastery of St. Kirik to conduct a seminary for the training of priests to work among refugees in the Balkans and elsewhere. St. Kirik's, whose four-year course is practical, up-to-date, and in the best Orthodox tradition, was with the college at Paris the principal source of young clergy for Russian emigrant parishes in Europe.

America. (See p. 150.)

The Far East. There are about 100,000 Russians[37] in Manchuria and 50,000 in China proper, many of them living in compact groups in localities where Russians have been settled since long

---

[37] About one sixth of them are citizens of the U.S.S.R. employed in soviet establishments; they seem mostly to be neither enthusiastic bolshevists nor faithful Christians.

before the revolution; their national manner of life is therefore to a considerable extent retained. Those in China are in the ecclesiastical care of the archbishop of Peking and his episcopal vicars.

The chief Russian centre in Manchuria is at Harbin (about 75,000 souls), and it is here that the lot of the refugees was more atrocious than anywhere else in the world: the record of their sufferings is almost beyond belief in what is supposed to be a civilized era. Two archbishops, Methody Gerasimov (d. 1931) and his successor Melety Zaboruskny, were true fathers in God to these unhappy people. The last named was even able to establish in 1934, with the help of members of the Brotherhood of St. Vladimir mentioned above, a university, with faculties of theology, economics, civil engineering, electrotechnology, and medicine; the Japanese Orthodox induced their government to give financial assistance to this enterprise.[38] That government indeed helped the Orthodox Church in Manchuria, but at its own price, which, as in Japan proper, was strict supervision and control. The metropolitan of Harbin has two assistant bishops, at Hailar and Sitsichar.

There are seventy Russian churches and three monasteries in Manchuria, and the metropolitan of Harbin has a certain jurisdiction over all the episcopal vicars in the Far East (Kamchatka, Tientsin, Dutch East Indies, etc.), who have care of emigrants. The faithful in this part of the world show a tendency to reunion with the Catholic Church, and a society has been formed to oppose this "leakage" and to help the formation of an Orthodox primary school in every parish.

The monastery of Our Lady of Kazan at Harbin was established in 1924. It has a community of 60 monks, who run a printing press, workshops for several trades, pharmacy and dispensary, and a hospital. The convent of St. Vladimir has thirty nuns, who lead a very penitential life and care for orphan chil-

[38] The first professor of English was an Englishman, the archimandrite Nicholas Gibbs, formerly tutor to the grand-duke Alexis, heir of the tsar Nicholas II.

dren. It has made much progress under the saintly Abbess Rufina.

Other Russian colonies in Asia and Oceania are in Chinese Turkestan (under a bishop), in Persia (with an archimandrite in charge at Teheran), India, and Australia.

The great task of Russian Orthodoxy in the emigration is to give a solid foundation to religion among the young, menaced on the one hand by indifference and on the other by a hazy eclecticism which for want of a better descriptive term must be called Protestant. One of the biggest problems in this task is presented by the Young Men's Christian Association, a wealthy body which has given much generous and valuable help to the Russians in France, U.S.A., Manchuria, and elsewhere, and is extremely active on behalf of the young emigrants. Unfortunately the undenominationalism of the Y.M.C.A. works in such a way that it becomes in itself a Protestant principle and, whether accompanied by direct proselytism or not, tends to undermine the faith of those Orthodox whom it sets out to help. From time to time the Orthodox authorities have reluctantly moved against their benefactors: the University of St. Vladimir at Harbin, for example, was designed to remove dangers arising from attendance at Y.M.C.A. educational centers as well as at the communist polytechnic institute.

THE MISSIONS

Reference has already been made (p. 15) to the unfairness of criticism of the Orthodox Church on the ground of her deficiency in foreign missions. Only the Russian Church was free to undertake such work in later times, and with her it vegetated during the eighteenth and early nineteenth centuries. Then there came a revival. The main object of the Kazan theological academy, when it reopened in 1842, was to train missionaries for Asia, and in 1870 the Orthodox Missionary Society was established by Metropolitan Innocent Veniaminov, the greatest Russian missionary of the century. By the beginning of World War I this society had 20,000 members and a large income, not only from private subscriptions but also from government grants — for in Russia as elsewhere the civil power was glad to subsidize Christian missions for its own ends. The missionaries (again as elsewhere) were both helped and handicapped by this official interest: among the Tartars, for example, the privileges given by the government to converts led to mass conversions, and these "rice-Christians" later relapsed to Islam just as easily.

Whether the achievements of the Russian missionaries were commensurate with their heroic devotion and energy is difficult to say. It is said that before the revolution converts from Islam and heathenism within the Russian empire numbered some five thousand yearly, and that the total number of "native" Christians was over two million. Since the revolution all missionary work has been forbidden. Such work, however, cannot properly be judged by statistics, but by the quality and faithfulness of its converts, whether few or many — and these things cannot be weighed or easily known. But it may be noted that the Orthodox Tartars themselves produced many missionaries and, at the time of the bolshevik persecution, martyrs as well.

There is no doubt that the Russian missionary "technique" is of great interest, and it has received very little attention in the West. Among its methods was the ordination of "native" priests at the earliest possible moment and the use of the local vernacular language in public worship; it was found by experience, e.g., among the Tartars, that until this last was introduced no solid progress was made at all. In this matter a great modern worker was Nicholas Ilminsky (d. 1891), a layman who was a most remarkable linguist and a collaborator with the Metropolitan Innocent. In fifty years his translation committee published over 1½ million copies of religious books in twenty-two non-Russian languages.[39]

The first claim on Russian missionary effort of course came from the Mohammedans and the heathens (still numerous) in their own country: the Tartars, Finns, Kalmucks, Lapps, Kirghiz, Buryats, Yakuts, and others in the far parts of that huge land.

[39] A striking picture of Russian missionary life is given by Lyeskov's "On the Edge of the World" in *The Sentry and Other Stories* (London, 1922).

These showed varying degrees of receptiveness of Christianity; but in any case the Christians among them can be regarded as part of the Orthodox Church in Russia itself. Outside of Russia, the following was the state of the missions in 1939, at which time they recognized the Synod of Karlovtsy; since 1943 many have returned to the Moscow jurisdiction.

China. Orthodoxy in China may be said to date from the last years of the seventeenth century, when there was a company of Cossacks in the imperial guard at Peking (the "Albazinians"). A small regular mission was established in 1715. Its head was both chaplain to the Cossack guardsmen and Russian ambassador to Peking: he was therefore both a diplomatic representative and a paid Chinese civil servant. The mission did not become a purely religious undertaking till 1861.

Its evangelizing work was necessarily very slow, but it produced a number of celebrated orientalists, including the remarkable Father Hyacinth Bichurin (d. 1853) and the Archimandrite Palladius Katharsky (d. 1878), whose character was as saintly as Bichurin's was equivocal. Up to the Boxer rebellion of 1901, when four hundred Chinese Orthodox were murdered, the Russian mission was never molested; in times of trouble Catholic and other missionaries and their flocks used to receive shelter within its walls.

The number of Chinese Orthodox today is only about 5000. They are under a Russian archbishop at Peking who, since the increase of Russian emigrants, has had auxiliary bishops at Shanghai and Tientsin. There are several Chinese among the clergy and the Chinese language is used in the liturgy.

Japan. (See page 146.)

Korea. The mission of Korea, founded in 1897, is in charge of an archpriest who depends on the metropolitan of Harbin. There were nine stations and 820 faithful in 1934. Korean is used in the liturgy, and there are several Korean priests.

Persia. In 1898 a Nestorian bishop went to Petersburg and there abjured his heresy; he then returned to his own country with Russian missionaries (whom the imperial government was only too glad to subsidize as part of its peaceful penetration in the Near East) and for a time there were many Nestorian converts to Orthodoxy. The headquarters of this mission, with schools and a printing press, was at Urmia, and a bishop was appointed in 1905, when his flock was said to number 70,000. During the first Great War these Orthodox "Assyrians" suffered equally with the other Chaldeans (see p. 190) and the mission of Urmia was destroyed; some of them took refuge around Bagdad and for these, and others remaining around Urmia and Salmas, the Synod of Karlovtsy appointed a bishop in 1931. He is called bishop of Urmia but he lives at Bagdad; his flock, which can now hardly number a few thousand, seems to be gradually returning to the Nestorians or to the Catholics of the Chaldean rite.

It is worth noting, in view of charges of "latinizing" so often made by the Orthodox against Rome, that the Russian missionaries deprived the Assyrian converts of their Chaldean liturgy and substituted the Byzantine rite in Syriac.

Alaska. (See p. 150.)

Palestine. In the days of tsarist ambition in the Near East the Russian Church exercised great influence in Syria and Palestine, and by 1913 the Imperial Orthodox Palestine Society had over a hundred establishments in the patriarchates of Antioch and Jerusalem. Of these nothing remains except the pilgrims' hostels and church at Jerusalem, where there is a prelate, two small monasteries of men and two larger ones of women, and a few Russian lay people. One of the convents, at Bethany, has an English, or rather Scottish, abbess, Mother Mary Robinson. The Palestine mission still owns a lot of property in that country. Archbishop Anastassy, who was greatly respected by people of all religions in the Holy Land, came to Europe in 1932 and was succeeded by Abbot Antony Sinkevich.

NOTE ON THE ORTHODOX OF HUNGARY AND CZECHOSLOVAKIA

In 1939 the Orthodox resident in *Hungary* numbered about 150,000, more or less magyarized[40] Slavs and Rumanians. When the Serbian patriarch, about 1925, announced his intention of governing the Slav faithful in Hungary by means of a bishop at Budapest, the local clergy, prompted by the government, asked the patriarch of Constantinople to take them under his jurisdiction. The Serbian Church protested vigorously, and for long Constantinople did nothing definite, leaving the Hungarians a prey to the mischievous activities of a priest, one Stephen Nemetz, who, after getting himself consecrated bishop in Syria, was eventually excommunicated both from Constantinople and Belgrade. The position was still unsettled at the outbreak of World War II. In 1946, however, these Hungarian Orthodox were brought under the higher jurisdiction of the Moscow patriarch, who sent a Russian bishop as his exarch, with a Hungarian auxiliary to succeed him.

The formation of the preponderatingly Catholic state of *Czechoslovakia* after World War I was soon followed by a serious nationalist schism among the Latin Czechs. Most of these schismatics, under Dr. Farsky (d. 1927), formed themselves into an organization that was, to put it mildly, protestantizing in tendency, and are no further concern of ours here; the remainder declared themselves Orthodox, under a bishop, Pavlik Gorazd, provided for them by the Serbian patriarch Dimitry. There were at this time some 40,000 members of his flock.[41] An attempt was made to bring them into the jurisdiction of Constantinople, which provided a new bishop for them; but this failed, and Bishop Gorazd was confirmed in office. In 1942 he, with several of his clergy, was shot by the German invaders, on the charge

---

[40] *Magyar* (pronounced "modyar"), people and language of the Mongoloid race predominant in Hungary.

[41] The Orthodox Czechs use the Roman rite, a thing unique in Orthodoxy except for a group of similar schismatics in Poland; these last had the Roman liturgy in Polish.

(probably false) of sheltering the assassins of the notorious Heydrich. The Orthodox of Czechoslovakia too have now been transferred from the jurisdiction of the Serbian patriarch to that of Moscow. There is a bishop as patriarchal exarch at Prague, and displaced persons and others have increased the number of faithful to some 146,000.

BIBLIOGRAPHY

Berg, *Die römische-katholische Kirche und die orthodoxen Russen* (Berlin, 1926).
*Conybear, *Russian Dissenters* (London, 1921).
Danzas, *The Russian Church* (London, 1936).
*Dobbie-Bateman, *St. Seraphim of Sarov* (London, 1936).
*Poole, *Religion in Russia under the Soviets* (New York, 1924).
d'Herbigny, *Vladimir Solovyev* (London, 1918).
—— *L'âme religieuse des Russes* (Rome, 1924).
†*Life of the Archpriest Avvakum, by Himself* (London, 1924).
Palmieri, *La Chiesa russa* (Florence, 1908).
Pierling, *Rome et Moscou* (Paris, 1883).
Solovyev, *La Russie et l'Eglise Universelle* (Paris, 1889).
†Zernoy, *St. Sergius, Builder of Russia* (London, 1939).
—— *Three Russian Prophets* (London, 1944).
—— *The Russians and their Church* (London, 1946).
*Anderson, *People, Church and State in Modern Russia* (New York, 1943).
Bennigsen, *et al.*, *Religion in Russia* (London, 1940).
†Bolshakov, *The Foreign Missions of the Russian Orthodox Church* (New York, 1943).
†Gorodetska, *The Humiliated Christ in Modern Russian Thought* (New York, 1938).
Koncevicius, *Russia's Attitude Towards Rome* (Washington, 1927).
†Macarius, *Russian Letters of Direction* (London, 1944).
†Timashev, *Religion in Soviet Russia* (New York, 1943).
†Arseniev, *Holy Moscow* (New York, 1940).
Isvolsky, *Soul of Russia* (New York, 1943).
†Fedotov, *The Russian Religious Mind* (Harvard, 1946).

2. THE SERBIAN PATRIARCHATE (YUGOSLAVIA)

During the sixth and seventh centuries of our era the Serbs, a Slav people from the land between the Carpathians and the Dniester, established themselves in southern Dalmatia, Herzegovina, Serbia proper, and neighbouring parts, being encouraged especially by the Emperor Heraklios (d. 641) as a bulwark against the Avars. Missionaries were sent to them from Rome, apparently without much success, and their definitive evangelization was effected from Constantinople during the ninth century and after. The Serbs were unified into a single state between 1159 and 1195 by Stephen I Nemanya, and his son Stephen II became the first Serbian king. He established a metropolitan see for his people in 1219, to which he appointed his brother St. Sabas, who had been a monk on Mount Athos and founded the Serbian monastery of Khilandari there. Sabas organized the church of the Serbs, erecting several eparchies, and after he had been consecrated by the patriarch of Constantinople, Manuel, at Nicaea (whither Manuel had been driven by the Crusaders) wrote to Pope Honorius III asking the pope's blessing and requesting him to send a royal crown with which he might crown his brother king. This the pope duly did, and in 1221 St. Sabas crowned King Stephen therewith at the monastery at Zitcha.[42]

[42] The position of St. Sabas between the Holy See and wavering Constantinople would seem equivocal in these more sophisticated days. But he is looked on by Catholics and Orthodox alike as the spiritual founder and patron of the Serbian kingdom. The Orthodox Yugoslav professor, Arnautovich, and other scholars of both communions have shown Sabas, his brother, and their subjects to have been in communion with neighboring Latin bishops and loyal to the Supreme Pontiff. St. Sabas figures in the Bollandist *Acta Sanctorum* and in several Latin kalendars of Illyria and Dalmatia. See Attwater, *Book of Eastern Saints* (Milwaukee, 1938).

But with the disappearance of the Crusaders' domination from Constantinople contact with Rome was lost. In 1346, under the great Stephen III Dushan who raised the Serbian kingdom to the height of its power, a synod at Uskub proclaimed the church autocephalous, giving to the archbishop of Ipek the title of patriarch.[43] Stephen III repudiated the communion of Constantinople and professed obedience to the Holy See, but his actions did not bear out his profession and Serbia gradually slipped into schism.

The country became a Turkish province after the disasters of Kossovo in 1389 and Smederevo in 1459, and for a century the patriarchate of Ipek was subjected to the Greek archbishops of Okhrida; but in 1557 its independence was restored by an apostate grand-vizier, Mohammed Sokolovich,[44] and was preserved till 1766 when the Phanar obtained a *firman* from the Sultan Mustapha III bringing all eparchies under the direct control of the Oecumenical Patriarch.

From 1806 to 1829 the Serbs, first under George Petrovich (Karageorge) and then under Milosh Obrenovich, were in conflict with their Turkish overlords, and by the Treaty of Adrianople gained internal autonomy under their own prince. The organization of a national church, with its metropolitan see at Belgrade, followed, and when Serbia was recognized as a sovereign state in 1879 her church became completely autocephalous; with the exception of violent disputes about the appointment of Greek bishops over the Serbs in Macedonia, its relations with the patriarch of Constantinople were amiable.

When the kingdom of the Serbs, Croats, and Slovenes, or Yugoslavia, was formed after World War I, four small autonomous Orthodox churches were involved in the consequent changes of political and national frontiers. These were:

1. *Karlovtsy* (Karlovitz). This had its origin in 1690 and 1737,

---

[43] Though frequently referred to as patriarchates, these mediaeval independent churches of Ipek, Okhrida, and Tirnova were never regarded as being on a level or comparable with the ancient patriarchates.

[44] He had a brother who was a monk and Mohammed had him appointed patriarch.

when numerous Serbian families were invited by Emperor Leopold I and Empress Maria Teresa to take refuge from the Turks in the southern part of Hungary. They formed an autocephalous Orthodox church under the protection of the Catholic emperors, and their primate at Karlovtsy was granted the title of "patriarch" by Francis Joseph in 1848. This church in 1918 numbered over a million faithful, with six episcopal sees.

2. *Montenegro* (Czernagora). The Montenegrins are simply Serbs who have always kept their small province from Turkish domination – the only Balkan people to do so. When the patriarchate of Ipek was suppressed in 1766 they became a single autonomous diocese depending, not on Constantinople, but on the holy synod of the Russians, their supporters against the Turks.

From 1516 till 1852 their hierarch was at the same time their temporal ruler, Vladyka of Montenegro as well as Archbishop of Cetinje, the offices passing from uncle to nephew in the family of Daniel I Petrovich from 1737 until another Daniel, nephew of Peter II, married and separated the two powers.

In 1918 there were about a quarter of a million Orthodox Montenegrins, the archbishop then having two suffragan sees.

3. *Czernovitz.* As part of the administrative reforms of the Dual Monarchy in 1873 the Orthodox of various races living in various parts of Austria were separated from the Church of Karlovtsy in Hungary and formed into another independent church, whose primatial see was at Czernovitz in the Bukovina. This curious agglomeration included two dioceses of Serbs in Dalmatia, Zara, and Cattaro, whose 100,000 or more faithful are now in Yugoslavia, the rest of the Czernovitz Orthodox (who were at the other end of old Austria) belonging to the Rumanian patriarchate (to Moscow since 1940).

4. *Bosnia and Herzegovina.* After Austria occupied these provinces in 1878, her government concluded a concordat with the Phanar (the only thing of its kind in Orthodox ecclesiastical history) whereby Constantinople recognized the autonomy of the eparchies concerned, with a nominal dependence on the

patriarch; the principal see was Dabro-Bosnia at Sarajevo. In 1918 there were some 830,000 faithful in four dioceses.

It was a difficult task to bring together these diverse elements, accustomed to varying systems of administration and to the enjoyment of local autonomy. But after eighteen months of negotiation it was done, and in August, 1920, the four and a half independent Serbian churches were united in the revived patriarchate of Ipek (Peć). It should be noted that this action was taken by the Serbian bishops on their own authority; but in 1922 it was recognized by the patriarch of Constantinople, Meletios IV, who gracefully gave up the suzerainty of his see over the Serbian eparchies in Macedonia[45] and Bosnia-Herzegovina.

But World War II brought disaster to the reorganized church. Virulent attacks were made on religion and its faithful; religious institutions were destroyed; communist-inspired partisans put to death numerous innocent clerics and others on the excuse of "fascism" and other political crimes; and the church has had to accept the new government's decision to abolish all official links between religion and the state. The aim seems to be to break up the Orthodox Church of Yugoslavia into four autonomous bodies, on a regional basis, which would have the effect of completely disorganizing and seriously weakening the church built up so laboriously after 1918. The following pages therefore must be taken as referring to conditions in 1939.

ORGANIZATION AND PRESENT STATE

Patriarch. "His Holiness the Archbishop of Ipek, Metropolitan of Belgrade and Karlovtsy, Serbian Patriarch" resides at Belgrade. He was formerly nominated by the government (now republican) from three names presented by an electoral assembly, a large body in which the civil power was represented. The patriarch is perpetual president of the episcopal assembly and holy synod; he has the right to consecrate all bishops and the holy chrism. The third patriarch of the new line was Gabriel

[45] These had shared the troubles of the Bulgars and Rumanians under the Greeks in Macedonia at the end of the nineteenth and beginning of the twentieth century.

(Gavrilo) Dozich, who during World War II was a prisoner of the Germans for four years for refusing to lend his influence to Nazi designs. Not till the end of 1946 was he allowed to return to Belgrade.

Bishops. In addition to the patriarchal eparchy of Belgrade there are four metropolitan sees, Cetinje, Skoplje (Uskub), Sarajevo, Zagreb, and sixteen episcopal sees, including Novi-Sad, Split (Spalato), Mostar, and Bitolj (Monastir). There are bishops also for the Serbs in the Rumanian Banat (Temesvar), Italy (Zara), and North America (Cleveland, Ohio). A vacant see is filled by the episcopal assembly.

Episcopal Assembly. This consists of all ruling bishops of the kingdom and has supreme legislative powers in all matters of doctrine, worship, discipline, and administration; it is a court of appeal in some matters and the sole court in others. Its external decisions must be confirmed by the council of civil ministers.

Holy synod. Six bishops, variously chosen, with the patriarch as president, form the synod, which is the supreme executive and administrative body. It is a court of first instance in certain matters and judges appeals from the permanent ecclesiastical high court. The *chancellor,* chosen by the bishops, represents the civil power at the meetings of both assembly and synod and is responsible for the organization of their work.

Lower clergy. There is a principal seminary at Belgrade, with a faculty of theology in the university, and five other theological schools. These are insufficient to give the church in Yugoslavia the clergy it needs, either in number or quality, and only a minority of the priests have studied in them. Like those of Bulgaria, the Serbian clergy are organized in strong associations, and for years have agitated for such innovations as the re-marriage of widowed priests and the use of the modern Serbian tongue instead of Slavonic in the liturgy; many of them, too, ob-ject to preaching oftener than at Easter and Christmas. Parishes are grouped into vicariates (deaneries) under a protopresbyter.

Monasticism. There are numerous Orthodox monasteries in Yugoslavia, almost as many as there are monks, who are becoming fewer and fewer. It was reckoned in 1933 that there were 204 monastic houses, with only 397 members, some of whom were employed in posts outside their monasteries. A monastic school to encourage vocations was started at Rakovitsy, near Belgrade. The principal monastery (founded *c.* 1512) is at Krushedol, near Karlovtsy, the Serbian "Westminster Abbey." Others are Studenitsa, founded by Stephen I in 1190, Milechevo (1230), Fruskagora, and Manassia, the last two of which are pilgrim shrines. There are only two convents of women, one of them occupied by Russian nuns. It is probable that Serbian monasteries have been still further depleted as a result of war.

The faithful. The Orthodox of Yugoslavia numbered 6,785,000 in a population of 14 millions; there were over five million Catholics, mostly Croats and Slovenes (census of 1931). All religions of the country were theoretically on an equal footing, but in fact Orthodoxy was given a specially privileged position, and the government exercised a careful surveillance over ecclesiastical activities.

Relations between Orthodox and Catholics varied from time to time, the hierarchs of the predominant religion at times showing themselves very ill-disposed towards the Catholic Church. On the other hand the respective authorities were on occasion able to combine for common ends, e.g., in the matter of education in 1927; religious instruction was made obligatory in all primary and secondary schools, but is unlikely to remain so.

After the patriarch Barnabas, following the example of the Holy See, had proclaimed the nineteen-hundredth anniversary of the Redemption (1933) a holy year of jubilee, a Belgrade newspaper declared that, "We are convinced of the strict obligation of the Slavs to do their best for the realization of unity between the Catholic and Orthodox Churches. . . . We know there are politicians and other public men in this country who want to see bad relations between them continue, but it is our duty to oppose such wicked policies." And the students of the Orthodox seminary at Belgrade in a manifesto condemned "those who are trying to sow enmity and discord between the Orthodox and Catholic Churches, especially at a time when the whole of Christendom is endangered by the advance of Bolshevism." Unhappily, the reply of the patriarch Barnabas to these expressions of good will was to forbid his theological professors to take part in a conference with the Catholic faculty of Ljubljana. In Yugoslavia, as elsewhere, World War II grievously harmed the cause of Christian unity. The terrorist *ustashis* of Catholic Croatia committed horrible outrages against Serbs, and the Serbs retaliated. Clergy were murdered, the Nazis sponsored an attempt to set up a Croatian Orthodox church, and the patriarch Gabriel and the revered Bishop Nicholas Velimirovich were carried off into captivity.

BIBLIOGRAPHY

†Hudal, *Die Serbisch-Orthodoxe Nationalkirche* (Graz, 1922).
Picot, *Les Serbes de Hongrie* (Prague, 1873).
†Yanich, *Lives of the Serbian Saints* (London, 1921).
*French, *Serbian Church Life* (London, 1943).
*Temperley, *History of Serbia* (London, 1919).

3. THE PATRIARCHATE OF RUMANIA

The Rumanians are in part descendants of the "veterans of Trajan," colonies of Romans chiefly from Illyria and Italy planted by him in the province of Dacia at the beginning of the second century of the Christian era; fusing with the Thracian natives and then overrun by Visigoths and others, they gave rise to a new people, predominantly Latin in language and some characteristics, but modified by Greek, Slav, and other influences. The language is almost an Italian dialect, with a large Slavonic vocabulary: the name "Romania" explains itself.

The first Dacian Christians were of Latin rite, and so remained till they were conquered by the Bulgars. Then, in the ninth century, they were subjected to Byzantine bishops, who imposed their own rite, and in due course the Rumanians were drawn into the schism of Constantinople. For long the Rumanians (or Vlachs) were dependent on the prelates of the Bulgarian and other churches; it was not till the fourteenth century (when Rumanian principalities independent of Turks, Hungarians, and Poles began to be formed) that three separate metropolitans were given to Valachia and Moldavia; namely, Ungro-Valachia (Bucarest), Western Valachia (Turnu-Severin), and Mavro-Valachia or Moldavia (Jassy).

Latin missionaries were active from the thirteenth century, attracted particularly by the pagan Kumans in the Danubian plain, and dioceses were erected; but the majority of these Catholics turned Orthodox or Calvinist at the time of the Reformation. Damian, the Moldavian metropolitan, signed the act of union at the Council of Florence, but it was not acceptable to most of his church and he and his successor had to seek refuge in Rome.

After the Turkish conquest of Bulgaria the two Valachian eparchies shared in the hellenization that was the lot of the Church of Okhrida (see p. 128), of which they are believed to have formed part; but Moldavia did not suffer in this way until the patriarchate of Constantinople finally suppressed the Churches of Okhrida and Tirnova in 1767. But by the seventeenth century the imposition of Greek as the liturgical language in the monasteries and larger churches had led to a loss of knowledge of the hitherto used Slavonic: this was met in the smaller churches and rural districts by the adoption of vernacular Rumanian, a usage that spread and became general by the end of the eighteenth century.[46] Later, in addition, the roman alphabetical characters were substituted for the cyrillic in the liturgical books. Thus, having started with Latin as their liturgical language, the Rumanians after a thousand years and many vicissitudes returned to a dialect of the same tongue in the worship of God.

From 1712, "the era of the Phanariotes," was the gloomiest period of Rumanian history; it came to an end when the internal autonomy of Valachia and Moldavia was conceded by the Treaty of Adrianople in 1829; complete independence was gained under Prince Alexander Cuza in 1864, and in 1881 Charles von Hohenzollern-Sigmaringen was crowned king of Rumania.

Nevertheless not all was darkness in that period, and there was considerable cultural activity. So much, that at the beginning of the eighteenth century Prince Constantine Brancoveanu was able to present a printing-press and Arabic type to the Orthodox patriarch of Antioch. It was set up at Aleppo. The same thing had been done, with Greek type, for Jerusalem some time before.

National independence inevitably led to ecclesiastical independence. Cuza, having secularized all landed property held by churches and monasteries (mostly by Greek monasteries

---

[46] It was made compulsory for all churches in Mavro-Valachia by Prince Alexander Cuza in 1862.

abroad),[47] proclaimed an autonomous Rumanian Church, to which the Oecumenical Patriarch replied by a solemn protest which, as usual in these circumstances, was ignored. For twenty years Constantinople looked on the Rumanians as being in schism, till in 1885 their autocephalous status was formally recognized by the patriarch Joachim IV. This "church of the Old Kingdom" had a primate, the archbishop and metropolitan of Valachia, at Bucarest, with a metropolitan of Moldavia and six other bishops.

As with the Bulgars and Serbs, there was a large number of Rumanians in Macedonia whose persecution at the hands of the Greeks in the early years of the present century left a bitter legacy of mutual hatred: this and its struggle with the encroachments of a liberalizing state were the outstanding features of the history of the Rumanian national church of the Old Kingdom.[48] Both difficulties still subsist, Serbs and Greeks doing all they can to absorb the Macedonian Rumanians.

The formation of the kingdom of Greater Rumania after the war of 1914–1918 brought about a situation very similar to that in Serbia, the following ecclesiastical groups being brought within its frontiers:

1. *Transylvania* (The Ardeal). The Rumanian province of Transylvania was occupied by the Emperor Leopold I in 1688 and remained part of Hungary until 1918. The Orthodox there became an autonomous church in 1864 under the metropolitan of Sibiu (Hermannstadt), with two suffragan sees, and at the time of their union with the kingdom of Rumania numbered 2¼ million souls; another 1½ million were Catholics of the Byzantine rite, fruit of the reunion of 1701.[49]

---

[47] He offered an indemnity of £1,125,000 ($5,625,000), which the monks refused to accept — not in generosity but in protest.

[48] A very bad effect was had, too, by the primate Athanasius Mironescu. He presided over an ecclesiastical court that acquitted him on a grave moral charge, and was then forced to resign by public opinion. This was in 1910–1911.

[49] The Protestant Reformation wrought havoc in Transylvania both among Latins and Orthodox, who became "Calvinist by creed, Eastern by certain externals." There was even a Calvinist "superintendent" for the Orthodox

2. *The Bukovina.* The southern part of the Bukovina was transferred from Austria to Rumania in 1919. From 1873 the Rumanian Orthodox here had formed the metropolitan eparchy of the Church of Czernovitz (see p. 97); they numbered some 250,000, with the same number of Orthodox Ruthenians.

3. *Bessarabia.* From 1812 till 1918 the Rumanian Orthodox of this Russian province (adjoining eastern Moldavia) had simply formed part of the Russian Church, and were subjected to an intensive process of russification; there were 1½ million of them in two eparchies.

The organization of these diverse elements into one with the church of the old kingdom of Rumania was a troublesome business and took over six years; even then the Transylvanians had to be allowed to retain a good deal of their own special constitution (Statute of the Metropolitan Saguna, 1869), which, indeed, has influenced that of the whole church. A patriarchate of Rumania was set up in February, 1925, and a few months later the unification was completed. As in Yugoslavia, this momentous step was taken on the authority of the Rumanian bishops themselves, but was at once recognized by the patriarch of Constantinople, Basil III, and the other Orthodox churches.

This organization will now have to be modified, as since 1940 the whole of Bessarabia and the northern part of the Bukovina have been annexed by the U.S.S.R.

Rumania is the second largest Orthodox church, and since 1925 there has been a lot of talk of Bucarest being the heir of Constantinople and Moscow as the leader of Orthodoxy: "Imperial Russia has disappeared and Rumania inherits her religious mission; on her falls the honour of taking the leadership of Eastern Christianity," declared Father Delattre, S.J., in the *Correspondant* (May 10, 1927). "The buttress and pillar of Orthodoxy was once at Constantinople or in other countries of eastern Europe. Now our land is her centre, and Bucarest has the part in the life and direction of Orthodoxy that formerly belonged

in the seventeenth century, and resisters were persecuted by their Hungarian and German masters.

to Constantinople" (*Missionarul.*, June, 1925; see also Mr. Savin in *Universul*, November, 1933). The civil power in Rumania will do nothing to discourage this ambition and is only too anxious to keep a hand on so powerful an institution: this it does through the large lay element in ecclesiastical affairs and by insisting that the appointment of all bishops shall be approved by the government. Nevertheless, officially, Orthodoxy is only the "dominant" religion of the country.

Organization and Present State

Patriarch. He is "His Holiness the Archbishop of Bucarest, Metropolitan of Ungro-Valachia, Patriarch of Rumania," and he is appointed by an electoral assembly of clergy and laymen, and confirmed in office and invested by the king. The patriarch is president of the holy synod, national church assembly, ecclesiastical appeal court, etc., and consecrates the holy chrism. The first patriarch was Miron Cristea, who died in 1939.

Bishops. The church is divided into five metropolitan provinces: Ungro-Valachia, consisting of the archbishopric of Bucarest (the patriarchal see) and four episcopal sees; Moldavia, consisting of the archbishopric of Jassy (Iasi) and three suffragans; the Ardeal, formed by the archbishopric of Sibiu and four suffragans; the Bukovina, with the archbishopric at Cernauti (Czernovitz) and two suffragans; and Bessarabia, with the archbishopric of Chisinau and one suffragan. As has been mentioned above, one of these provinces, Bessarabia, and part of another, Bukovina, are now outside the borders of Rumania. There is a bishop for the military forces, one for the Americas, and several auxiliaries, as well as a patriarchal vicar for the Serbs of the Banat.

A vacant see is filled by the national church assembly and the assembly of the eparchy concerned; certain laymen and others have the right to vote *ex officio*. The election must be confirmed and the bishop invested by the king.

Holy synod. This is the supreme authority in all spiritual matters and consists of the whole bench of bishops, ruling and auxiliary. It has a permanent committee of four bishops, renewed every four years, for urgent affairs.

National Church Assembly. This body consists of two clerics and four laymen from each eparchy, elected for six years, together with the members of the holy synod. It is responsible for church administration, schools, charities, and endowments, etc., and has a permanent executive committee of 15 members.

Every ecclesiastical unit in Rumania, from a metropolitan eparchy to a parish, is very highly organized, with its own assemblies, councils, and committees.[50] Indeed, the church is overorganized and there has been a good deal of agitation to reform and simplify the ecclesiastical constitution settled in 1925.

Lower clergy. There are faculties of theology in the universities of Bucarest, Cernauti, Cluj and Chisinau, a central seminary and another at Bucarest, and a score of seminaries in other places. The standard of training of the clergy has risen notably of late years, but it still leaves a good deal to be desired, especially within the old kingdom. Some clerical students were sent to Protestant universities, but as it was found that they were subjected to propaganda and imbibed dangerous notions the patriarch Miron approached the authorities of certain Catholic universities; some of his students went into residence at Strasburg and, at the request of their bishop, Cardinal Pacelli (now Pope Pius XII) arranged scholarships for two Rumanian Orthodox students in Rome. In 1932 the holy synod decreed that in future only licentiates in theology[51] should be admitted to the priesthood, but it will be long before this takes effect outside the old kingdom.

The Rumanian clergy do not enjoy a particularly good reputation, even among their own bishops, but a strong desire for improvement is manifest; there are some very capable men

[50] This is unusual in an Eastern church. Historically it is partly due to the example of Transylvania, whose constitution was drawn up under Western influence and to meet the pressure of Catholicity, on the one hand, and Protestantism, on the other.

[51] It is interesting to note that a number of women teachers in Rumania have this degree (*O si sic omnes!*), and claim the right to be nominated religious instructors in primary and secondary schools.

among them who are active in the cause of reform.[52] In particular, more frequent preaching is being advocated.

Eastern clerical costume is less and less worn in Rumania outside of church; long hair has disappeared, and some priests even shave their beards. Parishes are grouped into "deaneries," each under a protopresbyter.

Monasticism. All monasteries in Rumania are subject to the local bishop and they share the careful and complex organization of the rest of the church. There were 44 monasteries of men in 1939, with an average of 36 monks each, the communities ranging in size from 3 only to 400. Only one of these is in Transylvania, and nearly half were in Bessarabia, Noul Neamtu being the principal. There is a college for young monks at Sernika, near Bucarest, and another at the monastery of Ketatuïa, near Jassy, founded in 1930.

The 24 convents have an average of 75 nuns each. The best known is Horez, in the forests of Valsea in the Carpathians, founded for men early in the eighteenth century by Prince Constantine Brankoveanu.[53] It has been occupied by nuns since 1873.

The monasteries are strongly urged to establish printing presses, studios, training colleges for missioners, etc., and the patriarch Miron and Princess Kantakuzena have been very zealous in encouraging nuns to undertake teaching, nursing, and orphanages; but so far these activities have not been taken up with any great enthusiasm or success.

The faithful. In 1938 the Orthodox Rumanians numbered 13 million (including a number of Russians and Bulgars) in a total population of 20 million. The Russian annexations have reduced the total by nearly 3½ million, nearly all Orthodox but very mixed in nationality. In Rumania religious instruction was made compulsory in primary and secondary schools only in 1932, too lately to have had any effect yet on the religious ignorance of the people, who are, however, characterized by a notable care

[52] The well-known writer Gala Galaktion is a secular priest (Father Piskulescu) and a distinguished theologian.

[53] He was executed by the Turks at Constantinople in 1714 and canonized as a martyr by the Rumanian holy synod in 1934.

for their dead. On Saturdays the churches are crowded for the *parastases,* prayers for the faithful departed.

But some among the younger people are conscious of their responsibilities and the past few years has seen the growth of "Orthodox Action," admittedly inspired by "Catholic Action." Mention may be made of the Society of Student Missioners, for the instruction of children and encouragement of retreats, and the Patriarhul Miron society (rather like the Greek "Zoe"), which is specially concerned for personal good morality;[54] the first was founded by an old Oxford man, Professor V. G. Ispir, the second by the archimandrite Teofil Ionescu. A similar movement, called *Fratia Ortodoxa Romana,* began in Transylvania in 1933. The Oastea Domnului, "Lord's Army," organized by Father Trifa on the lines of the Salvation Army, is also important.

Unlike Yugoslavia, Catholicity in Rumania is predominantly Byzantine in aspect, but the attitude of the Orthodox toward the Catholic Church and reunion is equally variable in both countries. The open letter which a distinguished Orthodox theologian, Father Jeremias Chekan, protopresbyter of Chisinau, addressed to the bishop of Oradea Marc in 1933, declaring that the reunion of the Orthodox with the Holy See is a necessity, received much support as well as strong adverse criticism. But too much importance must not be attributed to that sort of thing, or to such incidents as the most amiable reception of Cardinal Tisserant by the Orthodox monks of Siganesti when he visited their monastery.

BIBLIOGRAPHY

†Iorga, *Histoire des Roumains* (Bucarest, 1922).
Netzhammer, *Aus Rumänien,* 2 vols. (Einsiedeln, 1913).
†Theodorian-Carada, *L'ame roumaine* in *Irénikon,* t. V. p. 10, t. VI. p. 643 (Amay, 1928–1929).
†Beza, *The Rumanian Church* (London, 1943).
*Seton Watson, *A History of the Rumanians* (Cambridge, 1943).
Disdier, *Une enquête sur l'union des églises en Roumanie* (Lyons, 1939).

[54] And also for what some Orthodox delight to call "proselytism" when it is exercised by Catholics. In 1930–1934 it claimed 1100 conversions, nearly a half of them being from Catholicism.

CHAPTER V

THE OTHER GREEK CHURCHES

1. THE CHURCH OF CYPRUS

THE apostolic church of Cyprus, founded by St. Paul and extended by St. Barnabas, was the second church to become extra-patriarchal and independent of all outside itself save the Supreme Pontiff (Armenia was the first). It was recognized as autocephalous by the Council of Ephesus in 431, and, in spite of the protests of the patriarchs of Antioch, this was confirmed in 488 by Acacius, patriarch of Constantinople, and decreed by the emperor, Zeno.[1]

For a few years after 691, under Emperor Justinian II, many of the clergy and people of Cyprus were transported to the mainland to be out of the way of the Mohammedan Arabs; they were settled around New Justinianopolis in Cyzicus, but soon returned home. The island was captured by King Richard the Lion-Hearted in 1191 and was under "Frankish" rule till the Turks seized it from the Venetians in 1571. During these four hundred years the local church was subordinated to the Latin hierarchy of the conquerors, and Catholic historians show that the ecclesiastical rule was extremely oppressive. In 1213 Pope Innocent III sent two cardinal legates to Cyprus, the Englishman Robert Curzon and Pelagius, a Portuguese. Curzon died but Pelagius lived "which was a great misfortune, for he did much mischief," says the continuer of the chronicle of William of Tyre; for example, in 1231 he had thirteen Cypriote monks tortured and burned to death for opposing the Western ecclesiastics. The Greek sees were reduced to four and their bishops made to live

[1] From the end of the sixteenth century till 1860 the Cypriote metropolitan applied to Antioch for the holy chrism; since then he gets it from Constantinople.

in remote villages, subject to the Latin archbishop of Nikosia; two of their own archbishops were banished, and after the death of Germanos Pesimandros (*c.* 1275) no other was allowed to be appointed.

The result was that no proper reconciliation of the Cypriote church with the Holy See was ever effected, in spite of the more conciliatory efforts of Popes Innocent IV and Alexander IV, except for a time after the Council of Florence; this temporary reunion had a curious and unlooked-for effect in Cyprus (and elsewhere in the eastern Mediterranean) – many Westerners, clerical and lay, without permission or canonical process embraced the Byzantine rite. Nevertheless Popes Leo X, Clement VII, and Paul III all had to insist on the Latin bishops of Cyprus properly carrying out the decrees of Florence and not treating the Byzantine church with contempt.

The taking of Famagusta by the Turks, in 1571, meant the extinction of the Western church in Cyprus, and the Byzantines at once took steps to obtain a new primate of their own. They got the freedom from Latin domination that they wanted, but at a price – for Turkish oppression, though of a different kind, proved as bad as Frankish.

For generations the history of the church was chiefly a tale of internal dissensions, but mention must be made of the Synod of Nikosia in 1668 which condemned protestantizing doctrines. In some matters where Catholics and Orthodox disagree its decrees showed a strong Catholic tendency (see p. 62). At the beginning of the seventeenth century the Cypriote archbishop, Athanasius, came into communion with the Holy See; he ended his life as parish priest of the Catholic Byzantine colony at Leghorn in Italy.

At the time of the Greek war of independence the Turks murdered Archbishop Cyprian (one of the best hierarchs the Cypriote Church ever had), with all three bishops[2] and many other

---

[2] So a complete new hierarchy was required. It was provided in these exceptional circumstances by the Oecumenical Patriarch through the patriarch of Antioch, who sent three bishops to the island to consecrate four Cypriotes.

clergy and lay people, for sending help to the Greeks, and it was not till the occupation by the British in 1878 that Cyprus got some measure of peace. But from 1900 until 1909 there was a disturbance (it convulsed all the Orthodox churches of the Near East) concerning the election of a new archbishop, which was eventually settled by the appointment of Cyril Papadopoulos, a supporter of the movement for the transfer of Cyprus from British to Greek control. There was a good deal of excitement when the Gregorian kalendar was imposed in 1924; in the following year Cyprus definitely became a British possession; and six years later another first-class upheaval began.

After World War I many of the Orthodox of Cyprus wanted their island to come under Greek government, and in 1931 an insurrection broke out: the rebels proclaimed "self-annexation" to Greece, and a mob set fire to the house of the British governor, the learned Sir Ronald Storrs; troops had to be sent from Egypt to restore order. Two bishops, Nicodemus of Kition (Larnaka) and Makarios of Kyrenia, were so foolish as to lead the insurrection in their respective eparchies.[3] They were promptly deported and a decree of banishment issued against them by the British authorities. Shortly afterward the archbishop of Constantia (Famagusta) died, leaving only the bishop of Paphos on the island.

For years all efforts to arrange for the election of another archbishop and bishops were unsuccessful. In 1937 an assembly was about to do so, when the British government declared (not surprisingly in the circumstances) that it must lay down certain qualifications for the elegibility of candidates and have a right of veto. The Cypriotes would not accept these conditions, and so nothing was done. It was not till 1947 that Leontios of Paphos was elected to the primatial throne; and as he died five weeks later the see at present writing is again vacant.

[3] The official organ of the Orthodox patriarchate of Alexandria, *Pantainos*, commented (December 10, 1931): "The Church may have the right to participate in nationalist movements, but she should not take the initiative when there are other organizations to do so: that is going outside her province."

ORGANIZATION AND PRESENT STATE

Chief hierarch. The head of the Cypriote Church is "His Blessedness the Archbishop of Constantia, New Justinianopolis and All Cyprus," who lives at Nikosia ("Constantia" is Famagusta).

Bishops. The suffragan eparchies are Paphos, Kition, and Kyrenia, whose bishops have the title of metropolitan.

Several attempts have been made during the past twenty-five years to draw up a constitution for the church, with definite regulations for the election of these hierarchs, but the events of 1931 seem to have put agreement farther off than ever. Meanwhile, the government of the church is theoretically in the hands of the bishops in synod, with a mixed council for temporal affairs which does not seem to function very regularly.

Lower clergy. There was a seminary, at the monastery of St. George at Larnaka, from 1910, but it has now ceased. Consequently the clerical standard is very low, though it has improved a little in recent years.

In every diocese there is an archimandrite (who formerly had charge of interior economy and finance, with an oikonomos to help him), an exarch (for external relations), and an archdeacon (whose concerns are strictly ecclesiastical).

Monasticism. There are seven monasteries in Cyprus, with an average of ten monks each. They are rapidly degenerating and will soon disappear altogether unless something is done to put new life into them. The chief of them are Kykko, founded near the end of the eleventh century, Makhaera, and Enklistra (both twelfth century).

The faithful. Of the 350,000 people in Cyprus, probably 280,000 belong to the Orthodox Church. They are of very mixed blood, but Greek is the vernacular tongue of all; they consider themselves to be of that nationality and are very annoyed at any suggestion that they are not pure Hellenes. There is a considerable number of Mohammedans, and a few hundred Latin and Maronite Catholics.

BIBLIOGRAPHY

*Hackett, *A History of the Orthodox Church of Cyprus* (London, 1901).
*Gunnis, *Historic Cyprus* (London, 1936).
*Hill, *A History of Cyprus,* 2 vols. (Cambridge, 1940).

Daphne

Tegea

GREEK CHURCHES

Courtesy, *Christian East*

DIONYSY VALEDYNSKY,

PORPHYRIOS III,
ARCHBISHOP OF SINAI

HERMAN, ARCHBISHOP OF FINLAND

Novgorod

Sergyevo

RUSSIAN CHURCHES

2. THE CHURCH OF SINAI

The monastery of St. Catherine of Sinai, "the God-trodden mountain," situated at the southern end of the Sinaitic peninsula, is probably the oldest existing monastery in the world, with the possible exceptions of the Coptic Dair Antonios and Dair Boulos in Egypt. Here, on and around the mountain where Almighty God gave the law to Moses, there were anchorites from very early times, and they had formed themselves into one or more communities long before the Emperor Justinian in 530 built a fortified monastery at the reputed spot where Moses saw the burning bush. That has been the monastic site ever since, and the church at least is of Justinian's building.[4] Among the early abbots was St. John Climacus in the seventh century, author of *The Heavenly Ladder,* an ascetical work very popular in the West in the Middle Ages. After the Arab invasion the monastery was at first respected but later suffered a great deal: this led to the loss of its "international" character, Syrians, Slavs, and others abandoning it to the Greeks; and to the sending of monks to Europe to beg alms and protection, e.g., from Pope Paul V and King Louis XIII, in 1620. Many popes befriended it after the Crusades, from Honorius III early in the thirteenth century to Urban VIII, who wrote affectionately to the archbishop-abbot Josephat in 1630.[5] In spite of the extraordinary wildness and remoteness of its situation, St. Catherine's was for centuries

---

[4] It contains the alleged relics of St. Catherine, supposed to have been transported thither by angels from Alexandria. None of the early travelers whose records are extant mention this marvel, and the history of Catherine herself is wrapped in mystery. "Angels" is undoubtedly here a metaphor for "monks."

[5] For a time during the Crusades and after there were Western monks and a Latin chapel there.

a great place of pilgrimage, and was from time to time a wealthy establishment.

The abbots gradually extended their jurisdiction over the neighbouring dioceses of Pharan and Raithu, and endeavoured to become independent of their patriarch at Jerusalem. Their autonomy was at length recognized by Constantinople in 1575 and confirmed in 1782, though Jerusalem in theory hardly recognizes it. In the nineteenth century the monastery became more secure from Bedu Arab depredations through the efforts of Mohammed Ali and of the British, and a number of European scholars found their way to its library, rich in ancient manuscripts, many of them still unexamined.[6]

One hundred years ago the monastery had eighty properties (*metokhia*)[7] in Europe and hither Asia; of these only sixteen remain (five of them close to Sinai), the rest having been impounded by civil governments (e.g., in Rumania and Russia) or sold as unproductive.

The autonomous Church of Sinai, then, consists now of a monastery, some outlying cells, and a handful of lay folk – the smallest complete and independent Christian church in the world.

ORGANIZATION AND PRESENT STATE

Archbishop. The only hierarch of the Sinaitic church is the Archbishop of Sinai, Pharan, and Raithu, who is also abbot of the monastery. He is elected by the assembly of senior monks and must be consecrated by the Patriarch of Jerusalem.[8] For sixty years the archbishops lived most of their time at the *metokhion* in Cairo, the monastery being run by the *dikaios*

[6] Here in 1844–1853–1859 Tischendorf found the Codex Sinaiticus of the Bible, now in the British Museum.

[7] A *metokhion* is equivalent to a monastic grange or cell in mediaeval times: a property situated at a distance from the monastery, administered by one or two resident monks.

[8] This dependence led to a dispute in 1867 when the monks purported to depose their archbishop, Cyril Byzantios. He appealed to Sophronios III of Constantinople, but Cyril of Jerusalem confirmed the deposition, whereupon there was a terrible row between Constantinople and Jerusalem. Orthodox public opinion was so strongly against the Oecumenical Patriarch that he resigned and Byzantios had to submit to the deposition.

(prior), but since 1928 he is again resident at Sinai. He is assisted by a *synaxis* or council, consisting of the *dikaios*, the sacristan, the procurator (*oikonomos*), and another monk; this council has almost complete control.

The monks. These numbered in 1936 twenty-six, fifteen resident and the rest in charge of *metokhia*.

As is mentioned elsewhere (see p. 183) St. Catherine's is the only Orthodox monastery that follows St. Antony's rather than St. Basil's rule of life. It is an austere existence, and a recent observer from outside, Professor E. G. Pantelakis, declares that the community can bear comparison with any of the great monasteries of Christendom: "The Sinaites are quiet and temperate, hard-working, well-disciplined, religious without 'putting it on,' and have the great monastic virtue of humility." Professor Pantelakis speaks especially of the personal goodness and of the work as a builder of Father Kallistos Tsilphoglou of Trebizond (d. 1916), whose labours were carried on by Father Moses Kapellos who, though over seventy, was a maker of roads as well.

The cells of the monks being small and unhealthy, and the 3300 manuscripts of the library being so inadequately housed that they would be in most serious danger should fire break out, the *synaxis* recently undertook the construction of a three-storied addition to the ancient buildings. To pay for it, drastic measures were taken to curtail living expenses, but the work progressed slowly owing to lack of funds, and help from outside was urgently needed.[9]

The faithful. The lay members of this tiny church consist of about fifty Arabs, mostly employed by the monastery,[10] and the same number of fishermen on the coasts. The monastic synaxis is the unofficial civil and criminal court of justice for all the neighbouring inhabitants, whether Christian or Mohammedan

---

[9] In 1933 the Smithsonian Institute, of Washington, sent Harlan Zodtner to Mount Sinai to carry out observations of the sun over a period of four years. He lived with his family in a house built for them near the monastery.

[10] Doubtless they are in part descended from the two hundred families from Trebizond and Egypt which Justinian planted near by for the defense and service of the monks.

(they are mostly semi-nomadic), and its decisions are enforced by the tribal chiefs. The monks dispense extensive and regular charities to these people (over 200 pounds of bread are distributed daily), all of whom without distinction of religion look on St. Catherine's as a holy shrine and gather together there at certain festivals.

BIBLIOGRAPHY

*Eckenstein, *A History of Sinai* (London, 1930).
Hofmann, *Sinai und Rom* in *Orientalia Christiana,* t. IX, No. 3 (Rome, 1927).
†Pantelakis, *Le monastère du Sinai* in *Irénikon,* t. XII, No. 1 (Amay, 1935).

3. THE CHURCH OF GREECE

Before the rise of Constantinople to civil and ecclesiastical power the country now called the Kingdom of the Hellenes was, as part of the Roman prefecture of Illyricum, within the patriarchal jurisdiction of the Roman pontiff. But eastern Illyricum was part of the Eastern Empire, and from the fifth century the patriarch of Constantinople claimed to have jurisdiction over it. The question was a source of never ending friction between Old Rome and New Rome, and it was one of the principal matters in dispute at the time of Photios. After 1054 what is now Greece was definitively involved on the side of Constantinople and was part of its patriarchate, sharing its political and religious history until the establishment of the modern Greek state in the early part of the nineteenth century.

During the Greek war of independence most of the clergy openly supported the insurgents, and at the national assemblies of 1821 and 1829 steps were taken toward the reorganization of the church in the freed land. President Capo d'Istria undertook negotiations with the Oecumenical Patriarch, but the president was assassinated in 1831 and two years later, without reference to the Phanar, King Otho I issued the charter of the autocephalous Church of Greece[11] under its own holy directing synod: it was felt that the clergy of that part of Hellas that was free could not be submitted to the jurisdiction of a hierarch who was still in the power of the Turks. The patriarch of Constantinople was, not unnaturally, very indignant and for seventeen years refused to recognize the new state of affairs. At length, in 1850, the Phanar issued a decree (*tomos*) acknowledging the auto-

[11] This is the only church that calls itself or can properly be called "The Greek Church."

cephalous Church of Greece, with certain reservations most of which have remained a dead letter; however, the Greek bishops still receive the holy chrism from Constantinople. This *tomos* was followed by a fresh charter from the Greek government, which *inter alia* imposed on the holy synod a civil commissioner whose consent should be necessary for the validity of its resolutions.

When Great Britain ceded the Ionian islands to Greece, the holy synod at Athens assumed control over their dioceses in spite of the protests of Constantinople, and the same thing happened in Thessaly and part of Epirus in 1882 – except that Constantinople suffered in silence. This brought the number of Greek eparchies up to thirty-two. The further provinces reconquered from Turkey in 1912 remained under the jurisdiction of the Oecumenical Patriarch until 1928, when an agreement was reached whereby he delegated his powers to the Greek holy synod, reserving his rights for the future: this, of course, means in fact not that they are in abeyance but that he has lost them entirely. The Greek eparchies are increased by another thirty-nine. Thus Greece has become (excluding Russia) the second largest Orthodox church and one of the four most important of these churches; her numbers were still further increased by the exchange of populations with Turkey (Greeks in Turkey, outside Constantinople, for Turks in Greece, outside western Thrace) in 1923.

Political upheavals in Greece from 1917 onwards had considerable repercussions in the church, the archbishop and certain other bishops being deposed or appointed accordingly as they supported Venizelos or King Constantine.[12] After the revolution of 1922 Chrysostom Papadopoulos became archbishop of Athens, and was able to maintain his position in very difficult circumstances.[13] Other bishops were not so fortunate. In 1923 the holy

[12] Meletios Metaxakis, afterward patriarch of Constantinople and then of Alexandria, was archbishop of Athens from 1918 to 1920 by the will of Venizelos.

[13] He was at one time director of the Jerusalem theological school of Holy Cross, and was strongly anti-Catholic. He died in 1938.

synod was suppressed and replaced by an assembly of all the bishops of the old kingdom; two years later this was revoked by Pangalos, and the synod reinstated; its members all were deposed during the Venizelist adventure in August, 1935, and their successors superseded after the restoration of the monarchy a few months later. Altogether it is clear that the state in Greece has every intention of trying to continue completely to control the church in order to use it as a political weapon. At the present time the church is constituted mainly under the law of 1931, a revision of those of 1923 and 1925.

The question of the kalendar, moreover, raised surprising difficulties. At the instance of the government the holy synod some years ago decreed the abandonment of the Julian kalendar for the reformed one. There was at once a furore of opposition, chiefly among the less-educated lower clergy and laity, who flatly refused to obey: but it was led by three bishops, who threatened a schism. The holy synod took energetic action and in 1935 two of the three bishops were deposed and sentenced to confinement in a monastery. The holy synod took the line that either the civil power should effectively suppress the opposition or else the Julian kalendar should be everywhere restored. But the partisans of the old kalendar (who have the terrific name of "Palaiohimerologites") are royalist in politics, and the royalists needed all the support they could get. After 1939, however, the people of Greece had something else to think about. Their sufferings during World War II were atrocious: by German reprisals alone 1600 villages were completely destroyed and two million peasants made homeless. Not the least of the problems confronting them is the rebuilding of hundreds of churches; and the disturbed internal politics of their country involves yet more disturbance for their national church, whose leaders set them so good an example during war.

ORGANIZATION AND PRESENT STATE

Chief hierarch. He is the "Blessed Archbishop of Athens and of All Greece," and is president for life of the assembly of bishops and of the permanent holy synod. When the throne is vacant the plenary assembly of bishops chooses three names by ballot, from which the Minister of Worship selects the new archbishop. This form of election was imposed by the civil power during the vacancy of 1938; before that the minister simply approved the choice of the assembled bishops. The present archbishop is the Lord Damaskinos Philippides.

Bishops. There are seventy-one[14] dioceses in the Church of Greece, and there is a very large number of bishops in the country, counting those who are auxiliary, retired, or deposed. Every bishop is called a metropolitan, but none of them have suffragans except the metropolitan of Crete, who has three. Among the principal other eparchies are Corinth, Patras, Larissa, Zante, Janina, Salonika, and Corfu; several of the sees have multiple titles, e.g., that of Syros, Tinos, Andros, and Kea. Since 1931 pressure has been applied by the state to reduce the number of these sees to forty, but progress with this reform is very slow; it was ordered to be carried out by 1934, but little seems to have been done.[15]

When a see is vacant the permanent synod sends the three names most favoured by all the metropolitans to the Minister of Worship, who himself makes a choice from the *terna.* Though technically a monk, a bishop has not generally been a member of a monastery but of an episcopal *curia.*

The island of Crete has a special ecclesiastical constitution of its own and is virtually antonomous. The metropolitan (of Heraklion) is selected by the Oecumenical Patriarch from three names submitted by the other Cretan bishops. Monasticism is more flourishing in Crete than in other parts of Greece.

Episcopal assembly. The supreme authority in the Church of Greece is all the ruling bishops assembled in synod; they have the safeguarding of faith and morals and of the discipline of the

[14] There are thirty-two in the old kingdom and thirty-nine attached from Constantinople as related above.

[15] It would save money, as well as have other advantages, for the state pays a small salary to every bishop, whether active or not.

church. Normally the assembly meets every three years; its acts must be approved by the civil power.

Permanent synod. This is the directing administrative body in the church and exercises full ecclesiastical powers, subject to the canons and to the assembly of bishops. It has the right to appeal for support to the secular arm. It consists, under the presidency of the archbishop of Athens, of some bishops from the old eparchies and others from those detached from Constantinople; these are renewed every year according to the order of their seniority, but in practice the synod has been "packed" by the government of the moment.

Though the government commissioner (procurator) must be present at meetings of the synod he no longer has the right of veto.

Cases concerning bishops are judged by a supreme court of twelve bishops elected by the synod, with the archbishop as president; a final appeal can be made to the assembly of bishops.

Lower clergy. The sacerdotal standard is slowly but steadily rising in Greece; there are now a dozen colleges (but with very short courses) for aspirants to the priesthood, and preaching and the systematic instruction of children is more and more widespread. Nevertheless, large numbers of the clergy are still undereducated, and the material conditions of many of them are very bad indeed. There is an insufficiency of institutions for their full-time formation; only a very small proportion of them have been to the theological school at the University of Athens or to the excellent Rhizarion seminary founded by the brothers Rhizares in 1843, and only about a quarter to the colleges above mentioned. The law of 1945 provided for the establishment of more seminaries and church colleges.

Parish priests are proposed by the parishioners: they must be at least thirty years old and married, and have to retire at seventy-five. The Greek dislike of young parish priests is a big factor in the problem of training them properly.

Monasticism. In 1833 there were nearly 400 monasteries in Greece, with an average of only five monks or nuns, and the government suppressed all those with less than six members. At the present day Hellenic monasticism is in a similar condition: the 1850 monks were distributed among so many monasteries (177) that the law of 1931 ordered all houses with less than seven members to be united with the larger ones. There are 32 convents of women, with 600 or so nuns, of whom a large proportion are in the convent of the Falling-Asleep of the Mother of God, a pilgrimage shrine on the isle of Tinos. Many of the monasteries have no novices at all, many of the monks are non-resident and many more are aged; it is, therefore, not surprising that there is a strong inclination in contemporary Greece to look on the monastic life with contempt.

The most famous existing monasteries are those of Meteora in the plain of Thessaly, built on the top of high, isolated crags like islets of rock. They first appear as cenobia in the fourteenth century, and seem now to be hastening to a most regrettable extinction: in 1931 there were left only five monks each in the Great Meteora, Holy Trinity, and St. Barlaam's, six in St. Stephen's, and a solitary hermit in Rossani. In 1941 Italian troops drove out the remaining monks (killing some of them) and looted the monasteries. The ancient and well-known monastery of Megaspileon in the Peloponessus was destroyed by fire in 1934.[16] Hosios Loukas in Phokis, south of Mount Helikon, which has fifteen or so monks, has a superb eleventh-century church and mosaics. An attempt is being made to establish a congregation of Sisters of Christian Instruction, for the education of girls.

The faithful. Practically all the inhabitants of Greece (5,961,000 out of 6,204,000) are members of the national church. Those in U.S.A. and elsewhere abroad are under the jurisdiction of the patriarch of Constantinople (see pp. 29 and 153).

In general, the countryfolk are more attached to their religion

---

[16] Many priceless manuscripts and lovely eikons were destroyed. Much of the damage was done by the explosion of gunpowder, which had been stored there, under the treasury, ever since the year of independence! Some clamored that all the monks should be shot summarily for their carelessness! What was left was destroyed by the German invaders in 1943.

than those of the towns, but of late years there has been a strong movement of revival among the younger people of the educated middle class, who realize that harmony has got to be established between their religious life, rooted in Byzantine culture, and the modern Western civilization in which they live. This movement centres round the weekly paper called *Zoe*, founded by the late archimandrite Eusebius Matthopoulos, who collected a body of lay and clerical workers. The *Zoe* brotherhood is concerned with preaching, the more frequent reception of the sacraments, the publishing of religious literature, and religious instruction of the young and the training of teachers therefor. Some of its preachers are laymen, and *Zoe* exercises a wide and enlightened influence. Among its publications are liturgical and patristic books and a new edition of the New Testament.[17]

Other similar activities are the Young Orthodox Association, the Society of St. Thekla for women, and the periodical *Anaplasis*. Among the leaders in these movements are the theologians Professor P. J. Bratsiotis and Mr. N. Trembelas, and there has been a real deepening of spiritual life and a notable increase in preaching and instruction by the clergy. The holy synod in 1933 formed an organization to second these efforts and to counteract communist propaganda. On the other hand, the irreligious section of young Greeks is very virulent, and their hatred for and credulity about their national church is almost as crude as their attitude toward Catholicity. In general the religious groups, though certainly having no "Romeward inclination," welcome the interest of and association with Catholics; but unhappily the Latin church in Greece emphasizes its "foreignness" and is not seen at its best, at any rate on the mainland, so that the Orthodox Church does not fear its influence. The tiny body of Catholic Byzantines is bitterly opposed by the Orthodox authorities, and

---

[17] Among general works it has published a translation of Cardinal Wiseman's *Fabiola*. Matthopoulos in early life withdrew from his master Makrakis because his methods threatened to provoke a schism.

the law of 1938 against "proselytism" is particularly directed against them. This law seeks to give a veritable monopoly to the dominant church in the country.

The events of the years just past have done much to aggravate Greek opposition to Catholicity. To the Greeks, Italy stands for the Catholic Church. On Good Friday, 1939, Mussolini forcibly annexed Albania; eighteen months later he invaded Greece. The outrages perpetrated by some of the Italian troops, especially in Albania, will not easily be forgotten. To a Greek it looks like the Fourth Crusade all over again – the representatives of the Catholic Church coming with fire and sword to destroy Greek freedom. It is illogical; it is untrue: but that is how a Greek sees it.

BIBLIOGRAPHY

*Finlay, *Mediaeval Greece* (Edinburgh, 1851).

—— *Greece under Venetian and Turkish Domination* (Edinburgh, 1856).

Fortescue, *The Orthodox Eastern Church* (London, 1911).

Max of Saxony, *Das christliche Hellas* (Leipzig, 1918).

†Papakosta, *Eusebius Matthopoulos, Founder of "Zoe"* (London, 1939).

CHAPTER VI

THE OTHER ORTHODOX CHURCHES

1. THE EXARCHATE OF BULGARIA

THE Bulgars are in origin a Finno-Turkish people, long ago thoroughly slavonized, who established an independent kingdom in their present country and its borders during the seventh century. About the year 865 their Tsar Boris, largely for political motives, accepted Christianity from Constantinople and imposed it on his people. But Boris wanted his church to be independent, and turned to Pope St. Nicholas I, asking him to give Bulgaria a patriarch. Nicholas sent a bishop; but he was not given the rank of patriarch. This precipitated a long contest for jurisdiction over the Bulgars, both Rome and Constantinople claiming that they were in their patriarchal jurisdiction, and this was part of the question of Illyricum that embittered relations and contributed to the Eastern schism. The Slavs, too, had a big part in the conversion of the Bulgars. When the Germans made things impossible for the followers of St. Methodius in Moravia and Pannonia, a number of them fled into Bulgaria about the year 885 and evangelized the heathen there. Their leader St. Clement and four of his clergy, together with SS. Cyril and Methodius, are venerated as the Seven Apostles of the Bulgars. The use of Church Slavonic in the Liturgy as a "national custom" seems to have begun when these followers of St. Methodius introduced the practice at the court of Boris, who adopted it as a sign of independence of Constantinople. Bulgaria is accounted one of the Slav churches, for although, as has been said, the Bulgars are not Slav in origin they are so in culture and perhaps spoke Slavonic before they entered the Balkans.

The emperor Basil II ("the Bulgar-slayer") conquered Bulgaria in 1018, and the Church of Okhrida (Akrida) was hellenized and eventually involved in the Byzantine schism of the later middle ages. But it continued to be an autonomous church till 1767, when it was reduced to complete dependence on the patriarch of Constantinople, the see of Okhrida being suppressed. Eastern Bulgaria recovered independence in 1185, and from 1204 to 1234 was in unambiguous communion with Rome, its primatial see being at Tirnova. Then the politics of the Tsar John Assen II dragged the Church of Tirnova into schism, and when Bulgaria was conquered by the Ottoman Turks in 1394 its territory was united to that of Okhrida, but ecclesiastically it managed to maintain a semi-independence, as part of the metropolitan eparchy of Mavro-Valachia, until 1767. There was the usual tragic story of Turkish oppression, during which some of the archbishops of Okhrida returned to communion with the Holy See. Some of these reconciliations were purely political and opportunist, but others were undoubtedly genuinely religious.

When in that year all the Bulgarian eparchies were brought under the direct control of Constantinople they were subjected to a ruthless process of hellenizing: Greek became the compulsory liturgical language and only Greeks were appointed to episcopal sees. National consciousness awoke in Bulgaria and when, in 1856, the Turkish government decreed the freedom and equality of its Christian subjects, Bulgarian representatives demanded for their church a number of far-reaching reforms. (Political freedom was their ultimate object; it was practically gained in 1878.) The patriarch of Constantinople made certain concessions, including the appointment of some bishops of Bulgarian nationality. But it was too late; by 1860 Bulgaria was demanding an autonomous national church, and in 1870 it was granted by an imperial *firman* from the Ottoman Porte: the Bulgarian Church was to be autocephalous under an exarch and synod. Whereupon the patriarch of Constantinople, Anthimos VI, excommunicated the exarch and his followers, an action that was confirmed by a synod at the Phanar in 1872, which condemned the heresy of "phyletism," nationalism in religion. But the Bulgars were solidly behind their leaders and ignored the synod, in which the patriarchs of Constantinople, Alexandria, and Antioch, four ex-patriarchs, and twenty-five other bishops had taken part.[1]

From that day on for seventy-three years the four ancient patriarchates and the other Greek churches regarded the Bulgarian Church as schismatic and refused communion with it; the other Orthodox churches, however, accepted the fact of independence and recognized the Bulgarian Church as lawfully constituted. At length in 1945, at the request of Archbishop Stephen and his bishops, the Oecumenical Patriarch, Benjamin I, received the Bulgarian Church back into communion as an independent body. The increasing influence of the U.S.S.R. in Bulgaria probably facilitated this decision at the Phanar. At the same time the archbishop asked that his throne be made patriarchal, to which Constantinople replied that the matter would be considered. This probably means that before long there will be a Patriarchate of Bulgaria. This multiplication of patriarchs is rather silly; to give one to a not-very-big and purely national church reduces the dignity of a very ancient and most important office by helping to make it meaningless.

In the days of the "Macedonian question" there was a continuous contest between the Greek and Bulgarian churches that was one of the most disgraceful and disgusting episodes of Balkan ecclesiastical history; rival bishoprics were set up by the exarchate, and the Greeks retorted by siding with the Turks in their bloodthirsty suppression of the Bulgars. This state of affairs was ended by the Balkan wars of 1912–1913, which almost emptied Macedonia and Thrace of Bulgars, and at the same time the exarch took up his residence at Sofia. Hitherto he had lived at Orta-Keuy on the Bosphorus, under the very

[1] At the beginning of their stuggle with Constantinople there was an influential minority of Bulgars who sought ecclesiastical independence of the Greeks by means of reunion with Rome. This was the origin of the group of Catholic Bulgars of the Byzantine rite.

nose of the Oecumenical Patriarch, for greater convenience in dealing with the Turkish government and looking after his flock outside of Bulgaria proper. After the death, in 1915, of the third exarch, Joseph, a very capable prelate who had occupied the position for nearly thirty-nine years, no successor was appointed, and the post was administered by a vicar until in 1945 the Metropolitan Stephen of Sophia was appointed exarch.

In spite of its active part in the winning of national independence, the relations of the Bulgarian Church with the state have been far from good. The violent reforming projects of the minister Stambulisky (1920–1923) and his seizure of church property caused considerable alarm, and in 1928 the metropolitan of Sofia, Stephen, openly and categorically advocated complete separation of church and state in the interests of both. This friction has greatly handicapped the church in its efforts to formulate for itself a new constitution in harmony with present circumstances. In 1936 it was proposed that legislation should be passed providing for civil marriages, which were then only an ecclesiastical concern; the opposition was led by the Stephen just mentioned, who protested to King Boris III in person.

ORGANIZATION AND PRESENT STATE

Exarch. This hierarch is little more than first among equals, the holy synod being the real governing authority.

Bishops. There are ten Bulgarian eparchies, whose bishops are all metropolitans without suffragans, viz.: Sofia, Tirnova, Varna, Plovdiv, Rustchuk, Nevrokop, Sliven, Stara-Zagara, Viddin, and Vratsa.

A metropolitan is chosen by the holy synod from two names submitted by the eparchy concerned; he must be approved by the government.

Holy synod. The governing synod has supreme authority in the church and consists of four bishops elected by itself for a period of two years, under the presidency of the exarch or the senior metropolitan for the time being. In 1936 it was decided that the archpriests should be represented on the executive council of all the bishops.

Lower clergy. There are senior seminaries at Sofia and Cherepich, a junior seminary at Plovdiv, and a faculty of theology in the University of Sofia. Though a great improvement on the past, this provision is still inadequate for requirements and over half the Bulgarian clergy have had hardly any ecclesiastical training at all, a condition of affairs of which the authorities are keenly conscious. The material state of many of the clergy, too, is very unsatisfactory. They form, nevertheless, an independent-minded body, being organized into unions, which gave a good deal of support to the innovations of Stambulisky before his fall from power in 1923.

Monasticism. The religious life is in a state of rapid decline. Monasteries are fairly numerous, but they have few or no religious and many of them (as in some other countries) are used as places for country holidays. They house only about 150 monks and the same number of nuns, and some years ago a monastic school was opened at Troian to encourage vocations. An attempt in 1926 to establish a congregation of "active" nuns was a failure.

Among the monasteries are Cherepich, Batchkovo, and, the principal one, Ryla, in the mountains of that name south of Sofia.

The faithful. Out of a population of nearly 6,000,000, 4,500,000 are Orthodox, the largest minority being 800,000 Mohammedans; Catholics number about 40,000, of whom 5500 are of the Byzantine rite.

The newspaper *Pravda,* of Vratsa, wrote in 1931: "We Bulgars today are without religion. Most of us go to church three times in our lives, and then because we must: to be christened, to be married, and to be buried. For twelve centuries the Bulgarian people has been officially Christian, but in reality it has not yet been spiritually penetrated by the religion of Jesus Christ." It went on to blame the foreign (Greek) clergy in the past and then the fact that the Bulgarian clergy had been a political body more concerned for national unity than for the Christian apostolate. But it would have been fair to add that the disturbed state

In 1783 the Georgian king, Heraklios II, allied himself with Russia for defence against the Persians, and eighteen years later Tsar Alexander I annexed the whole country. In 1811 the katholikos Antony was forced to resign by the Russian holy synod, which appointed an exarch in his place, an office always filled from 1817 by a Russian; Slavonic was forcibly substituted for Georgian in the liturgy (the vernacular was forbidden even for preaching and teaching), the sees were reduced to four, monasteries and churches were despoiled – the Church of Georgia in fact became an oppressed part of the Church of Russia.[5] After the decree of religious toleration of Tsar Nicholas II the Georgians presented a petition for autonomy; the only reply was the exile of the prelate who presented it. Shortly afterwards the Russian exarch, Nikon, was assassinated by Georgian insurgents.

At the revolution in 1917 an assembly of bishops, priests, and laymen at once declared the Georgian Church autocephalous again and a few months later Kirion (d. 1919) was elected katholikos; the Russian patriarch Tikhon protested, but no notice was taken. In 1921 Georgia became a socialist soviet republic, and the katholikos Ambrose was arrested for sending to the Geneva conference of 1922 a memorandum against the government's anti-religious policy; another bishop and several priests were also imprisoned. Ambrose was sentenced to death, but the sentence was commuted to nine years in prison, where he died in 1927. In the same year a council of the church threw itself into the arms of the bolshevists: it repudiated the memorandum of 1922, declared that Georgian Christians were quite free under the enlightened and progressive rule of their soviet republic, and denounced the (supposed) relations between Georgian emigrants of the one part and the pope and the archbishop of Canterbury of the other. This was signed in the name of the council by the metropolitan Christopher, who became katholikos on the death of Ambrose.

[5] One effect of this policy was to make the Georgian church colleges centres of revolutionary disaffection. In the closing years of the nineteenth century there was at the Tiflis seminary a young student named Joseph Iugashvily. He is now known as Joseph Stalin.

Partly on account of this subservience, partly on account of the insurrection of 1924, bolshevist persecution has not been so intense in Georgia as in Russia. But a dozen churches (out of twenty-two) were closed, and thirty priests apostatized in Tiflis alone.

ORGANIZATION AND PRESENT STATE

The *katholikos,* who has the title of "Archbishop of Mtshetis and Tiflis, Katholikos of All Iberia," resides at Tiflis; the other episcopal *sees* are Imeretia, Guria-Mingrelia, Gori, and Sukhum; and these five hierarchs form the *holy synod.*

There is not much reliable information about Georgia today available, and it is difficult to gauge the state of its church. Doubtless the two seminaries and thirty-four monasteries and convents that formerly existed have now been dissolved and the 1300 monks and nuns scattered; nor may we suppose that nearly 2500 churches and 1700 priests are any longer required. The number of Georgian Orthodox is nominally about 2¼ millions, but a century of exploitation by imperial Russian officials, civil and ecclesiastical, was no good preparation for the fresh religious and political troubles that were to come upon them. A Russian *bezbojnik* (*sans-Dieu,* atheist), Pavel Postnikov, in the course of a journey for study and propaganda in 1931, found that at Tiflis sufficient watch was not kept on religious movements; the secretary of the chief local anti-religious organization replied to his remonstrance that, "Experience has shown the religious spirit to be so weak here that there is no need for us to trouble about its manifestations." A more recent observer comments on the lukewarmness of Georgian Christians as contrasted with Russians in the same republic. Nevertheless in 1946 the Katholikos Kinkadze (Kallistratos) estimated that 80 per cent of the Georgians were believers.

BIBLIOGRAPHY

Tamarati, *L'Eglise Géorgienne* (Rome, 1910).
Karst, *Littérature Géorgienne Chrétienne* (Paris, 1934).
*Wardrop, *The Kingdom of Georgia* (London, 1888).

3. THE CHURCH OF ALBANIA

Albania is predominantly a Mohammedan country, having 615,000 Moslems (who still keep several Christian customs); but the Gheg tribe in the north is pretty solidly Catholic (100,000 Latins), and there are 185,000 Orthodox.

After the absorption of the Church of Okhrida by the Patriarchate of Constantinople in 1767 the Orthodox metropolitans of Albania were Greek prelates depending directly on the Oecumenical Patriarch. At the Young-Turk revolution in 1908 and again when their country became an independent state after the Balkan wars of 1912–1913, the Orthodox Albanians showed strong separatist inclinations, and these were translated into action when the kingdom was established after World War I. After a rather fantastic affair in which the chief part was played by Fan Noli,[6] an Albanian priest from U.S.A. (his enemies asserted that he had been a gangster in Chicago!), an Orthodox congress gathered at Berat in 1922 under the presidency of the priest Basil Marku (At-Vassil) and demanded recognition of the independence of their church. The Greek bishops fled, and the Oecumenical Patriarch sent an exarch of Albanian blood, Hierotheos, to examine the situation, but he joined the autonomists; his example was followed by another bishop, Christopher Kissis. After negotiations the Phanar in 1926 made an offer of autocephaly on very fair terms, but these were refused at the last moment by King Ahmad Zoghu,[7] and there

[6] He became president of the council of ministers in the government of 1924, after having been ordained bishop. He was a man of considerable intellectual ability, who had studied at Harvard.

[7] He was a Mohammedan, but he issued diplomas of investiture to his Orthodox bishops — quite like old times. For some obscure reason English-speaking newspapers agree to call him "King Zog" — apparently another example of the journalistic habit of trying to make appear ridiculous that which is not ridiculous.

is little doubt that the government of Italy was behind this refusal—and, indeed, an encourager of the whole agitation: Signor Mussolini had not yet got formal autocephaly for the Dodekanese eparchies (see p. 27) and wanted allies with a similar cause. The Greek government also had a hand in it. Finally, in 1929, with the assistance of a Serbian prelate (and apparently the connivance of the Yugoslav patriarch, Dimitry), two more Albanian bishops were consecrated, a holy synod formed, and their church solemnly proclaimed autocephalous at Tirana.

The Patriarch of Constantinople now lost patience at last, declared the members of the synod degraded from the episcopal office, and acquainted the other churches with what had happened. Thereupon the Albanian government expelled the patriarchal exarch, Hierotheos (who had refused to join the new synod), and the Albanians, at any rate in theory, became as schismatic as their Bulgarian brothers. But they were openly recognized by the Yugoslav patriarch, who had insisted on having an exarch in Albania to look after the Slavs in the plain of Skutari, and in 1937 Constantinople gave in and recognized the new autocephaly.

The church has not yet elaborated a constitution. Its hierarchs, who form the holy synod, are at present the Archbishop of Durazzo at Tirana and the bishops of Berat, Argyrokastro, and Korytsa. The first archbishop was the Christopher Kissis mentioned above.

The liturgical language is Greek or Albanian, according to the needs of the congregation. The bishops have to get the holy chrism from the patriarch of Constantinople.

The disedifying succession of ecclesiastical and political intrigues in Albania during those fifteen years turned the eyes of many religious Orthodox toward Rome, and there has been some talk of mass reunions. But the spirit of Albanian nationalism is exceptionally strong, and a note of spite against Constantinople can be detected in this talk. But, says Father Pascal Giardi, an Albanian Jesuit, many of his Orthodox fellow countrymen "are practically Catholics at heart. In spite of an unbelievable ignorance about religion and the insufficient training of the clergy they are solidly attached to all that the Church teaches. . . . They often come to our services and ask us to hear their confessions." There are a few reunited Catholics of the Byzantine rite in the Al-Bassan district.

BIBLIOGRAPHY

*Peacock, *Albania* (London, 1914).

4. THE CHURCH OF FINLAND

Nearly all of the 3¾ million inhabitants of Finland are Protestant, but there were, in 1939, 73,500 Orthodox, of whom a tenth were Russians and the rest mostly Karelians. When the country gained its independence of Russia in 1919 the government, being unable to come to terms with the patriarch of Moscow, approached the patriarch of Constantinople, who in 1923 issued a *tomos* in which, in view of the difficult state of the Church of Russia, which prevented it properly looking after its Finnish child, he recognized the autonomy of the Finnish Orthodox under himself. The archbishop in Finland being a Russian, he was forced to resign in 1924, and his Finnish auxiliary, Herman Aava (an Estonian by birth), was promoted to the primacy but with a new title, a second eparchy being erected in the same year.

The primate is entitled the "Archbishop of Karelia and All Finland"; he lives at Kuopio, where he has a seminary. Before convening a synod he must have the permission of the Oecumenical Patriarch, who must be prayed for in the Liturgy; the choice of a new archbishop must be submitted to him and the holy chrism obtained from him. The language of worship is Finnish, except in Russian churches.

There were four Russian monasteries in Finland: Valamo (Valaam) and Konoveto (Konievietsky laura) in lake Ladoga, and Petsamo (Trifonopetchiensky laura), with 500 monks between them, and a convent of 30 nuns at Lintula. No new monasteries of any obedience were allowed to be established, and only Finnish subjects might be received in those that already existed.

Valamo was in 1939 the most important Russian monastery existing and functioning in the world. It was founded in an unknown year by SS. Sergius and Germanus, and its history has been as eventful as long; in 1575, for example, forty of its monks were murdered by the Swedes, who burnt it down in 1611. The monastery had an excellent library and numerous well-equipped workshops and studios. The community numbered about 300 and the sacred liturgy was celebrated with the most impressive solemnity.

Friction between Finns and Russians was aggravated by the extreme nationalist particularism of the Finns. Some of it was simply the natural enthusiasm of a newly independent people: a less respectable manifestation of this spirit was the making of ecclesiastical vestments on the pattern of the national flag, a blue cross on a white ground. This nationalism was, of course, very pleasing to the government, which subsidized clergy, churches, and schools, and officially promulgated the decisions of the five-yearly assembly of Orthodox clergy and lay delegates. But in spite of the many difficulties of his position, some of them due to his insistence on the less important manifestations of "progress" (the Gregorian kalendar and clean-shaven clergy, for example), Archbishop Herman led the Church of Finland through a period of encouraging development. Then came war, and the whole thing was smashed.

By the armistice terms of 1940 and 1944 the Finnish Church lost to the U.S.S.R. nearly all its churches, and many of its schools and other institutions, including the seminary at Serdobol, which was rather inefficient but had an excellent library. The suffragan see of Viipuri (Viborg) was also lost. Indeed, the church would have practically disappeared had not some thousands of its faithful emigrated into the interior of Finland, rather than become soviet citizens. The four Russian monasteries have all been lost too. But the community of Valamo has happily been able to re-establish itself near Kuopio in Finland, to form the monastery of New Valamo. The Patriarch of Moscow continues to make efforts to bring the Church of Finland within his jurisdiction; so far Archbishop Herman has been able prudently to avoid this.

BIBLIOGRAPHY

†Bolshakov, *The Foreign Missions of the Russian Orthodox Church* (London, 1943).

St. George, "The Russian Monasteries of Valamo. . . ." in *Eastern Churches Quarterly*, Vol. III, No. 3 (Ramsgate, 1938).

†James, "The Cultural-Ecclesiastical Problem of Finland" in the same, Vol. IV, No. 3 (Ramsgate, 1940).

5. THE CHURCH OF POLAND

When Poland was restored as a sovereign state after World War I there were included in her population nearly four million Orthodox, mostly Ukrainians and Byelorussians (White Russians) on her eastern borders, between Vilna and the Carpathians. In the years immediately following the formation of the new Poland these Orthodox continued under their former jurisdiction, that of the Russian Church, but the Polish government was urgently anxious to detach them from this obedience. The patriarch of Moscow, Tikhon, would do no more than grant a measure of autonomy, under the Metropolitan George Zoroszevsky. This bishop was a supporter of the policy of complete independence, and in 1923, unbelievable as it must appear, he was assassinated by a Russian monk of opposite views. The Polish government then appealed to the patriarch of Constantinople; and the Phanar, after carefully examining the whole matter, issued a *tomos* at the end of 1924 granting autocephaly to the Orthodox of Poland, under Metropolitan Dionysy Valedinsky, successor of the murdered George. The Russian patriarchate refused to recognize this proceeding, which Constantinople claimed to be based on sound canonical and historical grounds.

The head of the new autocephaly was called The Metropolitan of Warsaw and All Poland, and there were four other sees. The bishops were appointed by the holy synod, and had to be approved by the civil power. The synod consisted of these five hierarchs, and it had a lay procurator representing the Polish government. The relationship between church and state indeed reproduced in miniature the position in Russia in tsarist days — with the difference that the Polish government was not that of an "Orthodox power."

There were seminaries at Vilna and Krzemienik and a faculty of Orthodox theology in the University of Warsaw; but most of the clergy were insufficiently trained and in desperate material want, as were many of their peasant flocks, especially in Polesia. There were ten monasteries of men and six of women, the chief being the famous house of Russian monks at Pochaev, near Dubno.

Most of the Orthodox of eastern Poland were descendants of the Catholics of Byzantine rite who were forcibly aggregated to the state church of Russia during the nineteenth century. There was consequently a certain disposition toward reunion among them, a disposition which the Holy See sought to meet, as mentioned in the previous volume (page 127). But the Catholic appeal was rendered nugatory, largely by the obstructive policy of the Polish civil authorities, and by the attempts of some Catholic ecclesiastics to recover from the Orthodox, churches and other shrines alleged to have been formerly in Catholic hands – claims that were not always upheld in the civil courts.[8]

All this came to a head in 1938 when Metropolitan Dionysy made a strong protest to the government, stating that in places Orthodox priests were forbidden to preach except in Polish, that Orthodox churches were summarily closed and many destroyed, that pressure was put on Orthodox people to join the Latin church and to send their children to Catholic schools, and the like. In a pastoral letter to his clergy, the Catholic Metropolitan Szepticky of Lvov witnessed to the truth of the Orthodox bishops' statements, and added his own protest to theirs. Leaders in the campaign of intimidation were the members of the Polish Defense Corps (KOP), to which local authorities added economic pressure. In such ways did representatives of the civil power in a Catholic country help to defeat the work of the Holy

[8] For example, in November, 1935, the court of appeal at Lublin dismissed the action brought against the Orthodox Church by the Catholic diocese of Luck for the recovery of fifty-eight sanctuaries, including the monastery of Pochaev. *See* further for all this unhappy business, *Eastern Churches Quarterly*, Vol. III, No. 4, pp. 245–251.

6. THE CHURCH OF JAPAN

The Orthodox Church of Japan had its origin in Father Nicholas Kasatkin, who was appointed chaplain to the Russian consulate at Hakodate in 1860. He made a number of converts, and a regular mission was established in 1871. Like all other Christians, the Orthodox found that the commendation of the gospel to the Japanese is no easy matter; but relatively they made remarkably good progress, and by the beginning of the Russo-Japanese war in 1904 there were 28,000 Orthodox Japanese, with thirty-nine clergy, all but three of them Japanese. The honourable behaviour of Bishop Nicholas (as he was by then) during this war increased the already great regard in which he was held in the country, and in 1906 he was made the first archbishop of Tokyo.

The mission in Japan received less material help from the Orthodox Missionary Society than other Russian missions: it was built up by the people themselves, under the quiet, tireless direction of Archbishop Nicholas, who never had more than two or three Russian priests to help him. So devoted was he to his flock that he revisited his homeland only three times, and his death in 1912 was an occasion of sorrow to Christians of all obediences.

In 1939 the Japanese government decided to bring the Christian bodies in the country under its control, and they were ordered to draw up and submit new constitutions. Those of the Orthodox Church were so heavily amended by the civil power that the Metropolitan Sergius resigned his charge in Japan, and it was decided to make the church virtually autonomous. Sergius conveyed the property of the Russian mission into Japanese hands, and appointed the archpriest Heikichi Ivazava

GREEK MOSAIC OF THE THEOTOKOS
(Fourteenth Century)

Courtesy, C. F. L. St. George

RUSSIAN EIKON OF THE FALLING ASLEEP OF OUR LADY
(Sixteenth Century)

OUR LADY OF VLADIMIR

Christ the King (Pantokrator)

St. Gregory Theologos

SEVENTEENTH-CENTURY SERBIAN EIKONS

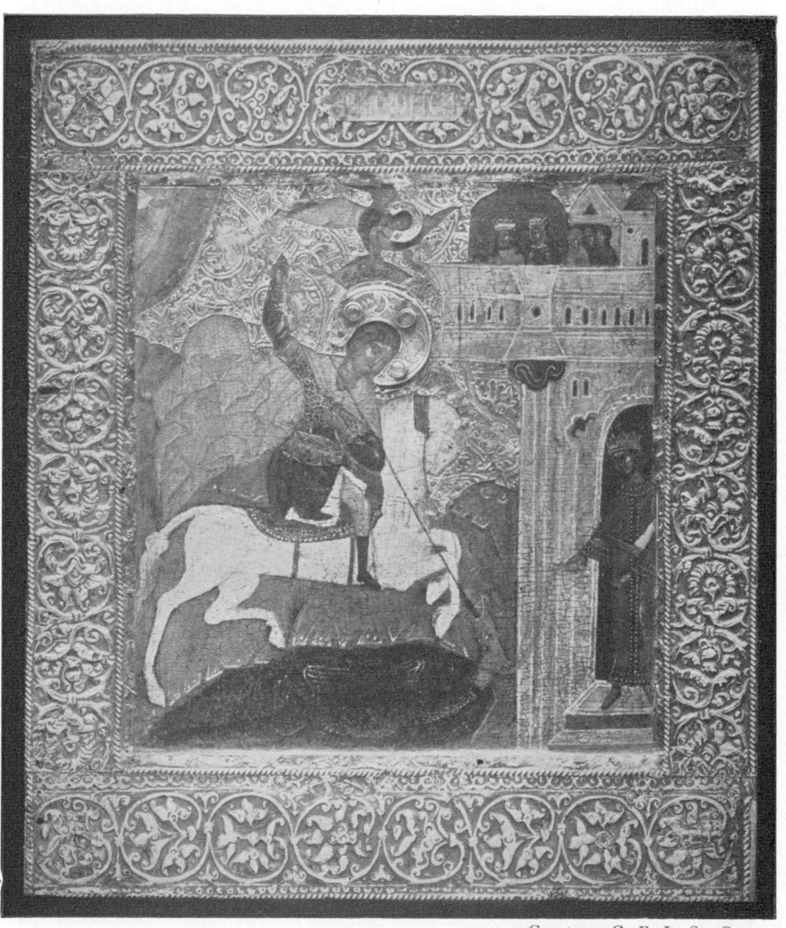

Courtesy, C. F. L. St. George

RUSSIAN EIKON OF ST. GEORGE

(Seventeenth Century)

ST. BENEDICT AND ST. BASIL

(A Fifteenth-Century Eikon)

EIKON OF ALL HOLY MONKS OF THE EAST

Copr., Mary Morton

Courtesy, Edward Bowron

GREEK MONKS

to be administrator of the church. In the following year, 1941, the Japanese government approved the new constitutions; they provide that the clergy shall all be Japanese (which was practically the case already), that bishops and some other office-holders must be confirmed by the government, and that all ecclesiastical activity shall be severely controlled by the civil power.

In the same year the archpriest John Ono became the first Japanese archbishop of Tokyo. He was married, but his wife (daughter of the first Japanese Orthodox priest, Paul Savabe) wished to become a nun, and both received the monastic habit on the same day. Father John took the name of Nicholas, and received episcopal ordination shortly after.

The Japanese Orthodox numbered 50,000 ten years ago, of whom rather less than half were classed as "fervent." They had about thirty priests, and 180 places of worship. In 1939 the numbers were said to have fallen to 41,000.

One of the principal needs of the Japanese church is a seminary. One was founded by Archbishop Kasatkin, but it was closed in 1918, and so far all efforts to get it going again have failed. From the early days of the mission the Japanese language has been used in public worship.

BIBLIOGRAPHY

†Bolshakov, *The Foreign Missions of the Russian Orthodox Church* (London, 1943).

†Gorodetska, "Missionary Expansion of the Russian Church" in *Eastern Churches Quarterly*, Vol. V, Nos. 5–6 (Ramsgate, 1943).

7. THE ORTHODOX IN AMERICA[10]

Excluding the rather special case of Alaska, the Orthodox Church in North America dates from 1812, when some Russians made a settlement in California, but the church remained almost unknown in the United States of America until the early years of the present century. Between 1905 and 1909 there were nearly 100,000 immigrants from Greece and Turkey, and then and at other times numerous Orthodox Syrians, Serbs, and Rumanians arrived from central Europe and hither Asia; the number of Russian immigrants was relatively small, but ecclesiastically they were increased by defections from among the Catholic Ruthenians (Ukrainians).

The tide of immigration having ceased, the Orthodox of North America are now trying to build up a permanent and solid organization. Their efforts are to a huge extent weakened, not only by factions imported from their home countries or started in America, but by their insistence on trying to develop sectionally along their respective national lines. Such particularism is inherent in modern Orthodoxy, and the pressure of national culture is easily understood (at any rate by a European); but it seems obvious to an outside observer that the good of religion in North America demands that the Orthodox of all races should co-operate in a single autonomous church. As it is, the various racial groups of Orthodox look to an outsider like so many unconnected, separate churches; occasionally the prelates of one nation assist at the services of another, especially at the ordina

[10] I have received special help in this chapter from the Rev. T. J. Collins of Detroit, from James F. Kane, of New York, and from Robert Cutler, c New York.

tion of priests and bishops, but even this is not often. And between the more ignorant of the Greeks and Russians there is an antipathy that has been compared with the ill feeling between Irish and Italians in America.

In 1927, on the initiative of Metropolitan Platon Rojdestvensky, a constitution for a North American autocephalous church was drawn up, with a Syrian archbishop, Aftimios, as president of the synod; but the project did not receive the general support of American Orthodox, and none at all from outside. So, when the Oecumenical Patriarch (Basil III) refused to recognize the new autocephaly, this well-meant and theoretically sound endeavour to unify the Orthodox in America collapsed.[11] In 1943 an attempt was begun to organize a "Federated Orthodox-Greek-Catholic Primary Jurisdiction in America," but it seems so far not to have made striking progress.

American Orthodox in general aim at the establishment of more organized parishes and schools, at reclaiming those who have fallen away from their church in a strange land, and at keeping the rising generation faithful to religion – a difficult problem. It cannot be a matter for surprise that they regard the existence of Catholic minorities among their people as a weakening of their forces, and make considerable efforts to detach them from their allegiance to the Roman centre of unity. On the other hand, there can be no question but that much of the cordiality shown by many of the American Orthodox toward the Episcopal Church, the Y.M.C.A., and other Protestant bodies is simply an acknowledgment of the financial and other help received from those sources.

In 1944 the Greek archbishop of New York stated that there are five million Orthodox believers in the United States. If by that is meant five million persons who by origin and descent are Orthodox the figure may be a fair one; but if practising Orthodox Christians is intended the figure is very heavily

---

[11] For a short time this body produced an interesting monthly publication called *The Orthodox Catholic Review*.

overstated.[12] In the statistics that appear below I have given in most cases figures taken from the official U.S.A. census of religious bodies for 1936; these figures are definitely on the low side, and perhaps refer only to adults or to those people sufficiently concerned about their religion to record it. B. Y. Landis, in the *Yearbook of American Churches* (Lebanon, Pa., 1943) gives much higher figures. Orthodox are most numerous in the states of New York, Pennsylvania, Massachusetts, Illinois, and Michigan; and there are many in Minnesota and Wisconsin. L. M. Gray in an informative article on "Eastern Orthodoxy in America" in *The Commonweal* of April 13, 1932, wrote: "American Orthodoxy is yearly losing from its active communicants more than three quarters of its baptized who reach the age of sixteen. Today not more than 5 per cent of Orthodox baptized in America actually confess to an Orthodox priest at Eastertime. Most Orthodox children attend no religious service whatever at any time. One half of all Orthodox born in America and now over fifteen years of age who are regular attendants or members of any religious body are no longer Orthodox but Protestant episcopalians."

THE RUSSIANS

The Russians are now the largest as well as the oldest Orthodox group in America. In 1794 a band of missionary monks from Valaam arrived in Alaska and built the first Orthodox church, on Kadiak island; the great figure of those early days was the hieromonk Innocent Veniaminov, afterwards metropolitan of Moscow. A number of Eskimo and Indian converts were made, and in 1840 a regular diocese was erected for "Kamchatka, the Kurile and the Aleutian Islands," with its see at Sitka, on Baranof island in Alaska. Father Innocent was its first bishop. In 1872

[12] It is extremely difficult to get accurate statistics of the dissident Eastern Christians in America. But it is beyond doubt that only a minority of them, sometimes a very small minority, practice their religion. For example there are probably 10,000 dissident Armenians in Detroit, but their one church will hold only 350, and it is not always full on Sundays. One and a half million would perhaps be a fair figure for effective Orthodox.

the see was moved to San Francisco, in 1890 an auxiliary bishop was appointed for Alaska, and in 1906 Sitka again became the centre of a separate diocese of Alaska and the Aleutians. It comprises some 8000 Indians, Aleutians, and Eskimo, and a number of Russians and Serbs, and is divided into three vicariates, Sitka, Unalashka, and the North (at Ikognut). There is a small monastery on the island of Elovy.

In 1905 Bishop Tikhon (later to be the ill-fated patriarch of Moscow) moved his see from San Francisco to New York,[13] and in the following year he was made archbishop, with suffragans in Alaska and Brooklyn. At this time the spread of Russian Orthodoxy was due to secessions from the Catholic Ruthenians, a movement led by the archpriest Alexis Toth; of the 29,000 Russian Orthodox in North America in 1909, over a half could be accounted for in this way.[14]

After the revolution of 1917 there was a big influx of Russians into North America (nearly all to U.S.A.), which caused extensive and frequent hierarchical changes and rearrangements; these were complicated by the internal divisions of the Russian Church in Europe and Russia. The chief American hierarch was Platon Rojdestvensky, who supported the party of Metropolitan Eulogius (see p. 83). The reconciliation in Europe of this hierarch with Metropolitan Antony led to a more easy state of affairs, but Russian Americans still divided between recognition of the Synod of Karlovtsy and of the Moscow patriarch. But at a council held at Cleveland, Ohio, in the fall of 1946, a majority voted for recognition of the Patriarch of Moscow as their spiritual head, but with complete administrative autonomy for themselves. A number of parishes, led by Archbishop Vitaly, still recognize only the Synod of Karlovtsy (Munich).

The head of the Russian Orthodox Church in North America

---

[13] The first Russian church in New York was opened *c.* 1870 on Second Avenue by Father Nicholas Bierring.

[14] When an Eastern Catholic parish was to be organized in Minneapolis in 1891 the local bishop refused to recognize its priest, Father Toth, because he was married. Father Toth then led his flock into the Orthodox Church. This was very wrong, but in the circumstances understandable, for up till then Father Toth was a priest in good standing.

in 1947 is Theophilus Pashkovsky (who administers the sees of San Francisco and New York). Other bishops have their sees at Sitka, Seattle, Chicago, Detroit, Pittsburgh, Jersey City, Brooklyn, and Edmonton, Alberta.

There is an important Russian monastery with a seminary, orphanage, and retreat-house, at South Canaan, Pa., and smaller ones at Jordansville, N. Y., Blufton, Alberta, and Sifton, Manitoba. St. Tikhon's at South Canaan is the great American centre of Russian Orthodoxy. There is an institute of theology (St. Vladimir's) affiliated to Columbia University and another seminary at Bridgeport, Conn.

There are over 200 Russian churches and chapels in North America, but the faithful are mixed and show a predominance of Ukrainians over Great Russians everywhere except in the West. Their number is very uncertain; it is said to be over half a million, but the 1936 census suggests that not more than 100,000 are effectively members of their church.

There is a movement among the American Russians to use the English language in the Liturgy, but this movement is far from unopposed. They are also divided as to whether they should encourage a *rapprochement* with the Protestant Episcopalians or with the Catholic Church. The second alternative has by far the weaker following, partly because it seems to have received little, if any, encouragement from the attitude of Catholics. On the other hand, seeing how much has been done by the Episcopalians and how little by Catholics for the Russians, the slight Romeward inclination is probably entirely religious: Catholics have a very serious responsibility to meet it with sympathy and understanding.

The first Russian church in South America was opened in the 'eighties of last century in Buenos Aires. There are now some tens of thousands of Russians there. The first episcopal see was set up in 1934 at São Paulo in Brazil, where there is the second most important establishment of the Brotherhood of St. Vladimir (see p. 87). There is a bishop also in the Argentine and one at Montevideo.

THE GREEKS

The first Greek church in America was opened in New Orleans in 1866, the first in New York in 1891, and after the influx of 1905–1908 many more were built; but they did not have a bishop till 1918. The number of Greek Orthodox was given as 189,000 in 1936.

When they were withdrawn from the jurisdiction of the Church of Greece and returned to that of Constantinople in 1922, the Oecumenical Patriarch (Meletios IV), organized them into an autonomous American Greek church, with an archbishop at New York and suffragans at Boston, Chicago, and San Francisco. This was found to be premature, and after several years of disputes and difficulties the Phanar reduced the autonomous church to the status of a diocese dependent on Constantinople. The metropolitan for the two Americas, at present (1946), Mgr. Athenagoras of New York, has two auxiliary bishops. But this arrangement did not give satisfaction, political and personal rivalries were at work, and a new schism broke out. This was led by Bishop Christopher of Philadelphia, who consecrated several bishops with the avowed intention of creating an independent holy synod for the Greeks in America.

There are no Greek monasteries, and the seminary founded at New York in 1921 was closed three years after; but a new theological college was opened in 1936. Their churches number over 200.

Of all the Orthodox in America the Greeks are the most friendly with the Episcopalians and the most antagonistic toward the Catholic Church.

THE SERBS

Serbs are mainly found in Pennsylvania and the west, where their first church was built at Jackson, Calif., in 1894 by the archimandrite Sebastian Dabovich. Their numbers were given as 20,000 in 1936.

The first Serbian bishop for all America, subject to the patriarch at Belgrade, was Madary Uskokovich of Chicago. There is a Serbian monastery at Libertyville, near Chicago, with an imposing church in the national style. They have about a score of churches in U.S.A.

THE SYRIANS

The Melkites in America, mostly from the patriarchate of Antioch, leave that name to their Catholic brethren and call themselves simply Syrian Orthodox. Their first church, St. Nicholas', was built at Brooklyn in 1902 and is now their cathedral. They are said to number 85,000 or more in the Americas but very many are out of touch with their churches and those organized in parishes in U.S.A. were given as only 18,500 in 1936, with 60 churches. In spite of their troubles, these Syrian Orthodox have shown a good deal of activity and progress during the past twenty years.

Their chief bishop in North America (depending on the patriarch of Antioch) is Antony Bashir of Brooklyn. These Syrians have a convent of nuns in New York. There is another bishop for the Syrian Orthodox of Brazil and the Argentine, where they are fairly numerous.

THE RUMANIANS

The first Rumanian church in U.S.A. was opened at Cleveland, Ohio, in 1908. The people, about half of whom come from the "Old Kingdom" and the rest from Transylvania and elsewhere, were enumerated at 15,000 in 30 parishes in 1936.

The first bishop, Polycarp Morusca of Cleveland, was appointed by the patriarch of Rumania in 1935; he has jurisdiction over his people throughout both Americas.

In America, as in other places, the Orthodox Rumanians are found to be on the whole well disposed towards their fellow countrymen who are Catholics of the Byzantine rite; they readily attend their churches and mix with them in social and other work, but there is still a big gulf of mutual ignorance.

THE BULGARS

Bulgars in America are found mostly in New York, Missouri,

and Illinois, where their first church was built in 1908 at Granite City by the hieromonk Theophylact. Their five churches were attended by 1000 persons in 1936. They are in charge of a bishop appointed by the holy synod at Sofia, who lives at Indianapolis. It is historically to be expected that the Bulgars should hold aloof from the Greeks, but they hold a similar attitude toward the Russian Orthodox authorities in U.S.A. as well.

THE ALBANIANS

There are said to be 15,000 Albanians in the U.S.A., chiefly around New York and in New England, but in 1936 only 3000 were returned in their thirteen parishes. In the earlier days of their emigration they were befriended by the Russians, and it was Platon who, in 1908, ordained the first American Albanian priest, Fan Noli, who was afterwards very active in political and ecclesiastical affairs in Albania. He is now the Albanian bishop for America, and seems in some way to depend on the jurisdiction of the Russian metropolitan.

There are various other groups and organizations of Orthodox and pseudo-Orthodox in North America, such as the so-called autocephalous Ukrainian diocese, nearly all of whose 11,000 members are schismatic Catholics, and the similarly constituted "diocese of Carpatho-Russians" (about 1800 members). These and similar bodies have very doubtful canonical status in any church, and their organization, composition, and extent vary so much and so frequently that any useful account of them is as difficult as it is disedifying. They are therefore disregarded here.

BIBLIOGRAPHY

Shipman, "The Greek Orthodox Church in America" in the *Catholic Encyclopedia,* Vol. VI, p. 772.

Bensin, *Yearbook of the Russian . . . Church in America* (New York, 1941).

Bolshakov, *The Foreign Missions of the Russian Orthodox Church* (New York, 1943).

CHAPTER VII

THE FAITH AND RITES OF THE ORTHODOX

ORTHODOXY is something much more than a "static edition of Catholicism minus the Pope," or a "kind of golden mean between Catholicism and Protestantism," though what the particular essential quality of Orthodox Christianity is has never yet been satisfactorily defined and formulated. This fundamental uncertainty is in large measure due to the varied and often conflicting views of the Orthodox themselves.[1] In recent times Russia has commonly been looked on as the "world church" of Orthodoxy (not unnaturally, in view of her tremendous numerical majority), and the dispersal by the revolution of many of her teachers throughout the West has further increased interest in their doctrines; on the other hand, the Greeks are not inactive, and in the conflict between the "Hellenic mind" and the "Russian soul" the Slavs do not have it all their own way. It is impossible, therefore, to give in a short space an adequate account of the faith and spirit of Orthodoxy.

When compared with that of the West, Eastern theology is found to be mystical or contemplative, strongly patristic, un-

---

[1] Contrasted opinions: "The differences which separate [Catholics and Orthodox] are not irreconcilable. . . . With [Protestants] we Orthodox have essential and humanly irreconcilable differences" (Professor Trembelas, of Athens); "There is no real disagreement between the Protestant point of view and that of the Orthodox Church; their opposition is chiefly external" (Archpriest Bulgakov). A third opinion: "Although dogmatically we may differ but slightly from the Roman Church, nevertheless spiritually we are nearer to Protestantism, in freedom of thought and individualism" (an anonymous Greek theologian). But it must be borne in mind that these writers are not looking at Protestantism in its historical sense so much as at the "Catholic parties" in the Protestant episcopal churches today.

systematized, and undeveloped;[2] but the East maintained its superiority in the pure theological field until the time of St. Anselm. While the West has paid far more attention to the relation of philosophy with theology, the East has excelled in the use made of the authority of the Fathers. For the Orthodox the patristic period (with certain reservations) lasted on till the first half of the last century, and this absence of a scholastic period accounts to a considerable extent for the lack of system and formulation in their theological ideas. Some of the most outstanding matters of belief in traditional Christianity, e.g., concerning our Lady and the saints, the problems of eschatology, have never been properly developed and set out – but that does not mean that they have no part in Orthodox religion. It is true that for most the doctrinal statements of the seventeenth-century theologians, approved by patriarchs and synods, have the force of dogma, but there has been a reaction against them (especially among the Russians), without doubt due in part to the pseudo-scholastic form – condemned as "Western rationalism" – in which those theologians presented their "confessions." An external characteristic of Eastern theology is its social quality, emperors and other laymen down to the "man in the street" taking an active and intelligent part in theological discussion.[3] An obvious danger from this is a degeneration into theological particularism, and that danger has not been avoided, whether in the form of referring religious questions to a "racial soul" for solution or of crude nationalism in religious controversy.[4]

---

[2] The only unassailable statements of Orthodox dogma are the Creed of Nicaea-Constantinople and the acts of the first seven oecumenical councils. Such statements as those of Gennadios Skholarios (1453), of Peter Mogila (1667), and of Dositheos of Jerusalem (1672), and catechisms of Platon and Philaret of Moscow (1766–1776, 1823–1827), are important and weighty, but their binding force is now contested by many.

[3] Many distinguished Eastern theologians have been laymen; Khomyakov (1804–1860) and Solovyev (1853–1900) in the past, Glubovsky and Androutsos at the present. Even preaching by laymen is not unknown. At the Orthodox theological congress held at Athens in 1936, the majority of those taking part were laymen.

[4] On the general aspects of Byzantine theology, see V. Grumel in *Echos d' Orient,* No. 164, Oct.–Dec., 1931, p. 385.

DOGMATIC DIVERGENCES

There is no need to go over that large body of dogma wherein there is no substantial difference between Orthodox and Catholic teaching (see pp. 4, 5), but reference must be made to the principal points of doctrinal divergence. In general I take as my guide the *Greek Orthodox Catechism* of Father Constantine Kallinikos, which is a reliable statement of traditional teaching, approved by the holy synod of Athens for use in Greek schools.[5]

The Church. The fundamental doctrinal divergence between Catholicism and Orthodoxy concerns the Church herself as such, what she is and wherein resides her teaching authority. Even here it is not possible to make a statement that will be valid and unquestioned among all Orthodox. What is certain is that, while Catholics often tend to emphasize the exterior, legal, and social aspects of the Church and her quantitative extension, the Orthodox are largely indifferent to such considerations and concerned almost exclusively with her spiritual aspects and the quality of her members and of their religious consciousness. This is one reason for their indifference to what appear to Western eyes as the ravages of ecclesiastical nationalism; these autocephalous churches find their unity in the common life of Christ's Mystical Body, confessing the same faith, sharing the same sacraments, without the addition of any unity of church administration or common visible authority. But, as has been pointed out (p. 6) the scope of their unity of faith must not be overestimated: they hold together doctrinally partly because their common body of faith is so small as to admit of a wide field of doctrinal disagreement.

The Church, says Chrysostom Papodopoulos, archbishop of

[5] Father Kallinikos was priest in charge of the Greek church in Manchester, and an excellent English version of his book was published in London (20 Newton Rd., W. 2) in 1926. It is not a catechism as we ordinarily understand that word, but rather in the sense of the Tridentine "Roman Catechism," a handbook for the use of instructors. It is concerned with "what we should believe, how we should behave, and in what way we should worship."

Athens, is the body of the faithful, founded by Jesus Christ, an organization and an organism, visible and invisible; its purpose is the sanctification of men and the building of the kingdom of God; it is one, holy, catholic, and apostolic; as a visible society it is an infallible teacher. Thus far no Orthodox would dissent, but the archbishop of Athens, even in the discussion of his definition (*Orthodox Catholic Review*, No. 7, Brooklyn, 1927, p. 286), leaves much unsaid. How, for example, does the Church speak infallibly? The Orthodox patriarchs in their answer to the apostolic letter "*In suprema*" of Pope Pius IX in 1848 (which is the point of departure of much recent discussion of the question) said, "The real guardian of religion is the body of the Church, that is, the people itself"; and so we find Khomyakov and his followers entirely dissociating the guardianship of truth from the hierarchical order and denying infallibility even to an oecumenical council. Its decisions are true, and its status oecumenical only if the faithful ratify and accept them; there is no *ecclesia docens* apart from the whole Church (*sobornost*). It is only a step from this to a denial that the Orthodox Church recognizes any external authority at all, and some have taken that step: our Lord, His apostles, the councils, bishops are not "authority"; they are part of "the infinite stream of the life of grace."

These opinions certainly do not represent traditional Orthodox teaching and, though popular, are less widely received than is often supposed. Most Greek and other more conservative theologians maintain oecumenical councils to be the highest authority in the Church,[6] made dogmatically infallible by the direction of the Holy Ghost; if a given synod is really oecumenical, then its decrees will receive the common recognition of the faithful. The "reunion council" of Florence would illustrate this view. It had every appearance of being oecumenical, but the Orthodox at large repudiated it. Therefore, they hold, it was not oecu-

[6] But, they say, the bishops as a body are infallible, whether meeting in a council or not. It must be remembered that they acknowledge only the first seven oecumenical councils, ending with Nicaea II in 787.

menical and infallible – but *not* as a result of recognition being withheld: the God-guided verdict of the people was the *test* of its objective status (Cf., the *communis fidelium sensus* of Catholic theologians). Even a "collective-conciliarist" like Father Bulgakov holds that a council to be oecumenical should be presided over by the pope, and the extremest innovations among the Orthodox are exaggerations of elements found in Catholicism, e.g., of the living part and priesthood of *all* members in the Church.

Kallinikos defines the Church as "the whole of those people who, united in the true faith of Christ and recognizing him, though invisible, as their supreme head, remain under the visible government of shepherds instituted by him and are sanctified by his grace which is imparted in his sacraments . . . the kingdom of Christ on earth. . . . The Church is composed of two parts, the one visible, the other invisible [non-Orthodox Christians]"; the Church is governed by Christ through the higher clergy: locally, a bishop; provincially, a synod; universally, an oecumenical council.[7]

Reference has already been made to how the Orthodox regard the Supreme Pontificate, but it may be useful to quote here the words of Photios II, patriarch of Constantinople, to a representative of the Athens newspaper *Proia* in 1931: "We Orthodox esteem and honour the Roman Catholic Church, an ancient and a great church, and we should never think of denying the supreme primacy of honour of her chief bishop, the Pope: in dignity he is the first of all bishops. . . . A universal council in which the Roman Church took no part would be only an oecumenical synod of the Orthodox churches." He then, of course, went on to deny the pope's primacy of jurisdiction and his infallibility as a religious teacher.

[7] There are still some who hold that the whole of the non-Orthodox world is wandering in the outer darkness of heathendom, and that Catholics and the rest must become Eastern Orthodox in all respects. At the other end of the scale are the Russian "progressists" (Arsenyev, Berdyaev, Bulgakov, Karsavin, Kartashov), for whom a definition of the Church seems almost impossible, though they do not believe that she is purely invisible.

The Holy Trinity. Kallinikos says, "The phrase in the creed, 'Proceeding from the Father' is quite right and does not present any void to be filled. . . . Nowhere in the Bible is it said that the Holy Ghost proceeds from the Son. The Son sends him only. But the sending of the Holy Ghost in time is one thing, his procession or emanation from the Father before all ages is quite another."

Photios was the first to declare that the Western church had corrupted the Faith by adding a word, *Filioque,* to the liturgical creed, affirming that the Holy Ghost proceeds from the Father *and the Son.* This word became representative of the differences between the two churches and caused endless controversy; but that the theological disagreements can be reconciled has been shown by the councils of Bari, Lyons, and Florence, and by eminent theologians on both sides. The Catholic doctrine is explained and justified by Dr. Fortescue in *The Orthodox Eastern Church,* pages 372–384. It is interesting to note that this addition to the text of the liturgical creed was first made in Spain, in which country the creed was first sung in the Latin Mass. Pope St. Leo III (d. 816) forbade the addition of the *Filioque* as unnecessary, of course without questioning the theological doctrine involved; the disputed phrase was first sung in the creed at Rome itself only under Pope Benedict VIII (d. 1024).

Purgatory. The Orthodox offer the Holy Sacrifice and pray for the dead, but their theologians frequently say that they deny the doctrine of purgatory. They certainly repudiate the word and disagree among themselves about the fact, but the teaching of many of them is substantially the same as that of the Catholic Church; they all strenuously deny any element of material fire, but then neither is this of faith for Catholics. Kallinikos defines the soul's intermediate state between death and the general resurrection as "A foretaste and pledge of its final condition after its resurrection and judgement"; but what he says on this matter appears both to assert and to deny a particular judgement at death.

Penance. Orthodox theologians maintain that absolution delivers the penitent not only from the guilt of sin but also from all temporal punishment incurred by it. For this and other reasons they deny the validity and efficacy of indulgences. "Penance is an admirable institution of psychotherapy," remarks Kallinikos in passing.

The Eucharist. The Orthodox Church teaches the real, objective presence of the body and blood of Christ in the Eucharist, and many of her theologians have described the change by the word "transubstantiation," which without doubt properly expresses her doctrine. Others refuse this word, through a misunderstanding of what Catholics mean by it. The synod of Jerusalem in 1672 (see p. 25) used an exact Greek equivalent for the word *transubstantiatio*, μετουσίωσις, and in the Russian translation of the acts of that council this is rendered by the astonishing-looking neologism *transsubstantsiatsiya.*

But also it is now quite definitely Orthodox teaching that this change is not effected by the words of institution *alone* in the Liturgy, but also by the subsequent invocation of the Holy Ghost (*epiklesis*): both forms of words are necessary. "From that most solemn moment [of the invocation]," says Kallinikos, "the mystery is completed."

However, it is interesting to note that the Cypriote synod against Protestantism held at Nikosia in the seventeenth century stated that consecration is effected "by certain specified words prescribed by Christ. . . . This is the orthodox faith of the Holy Eastern Church and it is upheld by the fourfold thrones of the all-holy patriarchs of the East, our brother worshippers and fellow workers."[8] Nicholas Kabasilas (d. 1371) was the first to affirm that the *epiklesis* is necessary for the consecration, and the Catholic teaching was still current in Russia in the seventeenth century, and later. The authoritative catechism of Philaret of Moscow (d. 1861) refers to the words of institution as "the

[8] The archbishop Philip Georgui remarked on this in 1875 that, "It may be observed that the compiler of these decrees appears surreptitiously to introduce in two places opinions of the Latin Church." The other refers to the wording of the decree on the state of the dead.

most essential part of the Liturgy. . . . At the moment of this act the bread and wine are changed or transubstantiated into the very body and the very blood of Christ."

The Immaculate Conception. The Orthodox have a very great veneration for the all-holy Mother of God and from early times her absolute sinlessness has been taught in the East. But since the Catholic Church has defined her Immaculate Conception spokesmen for the Orthodox have denied the doctrine, at any rate in those terms (the expression is admittedly a clumsy one): Anthimos VIII of Constantinople officially repudiated it in 1895. Father Kallinikos takes the common Orthodox view that our Lady was freed from original sin at the Annunciation.

Canon of Scripture. Although they continue in use for divine worship, the Orthodox Church now seems to deny the canonical status of the deuterocanonical books of the Old Testament.[9] This deviation first appeared among the Russians, and is of Protestant origin.

Marriage. Orthodox teachers (Kallinikos, for example) refer to marriage as "an indissoluble union," but for centuries the Orthodox churches have permitted divorce with freedom to remarry on account of adultery and other reasons, and there is a tendency to increase the number of causes for which such divorce is allowed. On the other hand, third marriages are frowned on and a fourth is forbidden. At a conference held at Karlovtsy in 1927 eleven emigrant Russian bishops, under the presidency of Antony of Kiev, declared marriage to be indissoluble, except by the death of one of the parties, but were not prepared to alter the long-established contrary practice of their church.[10]

Sacramental character. Their sporadic practice of reconfirming

---

[9] I.e., Tobias, Judith, Wisdom, Ecclesiasticus, Baruch, Machabees, part of Esther, and part of Daniel, which were admitted to the canon only after the other books.

[10] That the fathers of the Council of Trent were both aware of Greek practice regarding divorce and anxious not to annoy the Orthodox is shown by the wording of the council's canon 7, *de sacramento matrimonii.* See Denzinger, *Enchiridion Symbolorum,* edition 16–17, 1928, p. 321 and footnote.

penitent apostates and degrading clergy to a completely secular condition (*kathairesis*) suggests that the Orthodox have lost the doctrine of the indelibility of the character imprinted by the sacraments of Confirmation and Order.

Hesychasm. Although a consideration of this doctrine is far beyond the scope of this book, brief reference must be made to Hesychasm (ἡσυχία, quiet), as a matter of historical interest and because of a doctrinal point involved. Strictly speaking, hesychasm is simply the state of a life devoted completely to religious contemplation and any monk of the highest degree may be called a hesychast; but in the sense in which it convulsed the Orthodox Church during the fourteenth century it is a theory of mysticism and system of contemplation first practised by Athonite monks.

Ascetic training, according to its upholders, led to the beholding of the uncreated light of God, which accompanied our Lord's transfiguration; and it was taught that the "light of Tabor" and all divine operation is distinct from the divine essence: the contemplation of this light was the highest end of man on earth. To combat this doctrine and the pantheistic developments of hesychasm its opponents used the teaching of St. Thomas Aquinas and the scholastics, thus aggravating anti-Western feeling and widening the scope of the controversy. In 1351 a synod at Constantinople approved the doctrine, and another synod in 1368 canonized its chief upholder, Gregory Palamas (d. *c.* 1360); he was a monk of Athos and bishop of Salonika. His chief opponent was a Greek monk from Calabria called Barlaam.[11] It has been suggested that the spiritual teaching and life of the great saint, Sergius of Radonezh (founder of the Troitsa Laura and a father of Russian monasticism; d. *c.*

[11] He returned to Calabria in 1348 and Pope Clement VI made him bishop of Gerace; from him Petrarch, Boccaccio, and others learned Greek. An important figure who took first one side and then the other (that of Palamas) in the controversy was Nicholas Kabasilas, whom Bossuet called "one of the most solid theologians that the Greek church had produced for three or four centuries." He wrote an admirable treatise on the sacraments, called *Life in Jesus Christ.*

1392), owed a good deal directly to the contemporary Greek hesychasts.

To the extent, then, that the decree of 1351 is binding on Orthodoxy the real distinction between God's essence and operation is one more divergence from Catholic teaching.

ORTHODOX RELIGION

It will be seen from the above that it is extremely difficult to gauge exactly the doctrinal and other disagreements between the Catholic and Orthodox churches. But time and again it is found that alleged differences between traditional Orthodoxy and Catholicism are a matter of different emphasis or way of expression,[12] and in fact what really separates Eastern dissidents from Rome is not so much theological dogma as the events of history and a fundamental difference of mind and temperament – deep-rooted variations between Eastern and Western consciousness that cause identical doctrines to be clothed in such a way that they appear mutually and subtly opposed.

The Oriental prefers an interior process before, often at the expense of, external discipline, juridicism in all its forms is foreign to him, his note is "passivity" rather than "activity." It is significant that the sacraments are administered by deprecatory forms, "The servant of God N., is baptized . . .," "May God, through me, a sinner, forgive thee. . . ." Confirmation is received passively by babes, there is no explicit contract between the parties to a marriage, the monk does not "make his profession" but "receives the habit" – and the rather "go as you please" life to which he is admitted is always and invariably what in the West is called purely contemplative, "the angelic life," and but rarely is he to receive holy orders.

Of course Orthodoxy recognizes episcopal authority and the force of canon law, and its opposition to juridicism is not simply a partial making of the "order of authority" dependent on the "order of holiness." The principle of "economy" (see p. 3) is

[12] The Catholic reader will notice this repeatedly even in Zankov's protestantizing book (see bibliography).

a good illustration of these non-juridical ideas, and some modern Russian theologians seek to restate the doctrine of justification and salvation whose traditional presentation, they claim, is the result of too legalistic an attitude. Nowhere is Orthodox opposition to what it esteems legalism and authoritarianism more marked than in the sphere of personal conduct. Horror is expressed at the precise directions and careful distinctions of Western moral theologians as being manifestations of the letter which killeth; the spirit which maketh alive is the soul's love and worship of God, and these are the only true subject matter of Christian moral teaching. It follows that in a large measure the obligations of religion and morality are left to the individual conscience, rather than made the subjects of positive law. This does not operate entirely in favour of laxity. The absence of a distinction between venial and mortal sin is capable of being an aid to purity of conscience, and when there is no system of recognized dispensation the individual does not necessarily supply one.

Western man has his great mystics and contemplatives, but in general prides himself on being a "practical fellow"; among the Slavs, on the contrary, preoccupation with efficiency and order is little esteemed, and mysticism, in a broad sense, is the heritage of all. Holiness to them definitely means contemplation, and the complete recluse is the practical, as well as the abstract, ideal of a holy man. Benedict-Joseph Labre they understand at once, but how, they ask, could Francis Xavier or John Bosco, immersed in activities, be really men of God? Seraphim, a monk of Sarov who died in 1833 and was canonized by the Russian synod in 1903, was a typical figure and reminiscent more of the fourth century in Egypt than the nineteenth in Europe. It is true that in a few countries, e.g., Rumania, efforts have been made to extend the scope of the technically perfect life – monks and nuns are urged to conduct schools, for instance – but it is an exterior movement not rising spontaneously from the people's religion.

"God was made man," says St. Athanasius, "that we might be

made gods," and all traditional Christianity is essentially "divinizing." This is strongly emphasized in Orthodoxy. The primary significance of Christ is that He communicates a new, eternal, and divine life to the believer; this divinized man is head and epitome of creation, and our Lady is its greatest glory. The divine incarnation operates thus on humanity through the Church, which is the extension of it, particularly by means of the sacraments and especially the Eucharist. Communion is considered primarily objectively: it is "something which happens" to the Christian believer.[13] At Easter above all God enters into human life and transfigures it, it is a festival of "here and now" rather than the commemoration of an historical resurrection: "Christ *is* risen!" "Truly He is risen!" Moreover, it looks forward to that great *parousia,* never far away in the mind of the Russian Christian, "when the Lord shall come again, with thousands of archangels and hosts of angels, cherubim and seraphim, six-winged and many-eyed, who sing, cry, and announce the hymn of victory, saying, Holy, Holy, Holy."

It is significant that the most devastating schism the Russian church has known, that of the *Starovery,* was in a great measure occasioned by the liturgical reforms of the Patriarch Nikon (d. 1681). Eastern culture is based upon the liturgical expression of religion. Hence the Orthodox fear of "latinization" from association with the Catholic Church; and hence, too, something of their national particularism in religion and rites: *Pravoslavie* is "our Russian faith," Orthodoxy is "our Hellenic faith," and national egotism may claim in effect a monopoly of Christian faith and life. This spirit is not entirely unknown in the West, but it does not arise here from so remarkable a unity of civil and cultural life with the life of the Church, nor is it allied with that other Eastern element, dependence on the civil power.

Eastern transcendentality can and does produce superb examples of holiness and self-abnegation, and the wide freedom of

[13] They express surprise that Catholics do not have a more joyous demeanor when they receive Holy Communion.

personal responsibility in belief and conduct is grateful to the strong souled and the critically minded. But Orthodoxy affords little exterior support to the weak, to the doubting, to the spiritually maimed, halt, and blind, and its striking devotion may easily become superficial, whether from excessive emotionalism or from habit. So, too, morality decays, not so much from religious insufficiency in the soul of the people or in their faith, but chiefly from lack of instruction and example. The Slavs, for instance, are in general, as Berdyaev remarks, "less simply well-behaved, less 'decent,' than Westerners," though cupidity and hate are not Russian vices. The general spirit of detachment from the world so remarkable among many Russians, and of a kind diffused nowhere among Western peoples, is often manifested by an indifference to earthly sin (precisely because earthly) as well as by an indifference to earthly goods. And the believer, temperamentally overwhelmed by a sense of guilt, is likely to be so preoccupied with the internal struggle for righteousness that he overlooks the external manifestations of wickedness. Antinomianism and its other face, Encratism, seem to be not far away. And in fact they are not. Certain of the fanatical sects of Russian dissenters from Orthodoxy clearly show both their racial and their religious origins.

Far and away the best short and popular account in English of Orthodox spirituality is the book of that name published in England in 1945. Its author, an anonymous monk of the Orthodox Church, is extremely well informed about and in touch with Catholicism in the West, and he sums up his observations thus: "The fundamental principles of Christian spirituality are the same in the East and in the West; the methods are very often alike; the differences do not bear on the chief points. On the whole, there is *one* Christian spirituality with, here and there, some variations of stress and emphasis. The whole teaching of the Latin fathers may be found in the East, just as the whole teaching of the Greek fathers may be found in the West."

A very useful thing about this book is that it puts the distinctively Russian contribution in its proper perspective and does not exaggerate or overemphasize it.

Nevertheless, "there is a deep difference of religious mentality between the East as it has remained throughout the ages and the West as affected by the Renaissance, the Reformation and the Revolution. This difference narrows down very noticeably as one retraces the course of history. It makes one sick at heart to see how nearly related were the two Christian civilizations of earlier times, till the line of cleavage is lost in the perfect unity of primitive Christianity,"[14] and then turn to the gulf that now divides them in fact (though not in theory). What really separates Eastern dissidents from Rome is not so much theological dogmas as the events of history and that difference of mind and temperament – deep-rooted variations between Eastern and Western consciousness – which, aggravated by so many centuries of separation, causes identical doctrines to be clothed in such a way that they appear mutually and subtly opposed. But here it may be remarked that the term "temperament" must not be taken too literally or exclusively as an explanation of Eastern differences. Father I. Hausherr has put this warning very well: "If Eastern ascetics incline more towards passive than active virtues, does this come from an unconquerable inherited tendency? Or might it not rather be largely due to the fact that from Clement of Alexandria onwards all their spiritual teachers, especially the mystics (though also the ascetics, such as St. Basil), put before them, either as a moral ideal or as a necessary condition of contemplation, that *apatheia* which is always suspect in the West? Whence comes that exquisite charity that we are so happy to find in Eastern saints? And how does it fit in with the previous characteristic? Surely because brotherly love was taken to be a means of personal sanctification and a necessary remedy for the irascible passions considered as the great obstacle to a

---

[14] From a fine article by the late Metropolitan Szepticky in *The Commonweal* (New York) of Oct. 8, 1930; reprinted in *Pax* (Prinknash), Jan., Apr., 1933, and in *Orate Fratres* (Collegeville), Vol. xix, No. 8, 1945.

life of prayer. That is why charity took the special form of gentleness and forgiveness. Why did that charity not urge more towards active good works? Because, from Origen's time, it had been an axiom that only the 'perfect' were qualified to teach others. An active life like that of the Apostles presupposes for Orientals a holiness of life like that of the Apostles, which last is precisely what they understand by an 'apostolic life.' And it is that definite teaching of their doctors which has caused the infatuation of crowds by 'elders' and *startsy*" (see bibliography below).

The Eastern religious temperament (which, like the Western, is not one but many) is certainly in some respects radically different from that of the West. But it is not therefore itself at variance with Catholicity, which is not tied to any one temperament or mentality: the Universal Church is world-wide in every respect. It was "as a member of the true and venerable Orthodox Eastern or Greco-Russian church" that Vladimir Solovyev, on February 18, 1896, declared that he recognized "as the supreme judge in matters of religion . . . the apostle Peter, who lives in his successors, and who did not hear our Lord's words in vain."

ORTHODOX RITES

The Orthodox churches all use the forms and ceremonies of worship of the Byzantine rite. Among the dissidents, as among the Catholics, it has not the uniformity of celebration to which we are accustomed in the West, but the variations are not considerable or important (except the language used); there may be said to be two norms, the Constantinopolitan, or Greek, and the Russian. An account of this rite has been given in Volume I; and as the text and celebration of the various offices are, in their typical forms, practically exactly the same among Orthodox as among Catholic Byzantines, there are given here only a few notes pertinent particularly to the dissidents.[15] I remind readers

[15] Here and elsewhere it goes without saying that any specifically Western practice adopted by Eastern Catholics does not apply to dissidents unless expressly stated to do so.

that Orientals do not in their own languages call the eucharistic sacrifice "The Mass": they call it "The Divine Liturgy" or "The Offering"; and so in this book "the Liturgy" means the eucharistic sacrifice in one or other of its Eastern forms, unless the context obviously requires the more extended meaning of the word.

Liturgical languages. The Byzantine is sometimes called the "Greek rite," because that was its original language, but it is characteristic of it that linguistic uniformity is not required and in general it is celebrated in the vernacular, or a form of the vernacular, of the country. A priest may celebrate it at will according to circumstances in any of the admitted languages which he knows or for which he has the requisite books.

Old Greek (not classical, but the old common speech, ἡ κοινή γλῶσσα) is used throughout the patriarchate of Constantinople and the churches of Greece, Cyprus, and Sinai, by part of the patriarchate of Alexandria, and by the governing minority in Jerusalem.

Church Slavonic[16] is used by the Russians, Poles, Yugoslavs, and Bulgars, and by the various churches of Russian refugees.

Arabic is used throughout the patriarchate of Antioch, in most of Jerusalem, and increasingly in Alexandria.

Ukrainian is used by some Ukrainians in Europe and America.

Rumanian, Georgian, Albanian, Estonian, Finnish, and *Lettish* are used in the corresponding countries, *Tartar* in Siberia, *Eskimo* and *Indian* dialects in the missions of Alaska, *Chinese* and *Japanese,* and other tongues.

English will probably be increasingly used in churches of American-born Orthodox. In three churches in France, in Paris, the Liturgy is celebrated in *French* for French-born Russians, and in a few churches of congregations originating in the Baltic states *German* has been introduced.

Kalendar. A matter of custom that still causes upheavals in the East from time to time is the question of the annual kalendar. The reformed kalendar put forward by Pope Gregory XIII

---

[16] This is to the modern Slavonic languages roughly what Latin is to the Romance tongues.

in 1582, and at once adopted by most of western Europe except England, Wales, Scotland, and Ireland, gained no foothold in the East for a very long time. None of the Orthodox churches began to accept it before 1924, and none of the other dissident churches have done so yet. According to the Julian reckoning, fixed feasts fall thirteen days after the corresponding day by the Gregorian reckoning, and the two Easters and feasts depending thereon coincide only about one year in every three.

A conference at Constantinople in 1923 devised an annual reckoning which to all intents and purposes is the same as the Gregorian kalendar used in the West. This revision has been adopted for fixed feasts, the date of Easter and its dependent feasts being still reckoned by the Julian method, in the Orthodox churches of Constantinople, Greece, Cyprus, Finland, Rumania (1924), Georgia (1927), Alexandria (1928), and Antioch (1941). This reform met with a good deal of resistance, especially in Rumania, Cyprus, and Greece.

All the rest of the Orthodox, a majority, still use the Julian reckoning entirely, the traditional practice being energetically supported by the monks of Mount Athos, where only one monastery (Vatopedi) has succumbed to the reformed kalendar.

It is difficult for the Western mind to appreciate the passions aroused by this matter among the less educated in the East.[17] Those of the more educated who still oppose the new kalendar apparently do not question Pope Gregory's astronomy but resent his having reformed the kalendar without having consulted the East.

Penitential seasons. The practice of fasting is far more rigorous than in the West, and is considered to have more religious importance. Under the pressure both of modern conditions of life and of religious indifference the former careful observance

[17] But the Gregorian reckoning was greatly disliked by simple folk in the West when it was first introduced, so that fairs and other local festivities in Great Britain are often found to be still fixed by the Julian reckoning; and English tax returns and national accounts generally are made up to April 5, i.e., old Lady Day.

of the fasts is declining; but it is still true to say that, when an oriental Christian becomes lukewarm, fasting is the last religious practice he gives up, not the first. Eastern fasting, like many other of their religious usages, is the observance proper to monks gradually extended to the people at large, but by custom more than by law.

There is only one word, *nesteia,* to designate both fasting and abstinence and it is rather difficult to distinguish between them. Among the Greeks, fasting involves one meal only and that after sunset; strict abstinence forbids meat, milk, eggs, fish, oil, and wine; mitigated abstinence allows oil and wine, and sometimes fish: this is according to the old canons and customs, which envisaged strict fasting every Wednesday and Friday and in Lent, and abstinence on from 50 to 90 other days.

General observations. The Orthodox Byzantines have no such thing as a "low Mass": the Liturgy is always sung, though the assistance of a deacon is not necessary. It is the usual practice to celebrate the Liturgy only on Sundays and greater feasts in ordinary churches. In the larger churches concelebration is very common. The Orthodox have no "popular devotions" as we understand that expression in the West, though there is a measure of approximation to them in Russian veneration for the Holy Name and Holy Face and in the "Prayer of Jesus" – "O Lord Jesus Christ, Son of God, have mercy on me, a sinner." With this last is associated the "rosary" (*konbologion, chotki*), consisting of 100 beads on each of which the Prayer of Jesus or other short prayer is said, followed by a prostration. But this is a purely monastic practice.

The Akathistos Hymn, an office in honour of our Lady sung liturgically at certain times, is much used privately. Holy water (*hagiasma*) is in use to a limited extent, and it is solemnly blessed in the baptismal font (and sometimes in rivers or the sea) at the Epiphany, in commemoration of our Lord's baptism. Houses may be blessed on the first day of every month, grapes or apples on the Transfiguration, and flowers, especially sweet basil, on the two feasts of the cross. The custom of blessing and eating corn-cakes (*kolybes*) in memory of the dead is unquestionably a pagan survival.

To the devout Orthodox, especially the Slavs, religion is practically represented by intimate assistance in worship at the Eucharistic Liturgy (and other offices) and by personal austerity, whose principal form is fasting. The sacraments are primarily recognized as, and called, mysteries, and in the Eucharist this "hiddenness" is materially emphasized, by the *eikonostasis*, by the covered doors at the consecration. This instinct to cover holy things, and the stress put on the sacrificial aspect, together with the historical circumstance that there have been in the East no heresies attacking the Real Presence to necessitate its emphasis, result in complete absence of *cultus* of the Blessed Sacrament outside the Liturgy. It is reserved for the needs of the sick (otherwise communion "out of Mass" is almost unheard of), but receives no worship in the tabernacle distinct from the reverence that is accorded to the whole sanctuary as the hidden dwelling place of God. *Eikons*, indeed, hold a place in individual devotion similar in extent to that of the reserved Sacrament in the West; and these images of God and His holy ones, "channels of divine grace," as St. John Damascene calls them, seem almost to acquire a personality for the faithful, without their veneration collapsing into idolatry. This is part of that divinization which extends to everything in religious life and worship.

BIBLIOGRAPHY

†Arsenyev, *L'Eglise d'Orient* (Amay, 1928).

—— *Mysticism and the Eastern Church* (London, 1926).

†Bulgakov, *The Orthodox Church* (London, 1936).

*Gavin, *Some Aspects of Contemporary Greek Orthodox Thought* (London, 1923).

†'tHooft, *Anglo-Catholicism and Orthodoxy* (London, 1933).

Jugie, *Theologia dogmatica Christianorum orientalium ab Ecclesia Catholica dissidentium*, 5 vols. (Paris, 1926–1935).

†Khomyakov, *L'Eglise Latine et le Protestantisme au Point de vue de l'Eglise d'Orient* (Lausanne, 1872).

Kologrivov, *Pensées russes sur l'Eglise* (Rome, 1926).
Lev, *Les Orientations de la Pensée Religieuse Russe* (Amay, 1927).
†Tsebricov, *L'Esprit de l'Orthodoxie* (Amay, 1927).
Winslow, "Theological Thought of the Orthodox" in *Pax*, Nos. 129, 132 (Prinknash Priory, 1932).
†Zankov, *The Eastern Orthodox Church* (London, 1929).
†Anon., *The Story of a Russian Pilgrim* (London, 1931).
de Meester, *The Divine Liturgy of . . . John Chrysostom.* Greek and English texts (London, 1926).
Thompson, *The Orthodox Liturgy.* Translated from the Slavonic (London, 1939). Translations of other Byzantine offices are published by Williams & Norgate, of London.
†Nassar, *Book of Divine Prayers and Services* (New York, 1938). Orthodox Melkite usage.
†Gogol, *Meditations on the Divine Liturgy* (London, 1926).
Dirks, *Les Saintes Icones* (Amay, 1929).
Hausherr, "Les grands courants de la Spirualité orientale" in *Orientalia Christiana Periodica,* Vol. I, Nos. 1–11 (Rome, 1935).
†Anon., *Orthodox Spirituality* (London, 1945).
†Anon., *A Manual of Eastern Orthodox Prayers* (London, 1945).
†Beausobre, *Flame in the Snow* (Seraphim of Sarov) (London, 1945).
Gordillo, *Compendium Theologiae Orientalis* (Rome, 1937).
†Zernov, *The Church of the Eastern Christians* (London, 1942).
Lialin, "The Theological Teaching of Gregory Palamas" (Hesychasm), in *Eastern Churches Quarterly,* Vol. VI, No. 5 (Ramsgate, 1946).
See also bibliography on page 94.

CHAPTER VIII

ORTHODOX MONASTICISM

IT HAS been pointed out in the first volume of this work (pages 221–222) that traditional Eastern monasticism is purely contemplative; and that by comparison with the West it is rather unregulated and "easy-going," following various interpretations of the prescriptions of St. Basil the Great, who was not at all a monastic legislator in the sense of St. Benedict. This life is common to all Orthodox monasteries, and the following further particulars are in place here.

The Byzantine canons are not precise on the period of probation for the monastic life, and there is no novitiate and no formula of profession as we understand them. After a few days or weeks in the monastery, the aspirant is admitted to the lowest grade of monk (Gk. *rasophore,* Sl. *ryasonosets*), and he may if he wishes remain in that grade for the rest of his life, as many do. Or he may at the end of three years go a step higher and become a *stavrophore* (Sl. *skhimnik*), when he is tonsured again and takes four oral vows, of poverty, chastity, obedience, and stability. For this step a man must be at least twenty-five years old, and a woman forty. The maxims of St. Basil had in view only the cenobitical or community life, but the Orthodox conception of monasticism looks on the eremitical or solitary life as the end which the monk ought to have in view and for which community life is a training and preparation. (Cf., what St. Benedict says of hermits, in the first chapter of his Rule). When a soul has strengthened herself by obedience and austerity it is natural that she should draw nearer to God and wish so to remain in a life completely devoted to contemplation – and that, and not any special Athonite mystical theory, is the precise ordinary significance of the much abused term *hesychasm*. The third and highest grade of Eastern monk, then, renews his tonsure and his vows[1] in view of the greater asceticism of prayer, fasting, and silence that he undertakes, and lives a partly, and sometimes entirely, solitary life. Twenty or thirty years of community life are the normal preparation for this rank of *megaloskhemos*, to which only a small minority of the monks ever aim or attain. The discipline of this degree is extremely strict and penitential, and to it alone is permitted the full angelical habit. A bishop who attains to it is forbidden thereafter to exercise episcopal or sacerdotal functions (though a priest may celebrate the Liturgy), and if he is advanced to it in view of death but recovers his health, he must resign his see and retire to a cell. Bishops are chosen only from the monks, whether *rasophores* or *stavrophores* (rarely from the third grade).

There are frequently servants attached to an Eastern monastery, but there are no lay brothers, and just as St. Benedict legislated for independent, self-governing families of men not in holy orders, so it still is *the exception for an Eastern monk to be a priest*. But no distinction is made between the monk who is a priest (hieromonk) and the monk who is not.[2] The latter may be elected abbot and rule his ordained brethren, just as a monk of the lowest degree may be made abbot and rule over those of the higher degrees. The difference between *rasophore*, *stavrophore*, and *megaloskhemos* are personal, and affect the individual life; whatever the theory of beginner and proficient, imperfect and perfect monks, they are all in fact monks. The *rasophore*, though he has taken no vows, is considered equally

[1] The respective vows of *stavrophore* and *megaloskhemos* are not at all equivalent to our simple and solemn profession. The whole thing is different from beginning to end.

[2] Except that only a hieromonk may admit a man or woman to the monastic state, and then not to a degree higher than his own. For example, an abbot who is a priest and a monk of the second degree governs *megaloskhemoi*, but he cannot admit to that degree. Bishops who are monks have plenary powers in these matters. The colloquial word for any monk in the East is *kalogeros*, "good old man."

to have bound himself for life by entering upon the way of monastic perfection and assuming a part of the habit, and until a hundred years ago dispensations to leave the monastery were unheard of, though a monk could be expelled for misbehaviour. Even now the stricter non-Catholic canonists regard such a dispensation as opposed to the fundamental teaching of Eastern monasticism, but modern Russian monastic legislation recognizes its legitimacy.

The *rasophore* is so called because he receives the black wide-sleeved *rason;* this he wears over a girdled tunic, with a round cap (*skouphos*) on his head. The *stavrophore* is given a small wooden cross (*stavros*) and the "little habit," i.e., the above, with a black veil over the cap and a long black cloak (*mandyas*) which may be worn instead of the *rason.* The *megaloskhemos* ("great-habiter") has in addition a cowl (*koukoulion*) to be worn in church, consisting of a conical cap covered by a black veil on which are embroidered the instruments of the passion, and the *analavos;* this is made of wool or leather, and is in shape like the Western monastic scapular (with which it is quite unconnected), embroidered or painted all over with the instruments of the passion, crosses, and other symbols: the whole represents the cross which the monk has voluntarily taken up.

Monasticism in the past was even more influential in the East than in the West, and has left its imprint on every aspect of religious life, from the form of the Divine Office and the dress of bishops to the high ascetical standard and the fasts imposed on the laity. And if for many centuries now it has been the tradition (largely under the influence of Mount Athos) that intellectual and active work is not the concern of monks even within the cloister, it was not always so: some of the Syrian monasteries had schools, so did the early Russian ones, and the Stoudion at Constantinople during the ninth century was a brilliant centre both of monasticism and studies (and, especially under Abbot Nicholas, of Catholic unity).

The classical disposition of Eastern monastic buildings is about an open quadrilateral, as in the West – but there the re-

Courtesy, C. S. Cosby Oakes

ST. STEPHEN'S MONASTERY, METEORA

Courtesy, La Bonne Presse

THE LAURA, MOUNT ATHOS

Courtesy, La Bonne Presse

RUMANIAN NUNS SINGING OFFICE

Courtesy, C. S. Cosby Oakes

MONASTERY OF THE GREAT
METEORA, GREECE

BOAT OF MOUNT ATHOS IN
SALONIKA HARBOUR

Courtesy, La Bonne Presse

MAR SIMON XIX,
NESTORIAN KATHOLIKOS OF THE EAST
(d. at hands of Turks 1917)

Courtesy, *London C.T.S.*

KUDSHANES. SEAT OF NESTORIAN KATHOLIKATE

Courtesy, Fr. Eugene Hoade

COPTIC BISHOP OF JERUSALEM

COPTIC PRIESTS

Dair as-Suryani

Dair Anba Bishoi

COPTIC MONASTERIES

COPTIC CHURCH AT OLD CAIRO

CHURCH OF ST. GEORGE, ADDIS ABABA

ETHIOPIAN PROCESSIONAL CROSS

semblance ends. The main church (*katholikon*) is in the middle of the court, and the refectory is often opposite its west end, with a well or fountain in between. Around are grouped the guest house, the infirmary, the workshops, and the cells of the monks; the library used generally to be above the narthex of the church as being more secure from fire. Needless to say, this arrangement is modified at will to conform to the features of the ground.

As has been said above, each Orthodox monastery is independent of the others. It is normally under the jurisdiction of the bishop or metropolitan; an "exempt" monastery, depending only on the patriarch, is called a *stavropegion*. The *hegumenos* or abbot (*archimandrite* in a big monastery) is elected by the monks for life, and governs with the aid of an advisory council (*synaxis*).

The Eastern system of monasticism is considerably more "go as you please" (of course, within the canons and the rule) than the stricter development of the West, and it is only to be expected that the standard of observance should vary greatly from monastery to monastery, and even among monks of the same monastery. Reference to the state of local monasticism has been made under the various autocephalous churches, but mention must be made here of Mount Athos, which is the great stronghold of Orthodox monastic life.

Athos, or the Holy Mountain, is a steep narrow promontary (the most easterly of three) of the Khalkidike peninsula in the Aegean Sea; it is a ridge some thirty-five miles long, the outer end rising to a peak 6000 feet high, and is famous in early history for the canal which Xerxes dug across it. From an early date it was a haunt of hermits, and about 960 St. Athanasius of Trebizond, a monk from Kyminas in Bithynia, founded the first cenobitical monastery there, with the help of the emperors Nikephoros Phokas and John Tzimisces. This establishment still flourishes, the senior monastery of Athos, and is usually referred to simply as *Lavra*, "The Monastery." With the passing of the centuries many more monastic foundations of one kind or another were made, and Athos became a regular place of retreat for emperors, bishops, and others in days of misfortune. Its monks eventually followed their patriarch into schism,[3] obediently submitted to the Turks after the fall of Constantinople, and the purely monastic character and political semi-sovereignty of Mount Athos have been maintained for close on a thousand years.

Its establishments today consist of twenty *ruling monasteries;* twelve lesser monasteries or *sketes;* 200 *kellia* or cells, groups of hermitages ruled by an elder; and some 450 hermitages, either *ascetic kalyves,* organized like *kellia* but more austere, or *kathismata,* rented houses. All except the *kathismata* depend on one or other of the ruling monasteries.

Seventeen of the ruling houses are Greek, viz., Lavra, Vatopedi, Esphigmenou, Iviron (all founded during the lifetime of St. Athanasius; the last was originally Georgian), Dionysiu, Kouthoumousi, Pantokrator, Xiropotamos, Dokheiarion, Karakalou, Philotheou, Simopetra, St. Paul's, Stavronikita, Xenophon, Grigoriu, and Kastamonite; one is Russian, St. Panteleimon's or Roussiko; one Bulgarian, Zographou; and one Serbian, Khilandari, founded by St. Sabas about 1197. Seven of the *sketes* are Greek, three Russian, and two Rumanian.

These greater and lesser monasteries are divided into two classes, according to their form of life, the *cenobitic* houses, which have the ordinary common life, and the *idiorrythmic,* "on one's own." In these last each monk receives fuel, wine, some food, and a little money, and must then support himself by his work; they meet in church for the offices but dine together only at Christmas, Easter, and on the patronal feast. These idiorrythmic monks live in groups, the elders of the groups

---

[3] There was an abbey of the Latin rite there during the eleventh and twelfth centuries, whose archives are in existence but still unstudied. Pope Innocent III took the whole place under his protection when it was threatened by the crusaders. But Athonites today are prone to be rather anti-Catholic. They point out a cave where lie buried those who went to the Council of Florence — "blessed ground rejected them because they signed the union with the papists."

forming the monastery council whose president, elected annually, has the powers of an abbot.

Nine of the Athonite monasteries have this peculiar arrangement,[4] and these are the better off materially but they do not have the largest communities. A cenobitic house may not now become idiorrhythmic, but the opposite change is allowed; idiorrhythmism is more suited to the easy-going Greeks, and the Serbs at Khilandari are contemplating a return to communal life. There is great variation between the different monasteries, some of which are hidebound by unimportant customs and traditions: Vatopedi, where they have electric light and even the Gregorian kalendar for fixed feasts, is regarded as a centre of innovation.

The whole federation is governed by a council (with a president, *protos*), whose seat is at the village of Karyes, composed of one member from each of the twenty monasteries, so that the Greeks always are in a majority of seventeen to three. This has often caused trouble, especially with the Russians, but this element has become feebler and feebler since the revolution.[5] In 1905 there were 3276 Greek monks and 3496 Russians; in 1913 they had respectively 3243 and 1914; in 1928 the Russians had fallen to 464 in a total population of 4858 (Greeks, Russians, Bulgars, Rumanians, Serbs, Montenegrins, and a Georgian or two). The Russian houses are quickly becoming empty for lack of recruits; they had only about 250 monks in 1947. There is on the peninsula a certain number of lay servants and workmen and the staff of the representative of the Greek government, who lives at Karyes but has no particular duties to discharge. (No woman is allowed to set foot on Mount Athos, much less to reside there.)

There has been agitation from time to time for a reform of the constitution, the monks of the *sketes* demanding to be

[4] There are idiorrythmic monasteries in other places besides Athos.

[5] Of course the bolsheviks have deprived them of all their property in Russia. But the Greeks have suffered in this way too; they have been expropriated from almost all their *metokhia* in Macedonia and elsewhere and received only nominal compensation. The Greek government now requires that only subjects of the Greek state shall in future be received as monks on Athos.

represented on the governing council; and in 1928 a commission from the patriarch of Constantinople (who is the ecclesiastical superior) was very ill received when it arrived for the purpose of making a visitation; another commission, in 1935, was openly defied by many of the monks.[6]

Athos, remarkable alike for its unique history and life, its natural beauty, its buildings, and its still incompletely explored libraries, has been the subject of several books in recent years. The verdict of the author of one of them, Professor R. M. Dawkins, is impressive in its moderation: "The monasteries are probably in a state of decline; of the way of thought which we can see there, the keener, the more intellectual, element has for the most part disappeared; of the strength of the Byzantine mind we have not much left but its remarkable tenacity, with a good deal of its deliberate isolation and self-sufficiency."

The general principles governing Orthodox monasticism apply equally to nuns. Except to a limited degree in Russia before the revolution, "unenclosed" nuns engaged in "active" works were entirely unknown; and generally speaking female monasticism was (and is) even less widespread and flourishing than male. Just as in recent years the monks in Greece and Yugoslavia and Rumania have been urged by governments, and to a certain extent by public opinion, to undertake conduct of schools, agricultural colleges, printing works, etc., and to preach missions, so the nuns also have been looked to for corresponding activities; but with as little success. This must not be attributed to indifference to their neighbours' good, to laziness, or to lack of spiritual vitality: it must be remembered that Orthodox monastic life is governed by the unchanged tradition of over a thousand years and, however desirable it may be that some of those traditions should now be abandoned, it cannot be done

---

[6] An example of how the Orthodox ecclesiastical mind gravitates towards the civil power: When in 1936 there was a disputed election to the abbacy of Simopetra the matter was carried by the monks to the council of state at Athens. The council very properly referred them to the Oecumenical Patriarch.

in a day or even in a generation.[7] It is not likely that there will be in our time any considerable modification of Orthodox monasticism in the direction of greater "activity"; as Father Raymund Janin, A.A., justly remarks, "Attraction to a kind of life that is full of difficulties and quite out of accord with age-long ideas cannot be imposed by legislation; a serious religious formation to this end is first required." Indeed, such extension of work will probably come in the East as it did at first in the West, not by the modification of an existing institution but by the forming of entirely new organizations. On the other hand, chosen souls among Christian men and women will continue to be called to the purely contemplative life, and the system associated with the name of St. Basil the Great will continue to be one of the two outstanding forms of that life: nowhere is more likely to be the scene of reconciliation between Catholic West and Orthodox East than the common ground of our fathers among the saints, Basil and Benedict.

One Orthodox monastery only, that of Mount Sinai (see p. 115), looks to St. Antony rather than to St. Basil for its example, basing its life on the "sayings" and oral instructions of Antony which were put together by somebody else for the guidance of those living in a semi-eremitical rather than a cenobitical way. But in practice the result is much the same. This so-called rule of St. Antony is also the basis of the life of the Coptic, Ethiopic, and Syrian Jacobite monks and remotely of the non-Byzantine monasteries of Catholic Orientals.

BIBLIOGRAPHY

*Gardner, *Theodore of Studium* (London, 1905).
*Robinson, *Monasticism in the Orthodox Churches* (London, 1916).
*Hasluck, *Athos and Its Monasteries* (London, 1924).
*Riley, *Athos or the Mountain of Monks* (London, 1887).

---

[7] It is profitable to consider in this connection the early history of unenclosed congregations in the Catholic Church, e.g., of Mary Ward and the Institute of Mary.

*Dawkins, *The Monks of Athos* (London, 1936).
*Curzon, *Visits to Monasteries of the Levant* (London, 1897).
Belpaire, *Lettres du Mont-Athos* (in *Irénikon*, t. VI, Nos. 1–3, Amay, 1929).
Hofmann, *Athos e Roma* in *Orientalia Christiana*, t. V, No. 19 (Rome, 1925).
†Smolich, *Leben und Lehre der Starzen* (Vienna, 1936).
Wunderle, *Aus der heiligen Welt des Athos* (Würzburg, 1937).

CHAPTER IX

THE NESTORIAN CHURCH

WHATEVER may have been the beginnings of Christianity in Mesopotamia and Persia, there was a church in Edessa at the end of the second century; from that city the Faith spread eastward and another great centre was formed at Nisibis. At the beginning of the fourth century the Church in Persia was organized under his own direction by a bishop of Seleukia-Ctesiphon, Papa bar Aggai; and in 424 the synod of Markabta proclaimed the Persian church under its katholikos independent of the patriarch of Antioch, and the "Western fathers" generally (the hierarchical bond with Antioch through Edessa had always been tenuous). During this early period the church of East Syria and Persia produced a doctor of the Universal Church, St. Ephrem (d. 373), and it was made illustrious by the theological schools of Nisibis and Edessa and by hosts of martyrs at the hands of the Persians.

In 431 the Council of Ephesus condemned the teaching of Nestorius, patriarch of Constantinople (see Vol. 1, p. 4). Many of the Persian Christians and a party of the East Syrians, considerably influenced by anti-imperialist political considerations, refused to accept the condemnation, which resulted by *c.* 500 in the development of an heretical Nestorian Church under the protection of the sovereigns of Persia, who favoured Nestorians and Jacobites as a bulwark against Byzantine political and military aggression. At first they probably aimed at no more than a local autonomy like that of the recognized patriarchates and were moved towards Nestorianism by their strong antagonism to its opposite, Monophysism; but by the seventh century the schism had hardened and the Mohammedan conquest of

Syria and Persia confirmed their severance from the Catholic Church and their profession of the condemned teaching.

The Arabs followed the Sassanid monarchs in favouring the Nestorians and at the same time keeping them under strict control; from 987 the katholikos was even appointed by the khalifah. The cities of Nisibis, Beth Lapat, and Merv were great centres of Christian culture, and Nestorians were in demand for public offices on account of their education. On the whole, with the notable exception of the reign of the mad khalifah al-Hakim (1009–1020), the Nestorians were not seriously persecuted by their Arab governors, and for eight hundred years the Nestorian Church was, with fluctuations of prosperity, a mighty organization, one whose missionary enterprise is unsurpassed in the history of Christianity. It had 20 or more metropolitan sees with many bishoprics and monasteries, extending to China and India.

According to the Nestorian monument at Si-ngan-fu, Christianity was brought into China by a Syrian in 635. This monument was set up in 781 and gives evidence of a large Christian population in ten Chinese provinces, with a number of monasteries. These monasteries were dissolved by the Chinese emperor in 845, and a contemporary historian states that by 980 no Christians were left there. But Christianity continued to flourish in central Asia, and the European travellers of the thirteenth century speak of large Nestorian communities all over Eastern Turkestan and so far east as Manchuria, Korea, and Chin-Kiang-fu near the mouth of the Yangtse River: according to Friar William of Rubruck and others their standard of Christian life was not high. This second appearance of Christianity in China seems to have been due to converted Turkish and other tribes at the time of the Mongol invasion at the beginning of the thirteenth century. The connection of the Nestorians with southern India is referred to elsewhere (see Vol. I, p. 210).

When the Mongols under Jengiz Khan and his successors poured over China, Transoxiana, Persia, and Mesopotamia, they seem to have been even more tolerant of the Nestorians than were the Arabs. For a time there was a movement towards

Christianity among the Mongols themselves, till they found it was not the "success-religion" they supposed and that some of its professors represented it to be. As such an attitude suggests, the Nestorians as a body had become self-satisfied, a sure indication that they were religiously in decline.

During this thirteenth century Dominican and Franciscan friars were active among them, and the katholikos Yaballaha III had amiable relations with the Holy See; in 1304 his profession of faith was accepted by Blessed Benedict XI, several other katholikoi and bishops became Catholics, and soon after a number of Latin sees were erected, but they did not last long. Yaballaha III was a Sino-Turk, born in Pekin. He had sent another Mongol, the monk Barsauma, on an embassy to Rome and the West. Barsauma received Holy Communion from the hands of Pope Nicholas IV, and himself gave it to King Edward I of England in Gascony. For all that, the profession of faith he carried was only doubtfully orthodox.

But this period of relative prosperity was soon succeeded by utter ruin. At the end of the fourteenth century the Tartar hordes of the rebel Timur Leng devastated Asia, sweeping away the Nestorian Church in a cataclysm of blood and apostasy.[1] The remnants of the western part of his church gathered round their katholikos in northern Mesopotamia; of the eastern part, nothing remained (except in Malabar).

By the middle of the fifteenth century the office of Nestorian katholikos had become hereditary in a family, passing from uncle to nephew (it still does), and on the succession of Simon VIII Denha in 1551 a dissatisfied party elected a rival, John Sulaka. Sulaka went to Rome, where he made a profession of Catholic Faith and was appointed by Pope Julius III to be patriarch of those of his rite who should follow his example. The name "Chaldean" was adopted to distinguish such people, as to call them "Catholic Nestorians" was obviously impossible, and thus began the present Catholic church of the Chaldean rite.

---

[1] On the ruins of Isfahan, 70,000 human heads were piled; at Bagdad, 90,000.

There followed a period of extraordinary hierarchical confusion, with sometimes two patriarchs (or katholikoi) of the same obedience and sometimes none at all; for 250 years union with or secession from the Holy See was freely used as a move in Nestorian ecclesiastical politics. The upshot was that the Catholic patriarchs have since 1834 represented the original Nestorian line of Simon VIII Denha (of course not hereditarily), while the Nestorian katholikoi since 1692 have belonged to the formerly Catholic line of Sulaka.

In the sixteenth century the Nestorian patriarchal see was at Mosul, afterwards at Marga, just over the Persian border, and finally between 1662 and 1700 it was settled at Kudshanes, a village in the mountains of Kurdistan, where it remained till 1917.

Apart from the unremitting solicitude of the Holy See, modern Western interest in the Nestorians was kindled a century back by European archaeologists who had been working on Assyrian monuments, and by the terrible massacres of Nestorians perpetrated by Kurds in 1831–1843–1846. A number of Protestant missions to them were soon organized, with results of no particular importance except where the Anglicans were concerned.[2] "The Archbishop of Canterbury's Mission to the Assyrian Christians" was definitively established in 1886. Its object was not to make the Nestorians into Anglicans, but to educate, advise, and help them. In accordance with this, schools and a printing press for liturgical books were set up, and the Nestorians have benefitted from the labours of these Anglican clergymen, to whom they owe a great debt of gratitude.

During the past century the efforts of the Chaldean Antonian monks rallied nearly all the Nestorians in the dioceses of Akra, Amadia, Yako, Seert, and Gazireh to Catholic unity. The bearer of the invitation of the Holy See to the Nestorian bishops to attend the Vatican Council was Father Lemée, O.P. The then katholikos, a young man of twenty-eight, received the friar privately with great courtesy and informed him that he was "surrounded by people devoted body and soul to England, a nation

[2] For the Russian Orthodox mission, see p. 91.

from which we receive help and protection. . . . I would much rather be under the direction of the Pope than dependent on Protestants. I feel very attracted toward Rome – but I am not a free agent." He went on to promise Father Lemée that he would write to Pius IX stating that he would accept the acts of the council "in agreement with the other Eastern patriarchs." I do not know if this letter was ever sent.

Up to World War I nearly all the Nestorians were living in the plains around Lake Urmi and the frontier mountains in Persia, and in the hill country between Lake Van, Lake Urmi, and towards Mosul, under Turkish misrule. At that time they apparently numbered about 100,000, mostly in the Turkish district, and the katholikos, as well as being their religious ruler, was their civil head under the Porte. Thus was the mighty Nestorian Church of the fifth to the fourteenth centuries, with its memories of wholesale martyrdoms under Persian persecution and its far-flung missionary enterprise, reduced to an obscure body of a few tens of thousands of peasants, an unimportant *millet* of the Turkish empire, always at the mercy of fierce Kurds and Yazidis. They were soon to be reduced even further.

Here it may conveniently be noted that the Nestorians generally call themselves simply *Surayeh*, Syrians; formerly they had no objection to being called Nestorians, but have now learned from their Anglican benefactors that this is not a complimentary name. However, "Syrians" was ambiguous, and was, moreover, already in use for the Jacobites and their Catholic counterpart, and "East Syrians" was not much better, so the Anglican mission adopted the name "Assyrian Church" for them. The usage is difficult to justify since, as Fortescue points out, the Nestorians "are Assyrians in no possible sense. They live in one corner of what was once the Assyrian Empire"; but it has stuck, and plenty of people since 1917 have heard of the Assyrians without ever suspecting that they had anything to do with the fifth-century heresy of Nestorius. I shall continue to call them Nestorians, for the name is not without honour in history even though deplorable in theology.

In the earlier days of World War I the Nestorians gave military aid to the Russians in Kurdistan and to the British further south, and when the Russian army withdrew in 1917 Turks and Kurds fell on the Nestorians and Catholic Chaldeans of the Turko-Persian frontier and massacred 20,000 of them. Several thousand escaped to the neighbourhood of Baku and Tiflis. Others, besieged in the mountains, determined to cut their way out towards Bagdad and put themselves under British protection; and 10,000 armed men, with their wives and families and aged relatives, left houses and lands and set out. There was desperate fighting and the katholikos, Mar[3] Benjamin Simon XIX, was treacherously murdered by a Turk. The Nestorians retaliated by massacring all the Kurds they could lay their hands on, but they were hopelessly outnumbered in what had become an open struggle for the extermination of one side or the other. Altogether over half the Nestorians, men, women, and children, are said to have been slain, including six bishops and hundreds of clergy. The remainder mostly found refuge in Irak, where several thousand more died of cholera in the refugee camp at Baguba, near Bagdad. By 1919 the Nestorians numbered only some 50,000 souls.

Mar Simon XIX was succeeded by his brother, Paul Simon XX, who died after only a few months of office at Baguba, where he was succeeded by his nephew, Jesse Simon XXI, a youth of 13. He was subsequently sent to England for his studies.

Meanwhile, those Nestorians who had fled into the Caucasus made their way gradually, *via* Homs in Syria, to Mosul and Bagdad, in which they received much help from their fellow countryman, Father Tfinkji, the delegate of the Catholic Chaldean patriarch, Mar Emmanuel II Thomas. Some of them remained in Syria.

All the time the British held the mandate over Irak the interests of the Nestorians were reasonably well looked after, though the ill-will of the Mohammedan Irakis was aggravated by the

---

[3] *Mar* (Syriac, "lord"; fem., *mart*) is used in all Syriac rites, Catholic or dissident, as a title for saints and bishops.

recruiting from the Nestorians of a regular militia by the British military authorities. But in 1932 the British government gave up the Irak mandate, and made the childish mistake of being satisfied with verbal assurances that the Nestorians would be properly treated. At once the Iraki government moved against them, disbanding and disarming the militia and dispersing the people among several regions because they wanted to form a separate independent state (this had already been refused by the powers at the peace conferences). The katholikos, Mar Simon XXI, refused to collaborate with the representative of the League of Nations or to take the oath of allegiance to King Faisal; thereupon he was deprived of Iraki citizenship and eventually deported, the British giving him passage to Cyprus by air. At the same time France was involved by the action of a Nestorian leader, Yaku, who led a thousand men acrosss the Tigris to seek refuge in Syria, so the government at Bagdad sent Bakir Sidki Bey and a force of Kurds to "pacify" the Nestorian "rebels." The pacification inevitably took the form of murdering men, women, and children at sight (the report of the number of victims varied from 500 to 5000), and the League of Nations came to the conclusion that something ought to be done about it. Eventually, in October, 1933, the League accepted the suggestion of the Iraki government that, since the Nestorians were unwilling to be dispersed all over Irak, they should be given a home somewhere *outside* that country. This decision, that the Nestorians should be expatriated from Mesopotamia where they had lived from remote ages, has been called monstrous, and so in a sense it is. But their exact homeland is outside the borders of the state of Irak, neither Turks nor Persians would have them, and the alternative was probably rebellion in Irak and then their swift extinction.

But the thing was easier said than done. The first offer came from Brazil, to find room for 20,000 Nestorians in the state of Parana. This fell through. Then there was talk of Cyprus, of French Sudan, of British Guiana. Nothing could be done. Then France agreed to facilitate the settlement of 20,000 or more on the western bank of the Upper Orontes in the Ghab area of Syria; towards the expense of this the British and Iraki governments, the French mandated territory of the Levant, and the League of Nations agreed to contribute. This fell through too. But gradually relations between the Nestorians and their governors in Irak improved; and eventually they agreed to remain there as Iraki citizens, subject to the government's guarantee of fair treatment. Meanwhile there were some thousands of Nestorians temporarily settled on the Khabur river in the Dair az-Zor district of eastern Syria, east of the Ghab and between Irak and the Turkish provinces, where they have now settled down.

The Nestorians and the Catholic Chaldeans are racially one people, and it is often asked how it is that, while the first named are in such difficulties, the Chaldeans are comparatively (but only comparatively) contented citizens in Irak. The answer is that the Chaldeans were never recruited for that militia of Christian *rayahs* which gave such offence to the Mohammedans, nor did they clamour for autonomy or other preferential treatment under the Iraki government.

ORGANIZATION AND PRESENT STATE

Katholikos. The ecclesiastical and civil head of the Nestorian church and people is "The Reverend and Honoured Father of Fathers and Great Shepherd, the Katholikos and Patriarch of the East." He now always takes the name of Simon (*Shim'un*), and is chosen by the bishops and chief laymen from the patriarchal family, "holders of the throne," generally not without intrigue. The bishops are now again celibate (they were not always) and so the hereditary descent is usually from uncle to nephew, which often means that a mere child becomes katholikos: of the last three, Simon XIX was eighteen, Simon XX twenty-three, and Simon XXI thirteen at the time of their respective elections.

It has been mentioned above that Mar Simon XXI was educated and trained for his office under Anglican auspices in

England, and he was for long much under the influence of his aunt, Lady Surma. He does not enjoy considerable prestige among his subjects, and many of them now reject his authority and look to the other bishops, or even to none at all. This has been yet more so since Mar Simon was removed from Irak. The British government gave him a home in Cyprus, but since 1941 he has been in Chicago, organizing parishes among Nestorian immigrants in the United States.

Bishops. The other episcopal dignities are likewise hereditary, with the consequent abuses. The katholikos has the right to ordain, translate, and depose these bishops, who, like himself, are bound to lifelong abstinence from flesh meat; they were chosen by the clergy and chief laymen of the diocese, but since 1917 there are no dioceses except the Persian one of Urmia. The metropolitan of Ba-Shams-Din (called the *Matran*) administers the church in the absence of the katholikos, helped by one or more auxiliary bishops.

Lower clergy. The parish priests are all married, and the office often descends from father to son, though the nomination to a cure is made by the laity concerned. The priests may, moreover, marry more than once and with a widow, which is contrary to Eastern custom. There is no seminary or other organized means of training these clergy; they are often quite illiterate, and are not expected to be able to do much more than to celebrate the Liturgy, more or less decently, but they are in general very worthy men and respected by their flocks. Permanent deacons are (or were) numerous.

Dignitaries are the *archpriest* ("dean"), *chorepiscopos* ("rural dean"), and *archdeacon* ("vicar-general"). A dignity elsewhere unknown is that of *shahara,* "awakener," who presides at the night office and is usually a minor cleric.

Monasticism. There are no longer any monks or nuns among the Nestorians.

The faithful now number about 22,000 in Irak, 10,000 in Syria, a few thousand each in Persia, Russia, and Egypt, and perhaps (it is said) 25,000 in the United States of America, scattered from New York to California, notably at Chicago. They are a simple and, on the whole, amiable people, attached to their religion but modifying it with popular superstitions; they receive practically no religious instruction. Except for those who can send their children to Catholic or other schools there is no secular education either among them, and even before their recent misfortunes they were terribly poor. There are movements from time to time towards Catholic unity in their own rite, especially among the clergy: for example, there was a "group reunion" of four priests and 200 faithful at Homs in 1923. The Nestorians are outnumbered by the Catholics of their rite, who total 95,000.

The principal language of the Nestorians is a debased Syriac (*Sureth*), but Arabic, Persian, Turkish, and Kurdish are also spoken.

Dogmatic Divergences

It seems that the Nestorian Church no longer professes the errors associated with that word, and it is beyond doubt that none of them except a very few of the higher clergy understand or care anything about this heresy concerning the Incarnation; they believe that from the first moment of His conception our Lord was perfect man and perfect God: but they still refuse to call our Lady "Mother of God." Since their errors were condemned by the Council of Ephesus and they had no part in those that followed, they recognize only the first two oecumenical councils, and regard both Catholics and Orthodox, at any rate in theory, as heretics.

Like other Orientals the Nestorians now claim that the invocation of the Holy Ghost is necessary to the consecration of the Eucharist, and they reject what they think is the Catholic doctrine of purgatory, but nevertheless pray for the dead. Moreover, they show considerable uncertainty as to how many and what sacraments there are. Marriage is omitted from some lists, and divorce is allowed for adultery, but the indissolubility of marriage appears to be held in theory.

The words "and from the Son" are, of course, not sung in

the liturgical creed, but there is no reason to suppose that the Nestorian Church holds officially any strong views against this procession of the Holy Ghost.

LITURGY AND CUSTOMS

Nestorian worship is in origin just the same as that of the Catholic Chaldeans, which in many respects it still resembles (see Vol. I, pp. 204–208). The following are the most important divergences.

The Nestorians have no pictures or other images in their churches (or anywhere else), and use a plain cross instead of a crucifix, even on the altar. Great respect is shown to the cross, and the dislike of pictures seems to be a late development; it may be under Mohammedan influence. For many centuries a piece of ass's skin, covered with silk, has been used as a "corporal" on the altar during the Liturgy.

Vestments. These are similar to those of the Jacobites: *kotina* ("alb") with "cuffs"; *urara,* stole; *zunara,* girdle; *maapra,* a chasuble like a cope without a hood but not fastened in front, and embroidered shoes. Bishops wear the small hood, called *biruna,* and carry a pastoral staff of Byzantine pattern and a hand cross, but have no mitre (unless they borrow a Roman one) and no *omophorion.* Bishops, priests, and deacons respectively all wear their stole just as in the West. The ordinary clerical headdress is a flat black turban.

Altar-bread. The Nestorian Church emphasises the continuity of the Eucharist by the unity of the bread used. Each time it is baked (before every Liturgy, which is celebrated only on Sundays and feasts) it is leavened not only with some dough from the last baking but with a small portion of the "holy leaven," which has been handed on from age to age in each church. The baseless legend is that our Lord at the last supper gave an extra consecrated loaf to St. John, who later mixed it with water that fell from Christ's body at His baptism, and blood and water that flowed from His side at the crucifixion; the resulting dough was divided among the Apostles, and has been handed on by a process of leavening ever since. This leaven (*malka,* "king") is renewed in every church by the addition of dough, salt, and olive oil by a priest and deacon on every Holy Thursday. No Liturgy may be celebrated without it, and it is often numbered among the sacraments. An embroidery of the legend is that the West anathematizes Nestorius because when he fled from Constantinople he took all the *malka* with him and left the rest of the world without it.

Liturgical language. The liturgical Syriac is used with less admixture of the vernacular than in the western Syriac rite of the Jacobites.

The Eucharistic Liturgy is celebrated only on Sundays and feasts, and in the evening before Christmas, Epiphany, and Easter.

The astonishing thing about Holy Apostles' *anaphora* as used by the Nestorians is that in the manuscripts of it the words of institution are missing. This has provided a pretty problem for liturgiologists. Mar Ignatius Rahmani (in his *Liturgies Orientales et Occidentales,* Bairut, 1929) is satisfied that they were there in times past, and they have been supplied in the books printed by the archbishop of Canterbury's mission; but in spite of Anglican efforts it is alleged that some ignorant Nestorian priests omit the words from this anaphora. In the other two "hallowings" they are there, and said by the celebrant. It seems clear that the omission in the manuscripts was a form of the so-called "discipline of the secret" and did not imply an omission in celebration.

Confirmation. This sacrament was first confused with the baptismal rite (which it followed immediately), and was then dropped altogether.

Eucharist. Nestorians receive Holy Communion (but only rarely) in both kinds separately, the celebrant administering the Host, the deacon the Chalice. As the Blessed Sacrament is not reserved there is no provision for communion of the sick outside of the Liturgy.

Penance. This sacrament has gone out of use, except in the reconciliation of an apostate.

Anointing.[4] This sacrament also has quite gone out of use.

Kalendar. This is based on the Julian reckoning for months and on the "Era of the Greeks" (i.e., of the Seleucids, from 311 B.C.) for years, but the last has practically fallen into disuse.

THE MELLUSIANS

The "Church of Trichur," an unimportant schismatic sect in India, must be mentioned here as it is nominally Nestorian.

During his government of the Catholic Chaldeans from 1847 to 1878, the patriarch of Babylon, Joseph VI Audo, attempted to recover the former jurisdiction of his see over the Catholics of Chaldean rite in Malabar. In 1860, persuaded by an aggrieved Malabarese priest named Antony Thondanatta, he sent a bishop, Thomas Rokkos, to represent him in Malabar. Rokkos was peremptorily recalled by Rome, but a few years later Thondanatta, having been repulsed by Audo, received episcopal ordination from the Nestorian katholikos at Kudshanes and returned to Malabar as Mar Abd-Iso. Shortly after, he submitted to the Holy See and the nascent schism would probably have fizzled out, but unfortunately the relations of the Patriarch Joseph Audo with Rome were strained, and in 1874 he sent another bishop, Elias Mellos, to Malabar.[5] It is from him that the schismatics of Trichur get their colloquial name, for he organized the sect; but in 1882 he left Malabar suddenly and Thondanatta revolted for the third time and took his place, leading the Mellusians until his death in 1900. They were without a head till 1908, when the Nestorian katholikos sent them a bishop in the person of Mar Timothy Abimelech, who began a protestantizing policy, which was on the whole resisted by his flock.

The Mellusians today number a few thousand souls in the state of Cochin and are dying out. They conform more or less

[4] Note that Orientals call the seventh sacrament simply "Anointing." Dissidents sometimes err by giving it to those who are not sick at all.

[5] It must be clearly understood that Mar Joseph had no intention of provoking a schism in Malabar; he was imprudent and stubborn but acted in complete good faith. Mellos repudiated his schism before his death.

to the practices of the Nestorian Church, but their adherence to its heresy is purely nominal. They have a bishop at Trichur, who calls himself (without a shadow of justification) "Metropolitan of Malabar and the Indies"; in 1929 this bishop, Mar Timothy, went to the United States of America and stirred up trouble there between the Nestorian immigrants from Kurdistan and those from Persia.

BIBLIOGRAPHY

Fortescue, *The Lesser Eastern Churches* (London, 1913).
Labourt, *Le Christianisme dans l'Empire Perse* (Paris, 1904).
*S.P.C.K., *The Liturgy of Addai and Mari* (London, 1893).
*Mingana, in the *Bulletin of the John Rylands Library,* July 1925 (Manchester).
*Badger, *The Nestorians and Their Rituals,* 2 vols. (London, 1852).
*Maclean and Browne, *The Katholicos of the East and His People* (London, 1892).
*Browne, *The Eclipse of Christianity in Asia* (Cambridge, 1933).
*Hazell and Margoliouth, *Kurds and Christians* (London, 1913).
*Luke, *Mosul and its Minorities* (London, 1925).
*Vine, *The Nestorian Churches* (London, 1937).

For the Mellusians:

Panjikaran, *Christianity in Malabar* (Rome, 1926).

CHAPTER X

THE MONOPHYSITE CHURCHES OF THE ALEXANDRIAN RITE

OF THE churches that had their origin as schismatic bodies directly or indirectly in a refusal to accept the Council of Chalcedon (see Vol. I, pp. 4, 5) those of the Copts, Syrians, and Armenians are completely independent bodies; the Ethiopians have a certain dependence on the Coptic patriarch, and the Malabarese a nominal and much disputed dependence on the Jacobite patriarch. These churches are all in communion with one another and alike regard both Catholics and Orthodox as heretics, except that the Armenians have never declared themselves formally in communion with the others. Nevertheless an Armenian patriarch of Constantinople, Malachy Ormanian, says in his book, *The Church of Armenia* (Oxford, 1912, p. 211), that "the Syrian, Coptic, and Abyssinian Churches retain their autocephalic hierarchy without abandoning their communion with the Armenian Church" (it is really rather kind of him); and the relations between the Armenian and other monophysite churches are very cordial, at any rate nowadays, though not always in the past.

But there is not complete unanimity of doctrine and practice (quite apart from differences of liturgical rite) among the monophysites, and so a separate summary of the chief dogmatic divergences of each of these churches from the Catholic faith is given in its place: of the chief divergences only, for their theology is even more unformulated and difficult to specify than that of the Orthodox and on a number of points precision is impossible to obtain.

In as much as these churches continue pertinaciously to refuse to recognize the oecumenical council of Chalcedon and the "dogmatic letter" of Pope St. Leo I, they must on that count alone be accounted heretical, and this is not the place (even had this writer the ability) to consider how far their Monophysism (especially in the case of the Armenians) is due to misunderstandings engendered by the difficulty of rendering such philosophical terms as "essence," "nature," and "person" exactly equivalent in different languages, Latin, Greek, Armenian. But it should be pointed out that some Catholic theologians (e.g., Abbé J. Lebon, Father Jugie) claim that their Monophysism is more nominal or verbal than real. So long ago as 1610 Father Antony Fernandez, S.J., writing of the Ethiopians, said: "They are persuaded that we make two Christs, as if we claimed that his two natures operate separately. Their doubts were dispelled when I explained that His humanity and divinity operate conjointly, that there is one only Lord, one Son of the Eternal Father and blessed Mary, one single Messiah." Furthermore, Father Jugie emphasizes that these churches should not be called "Eutychian," and quotes the Russian theologian Bolotov: "Capable missionaries live for many years among the Ethiopian monophysites and yet do not realize that in fact there is no longer such a thing as an Eutychian in the world." "A clear example of the prejudice instilled by imperfect text-books of history," comments Father Jugie.[1]

But however doubtful the reality and formality of their Monophysism may be, these churches (under whatever theological misapprehensions, through whatever historical circum-

---

[1] Jugie, *Theologia dogmatica christianorum orientalium . . . dissidentium*, Vol. V, p. 545. Eutyches (d. *c.* 455) taught a very extreme form of Monophysism, which is *formally and officially* repudiated by the Armenian Church at least. He said that our Lord had two natures before the hypostatic union, which at His incarnation were fused into one. It may be noted that both the Armenians and Jacobites in the United States have officially declared that, while they do not adopt the Chalcedonian formula about the two natures in Christ, they explicitly believe that He was perfect God and perfect man.

stances and mistakes) still repudiate Chalcedon and all the following oecumenical councils, and hold aloof from communion with the apostolic see of St. Peter, though the average dissident Egyptian or Syrian, Ethiop or Armenian, cares little and knows less about either the council or the pope.

1. THE COPTIC CHURCH

From its beginnings Monophysism had its stronghold in Egypt, where the patriarch of Alexandria, Dioscoros, was its spokesman and leader. After six years of controversy and violence he was deposed and his teaching condemned by the Council of Chalcedon in 451. Practically all the clergy and people of Egypt refused to accept the decisions of the council, not altogether on account of religious enthusiasm but because political passions also were involved: it was bad enough to be subject to a foreign emperor without having "Byzantine theology" as well. The century that followed was an outrageous period of ecclesiastical quarreling, minor schisms, persecution, political chicanery, and physical violence. The see of Alexandria was bandied between hierarchs who were sometimes orthodox but more often monophysite, till in 567 two lines of patriarchs were definitely established: one for the mostly foreign minority of orthodox Catholics, the other for the solid mass of Egyptian monophysites, today called the Coptic Church.[2] With the modification that the orthodox line is now in schism from Rome, that is still the position.

The monophysite Egyptians continued to be troubled by domestic quarrels, by the Catholics, and in 616–628, by Persian invaders who bitterly persecuted them. Eleven years later the Arab conquest was begun, and the anti-imperialist Copts are said to have given aid to the khalifah against the Byzantines; but the deciding factor was the treachery of the Orthodox patriarch of Alexandria, Cyrus, who was also the imperial civil governor and handed the country over to the Arabs (he had previously

[2] A Copt is simply an Egyptian (Arabic *Kibti*=Gk [Ai] *gúpt* [ios]), in actual use a Christian Egyptian.

persecuted the Monophysites most bitterly). Then for century after century Egypt was oppressed by Arabs, Mameluks, and Turks; massacres were frequent and apostasies so numerous that today 93 per cent of the Egyptians are Mohammedan. But there were also many martyrs, and we must not forget the unforeseen part that our Western Crusaders played in the ruin of the Egyptian church. Their campaign in Egypt greatly embittered the Mohammedans, especially the common people, against all Christians, and the long process of attrition by which the Egyptians had gradually succumbed to Islam ended in a deadly persecution in the fourteenth century which reduced the Coptic Church to what it is today. This final catastrophe was brought about by the hatred incurred by the Crusaders and the military successes of those who fought against them.[3]

During the twelfth century the Coptic patriarch John V (1131–1146) defended the abuse which had grown up of ignoring the practice of confession. He was opposed by a priest named Mark ibn al-Kubar, who made a vain attempt to bring about reunion with the Orthodox, now themselves in schism. There was also a controversy about circumcision and the patriarch Cyril III (1235–1243) ordered that all boys be circumcised *before* baptism. Cyril, who had obtained his office by simony, made some half-hearted efforts toward reconciliation with Rome. It was under his rule that the only recorded apostasy of a Coptic bishop to Islam occurred. John IX (1427–1453) showed himself well disposed towards the Council of Florence and sent two abbots as legates who signed the act of union of the Syrian Jacobites, but it never became effective. Popes Gregory XIII and Sixtus V sent legates to the patriarchs John XIV and Gabriel VII and VIII, but with no more result. From

[3] A characteristic incident was in 1305 when the ambassador of the king of Aragon at Alexandria refused to pay a ransom justly due for a released prisoner, and, moreover, kidnapped the sultan's messengers who came for it. All the ancient restrictions on Christians in Egypt were at once revived in full force.

time to time during the Middle Ages (e.g., in 1320) the Friars Minor sent preachers from Palestine into Egypt.

Early in the seventeenth century Capuchin missions were established in the Levant by Father Joseph of Paris (Joseph Leclerc du Tremblay, "Grey Eminence"), and a foundation was made at Cairo in 1630. For a time it prospered, under the direction of Blessed Agathangelo of Vendôme. The Coptic patriarch, Matthias, who wanted reunion but was too old and feeble to do anything about it, opened all his churches to the friars, and Father Agathangelo gave spiritual conferences in the monasteries of the Lower Thebaid. Unhappily a great obstacle to reunion was the example given by the European Catholics resident in the country. Father Agathangelo eventually went off in despair to Ethiopia and was there martyred. It was not till 1741, when the Coptic bishop at Jerusalem, Anba[4] Athanasius, became a Catholic, that a body of Catholics of the Coptic rite was definitively organized.

With the irruption of Europe into Egypt in 1798 and the coming of Mohammed Ali in 1805 there opened an era of exterior tranquillity for the Copts. A promising move towards reunion, led by Moallem Ghali, a secretary of Mohammed Ali, was spoiled by one of the dissident bishops in 1815, and the arrival of Protestant missionaries created a diversion in the religious affairs of the country. The patriarch Cyril IV (1854–1862) was educated at a Protestant school, and subsequently showed himself sensitive in the matter of venerating holy images; but the superstitious excesses of some of his flock fully justified his short burst of iconoclasm. His successor Demetrios II received Mgr. Ciurcia as bearer of Pius IX's invitation to the Vatican Council. The patriarch was somewhat aloof and cold on that occasion, but discussed topics of theology with Mgr. Ciurcia and made at least one significant remark: "How can we Copts and you Catholics ever understand one another,"

[4] *Anba, abba,* father; a title used for priests and bishops by the Copts and Ethiopians.

salem (including part of northeastern Egypt), Bohaireh, Beni-Suef, Minieh, Sanabu, Kaneh, Esneh, Assiut, Abutig, Akhmin, Khartum, the Fayum, Dakalieh, and Manfalut. Several of these sees have longer titles perpetuating separate dioceses long since extinct. The custom begun some thirty-five years ago of raising the abbots of the four principal monasteries to episcopal rank is now being discouraged. A diocese is projected for immigrants in South Africa.

Lower clergy. The great reproach against the Coptic clergy is their lack of education – which is not their fault, for the only seminary has never yet functioned properly. Many of the priests cannot read their liturgical language (Coptic; they learn the Liturgy by heart), some even cannot read Arabic. Clerical education has been one of the concerns of the reforming party, but they want to send ecclesiastical students to England – where they run the risk of being protestantized; the late patriarch favoured Orthodox colleges. Priests are mostly drawn from the artisan class (for which reason alone the *bourgeois* laity despise them), and are always married before ordination. Deacons are very numerous, being often ordained in adolescence, though 25 is the age required by the canons.[6]

The *kummus* (also the title of an abbot, *hegumenos*) is a sort of rural dean or archpriest. The archdeacon has charge of ceremonies; he wears an iron pectoral cross.

Monasticism. Egypt was the birthplace of Christian monasticism: St. Antony, the father of all monks, St. Paul, the first hermit, St. Pachomius, the pioneer of the common life, St. Makarios, St. Ammon, St. Schenute, St. Pambo, all attained holiness and fame in the waste places on either side of the Nile between the Red Sea and the Libyan desert; Nitria and the Thebaid, the Wady Natrun and Skete are renowned forever in the history of Christian asceticism.

---

[6] Father Pachomius Hanna, who afterwards became a Catholic, was ordained in 1881 reader, subdeacon, and, as an afterthought, deacon all at once at the age of twelve, and with no more preparation than the learning by heart of the psalms and prayers of the office. He was made priest at nineteen. See bibliography.

During the fourth century the communal (cenobitic) life prevailed over the eremitical in upper and middle Egypt and got a footing around the delta, and before the Arab conquest in 639–641 monasteries were numbered by the hundred and monks by the thousand. Today there are only eight monasteries left, historically most interesting and strongholds of the Coptic Church. They are St. Antony's and St. Paul's (Dair Antonios and Dair Boulos) near the Red Sea, Moharrak in the province of Asiut, St. Simeon's in the Fayum, and four in the Nitrian Desert; namely Dair Makarios, Dair Amba Bishoi, Dair as-Suryani ("of the Syrians"), and Dair al-Baramus ("of the Romans," i.e., two young Greek hermits). These monasteries are mostly in very lonely places and the life is truly penitential, the staple food being bread and dried beans, but the monks have considerable freedom to roam about the country and stay with their friends. Some of the monasteries have considerable property (since 1928 a patriarchal commission controls its administration), but others, e.g., Suryani and Bishoi, give an impression of great poverty. The monks number some 300 in all.

While it is true that they are chiefly concerned for the preservation of their ancient houses and traditional customs, and have strenuously opposed even the good reforms mooted in their church of recent years, there is on the other hand an enlightened element among them. For example, a house of studies for young monks has been established of late years at Heluan, near Cairo, and a recent visitor to the Nitrian houses found that the monks of their own accord would raise the question of reunion—favouring the reconciliation of the Copts with the Orthodox Greeks as a first step.

There are three convents of women, not at all flourishing.

The faithful. The dissident Copts have a confusing habit of calling themselves "the Orthodox Copts." They number about a million[7] (there are some 50,000 Egyptian Protestants and the same number of Catholics of the Coptic rite), but an extremely

[7] There is only a handful of Copts in the United States of America, with no church or clergy.

first volume (pp. 136–141). The chief variations among the non-Catholics are as follows.

In the dissident churches the Blessed Sacrament is not reserved. Men do not uncover their heads in church but often remove their shoes; the people sit on the floor, though benches may now be found in city churches.

Vestments. Bishops have the Byzantine crown, pastoral staff, and hand cross, and wear the *omophorion* and the *sakkos.* Out of church the clerical hat is generally a turban, dark in colour; in church a round white cap, surmounted by a small cross.

The dissident priests wear a distinguishing vestment, namely, the *kidaris* or *ballin.* It is made of white linen, embroidered with two crosses, and one end hangs down the back under the chasuble while the other is wound round the head to form a hood; the bishop's *kidaris,* worn when he does not wear the crown, is of coloured silk. This vestment is for convenience referred to as a sort of amice, but historically it seems to be the same as the *fanon* worn by the pope when celebrating pontifically, and as the veil or hood worn in some form or other by all Eastern bishops and monks. Through poverty or carelessness Coptic priests in the smaller churches sometimes celebrate vested only in the *stikharion, kidari,* and *badrashain* (stole).

Altar-vessels. The vessels are similar to those of the Byzantine rite, without the spoon and lance, with three small and two large veils to cover the offerings. In many churches there is no crucifix or cross on the altar.

The Eucharistic Liturgy (*Korban*) is celebrated only on Sundays and feasts in most churches, and may be concelebrated.

Penance. Bishops, priests, and deacons are not required to confess their sins; lay people do so very rarely, and then receive absolution after vaguely accusing themselves in very general terms.

Eucharist. Communion is received in both kinds, either separately or by intinction of the Host, but reception by the laity is infrequent. Children are supposed to receive communion im-

Courtesy, *Catholic Herald*

ETHIOPIAN EIKON

ETHIOPIAN CLERGY ASSEMBLING FOR A PROCESSION

Courtesy, La Bonne Presse

SYRIAN JACOBITE CHURCH OF ST. JOHN MARK
AT JERUSALEM

Courtesy, La Bonne Presse

SYRIAN JACOBITE PRIEST AND DEACON

Courtesy, Dom Benedict Morrison

MAR ATHANASIUS QASIR, JACOBITE BISHOP OF MOSUL

MALABAR JACOBITE BISHOP

Courtesy, *London C.T.S.*

JACOBITE CHURCH AT KARINGACHERRY, MALABAR

Courtesy, *London C.T.S.*

CHURCH OF ST. HRIPSIME AT ETSHMIADZIN

Courtesy, La Bonne Presse

ARMENIAN PRIEST, DEACONS, AND CHOIR

mediately after baptism (circumcision before baptism is still practised, but without religious significance).

Anointing is administered by one priest instead of the seven called for by their ritual. It is administered in any sickness and even to the healthy as an absolution and for the avoidance of disease. In some places the prayers of this sacrament are said during Lent in every house, whether there is anyone ill or not, as a sort of blessing and prophylactic.

Kalendar. Easter is fixed by the computation of the patriarch Demetrios (d. 231). They commemorate on Mesore 7 (July 31) the Primacy of St. Peter the Apostle, together with the High-priesthood of Aaron.

Penitential seasons. The periods of fasting are long and severe, involving no food, drink, or tobacco between sunrise and sunset and abstention from eggs, cheese, and milk, as well as flesh meat. These are fairly seriously observed, as is the Mosaic forbiddance of eating certain animals, etc.

BIBLIOGRAPHY

Fortescue, *The Lesser Eastern Churches* (London, 1913).
Hanna in *Relations d'Orient*, 1908, p. 248; 1909, p. 176 (Bairut).
*Curzon, *Visits to Monasteries in the Levant* (London, 1897).
*White, *Monasteries of the Wadi'n-Natrun*, 3 vols. (New York, 1926–1933).
Maspero, *Histoire des Patriarches d'Alexandrie* (Paris, 1923.)
*O'Leary, *The Saints of Egypt* (London, 1938).
Strothman, *Die Koptische Kirche in der Neuseit* (Tübingen, 1932).

2. THE ETHIOPIAN CHURCH

Though historically the Syrian is the second in importance of the monophysite churches, I deal with the Ethiopic now because of its age-long association with the church of Egypt.

The Ethiopians[10] proper are partly of Semitic stock, and their ancestors of before the Christian era probably emigrated to Africa from southern Arabia. They now live in the mountainous land between the Sudan, Kenya, and the sea, their country being a huge tableland with a mean elevation of 7000 feet. They are homogeneous neither in race nor religion, but the nucleus is Ethiopic and Christian. The predominant race is the Amharic, others being the Gallas, Tigre, Danakils, and Somalis.

The first authentic evangelization of the Ethiopians of which there is record was towards the middle of the fourth century, when two youths from Tyre, Frumentius and Aedesius, spared from a massacre of their fellow-voyagers, attained influence at the Ethiopian court at Aksum and preached the gospel there. St. Frumentius was eventually consecrated bishop for his converts by the then archbishop of Alexandria, the great St. Athanasius himself. A more extensive evangelization was carried on some hundred and fifty years later by the "Nine Saints," who were monks and probably monophysites from Syria. In the time of Justinian there was lively competition between the Catholics and monophysites of Egypt for control of the Ethiopic mission; the last named won, and the Ethiopian Church remained hierarchically dependent on the Coptic patriarchate of Alexandria,

---

[10] "Ethiopia" and "Ethiopians" are to be preferred because those are their own names for their country and themselves, and there is nothing against them. The more usual "Abyssinia" and "Abyssinians" originated as an offensive nickname, "the mongrels."

and accordingly monophysite. Until the sixteenth century little is known of the history of Christianity in Ethiopia: especially after the Arab conquest of Egypt communication even with the oppressed mother church was difficult and often interrupted for long periods: the Ethiopians were a Christian island in a sea of Islam.[11]

From the earliest times the Copts did their best to provide that the head of the Ethiopian Church should not only be consecrated in Egypt but should be a Coptic monk, and this has been the rule and the fact at least since the twelfth century. This primate is called *abuna,* that is, "our father" (the ordinary style of address to a priest in Arabic). The *negus*[12] from time to time tried to get rid of this Coptic control, e.g., about 1140, when Gabriel II was patriarch in Egypt, and again in 1177 when a tentative appeal was made to Rome. But there were occasions when the Ethiopian kings protected the Copts against the Mohammedans.

The thirteenth century, in Ethiopia as in Europe, saw a veritable renaissance after a period of political unrest. About 1280 King Yakuno Amlak endowed the church with a large part of his territories at the instance of abuna Takla Haymanot, who exercised very great influence and is now ventrated as the patron saint of Ethiopia and especially of the monastic "congregation" of Dabra Libanos. Monasticism flourished anew, and theology was keenly studied, but the lives of the people did not support the enthusiasm of their clergy. At this time, it is said, a certain Mar Job, a bishop of Syrian rite, was sent into Ethiopia by the Jacobite patriarch of Antioch, Ignatius II, who had renounced Monophysism under the influence of the Friars Preachers. Mar Job was soon followed by some Dominicans, and a movement

---

[11] For nearly a thousand years there was a powerful Christian church in Nubia, also subject to Alexandria and monophysite; it was finally swept away by the Mohammedans in the fourteenth century. There are ruins of churches still in Nubia. See Monneret, *Storia della Nubia cristiana* (Rome, 1938).

[12] The title of the ruler of Ethiopia is *Negus neghesti,* "king of the kings"; "emperor" is a journalistic misnomer.

towards Rome began. This was short-lived owing to prompt action by abuna Salama. Mar Job was driven out and the friars and their followers murdered; their supposed relics are venerated to this day by the dissidents themselves, in the churches around Neebi. Coulbeaux in his history of Abyssinia says that there were other Dominican efforts, but his statements are questioned. Early in the fourteenth century the country was divided by a dispute between the monks of Dabra Libanos and those of Ewostatewos (St. Eustathius) on the subject of the observance of the Sabbath as well as Sunday: it was decided by the negus Amda Zion in favour of the double observance (such ecclesiastical action by the Ethiopian monarchs was common).

The Ethiopian Church was represented at the Council of Florence by the abbot of Dair as-Sultan in Jerusalem, who signed the act of union in the name of the negus Zara Jacob, but the union was even less operative in Ethiopia than in other places. The only concrete result was a royal deputation sent to Rome in 1481, as a result of which Pope Sixtus IV established a church, monastery, and hospice for Ethiopian pilgrims behind St. Peter's, San Stefano dei Mori, "of the Moors" (now the Pontifical Ethiopian College). Zara Jacob, mentioned above, who ruled from 1434 to 1468, was a reforming sovereign whose zeal outran his discretion, and some of his religious reforms were as bad as others were good; unfortunately he was himself in effect a polygamist, an endemic abuse among the Ethiopians.

At the beginning of the sixteenth century Ethiopia was engaged in a struggle with Mohammedan invaders, and there has already been related in my first volume (pp. 143–145) the disastrous and deplorable ecclesiastical results of the effort of the negus Labna Danghel to get help from the Portuguese. It led ultimately, about a century later, to the expulsion of all Catholic clergy from Ethiopia.

Controversies with Catholics had whetted the polemical appetite of the monks, and afterwards extravagant theological disputes again broke out violently between the two "schools" of monks. They were intensified by the arrival in 1634 of a Protestant physician from Lübeck, named Peter Heyling. For some years this man was the evil genius of the Ethiopian court and the inveterate enemy of Catholicism, but he came to a bad end, being beheaded at Suakim in 1647. Meanwhile the controversies of the monks dragged on, sometimes brought before synods, and the last embers died out only in our time.

The succession of Coptic abunas has been fairly regular since 1637 except for the vacancy of seventeen years which was ended by the appointment of Salama, in 1841, at the age of twenty-four; it is difficult to know which was greatest, the theological ignorance of this man, his hatred of the Catholic Church, or the corruption of his morals. It was he who persecuted Blessed Gabra Michael to death (Vol. I, p. 146). He misruled for twenty-six years and neither he nor his successor Athanasius appear to have made any reply to the invitation of Pope Pius IX to the Vatican Council (if they were asked separately from the Coptic patriarch).

Towards the end of the nineteenth century the procurator of the holy synod of the Russian Orthodox Church, the well-known Pobiedonostsev, sent an ecclesiastical mission to Ethiopia, and the Greek Orthodox of Alexandria also tried to make contacts. When in 1904 the Ethiopians claimed the monastery of Dair as-Sultan at Jerusalem[13] from the Copts and relations were temporarily broken off, the Russians strongly took up their cause and the conversion of Ethiopia to Orthodoxy was freely mooted. But Great Britain supported the Copts, and the whole affair fizzled out. Though there was for a time an Ethiopian representative at the court of the patriarch of Constantinople, these Orthodox advances never received serious encouragement, for the negus Menelik II (1889–1913) believed that they masked political attempts of Russia and Turkey to bring his country under their respective influence – in which view he was quite

[13] The Ethiopians have a small monastery on the roof of St. Helen's chapel of the Holy Sepulchre church at Jerusalem and a large church outside the walls of the city. Major D. V. Duff found the monks there about 1925 "quiet, peaceful, very poor and very pious" — they were also very rude about the Council of Chalcedon.

right. Abuna Matthew (Matewos) was at times not ill-disposed towards union with the Orthodox, and the *itshage* (see p. 218) was said to be definitely in favour of it; he had good relations with the monks of Mount Athos.

Attempts were made to establish Protestant missions in Abyssinia from 1830 onward, but even since the accession of Menelik II they have not had much success. Of one such missionary, in 1855, we read that he was "accompanied by his wife . . . several German gunsmiths . . . and afterwards by Bourgaud, a French gunsmith . . . and Moritz, a Polish soldier of fortune." They succumbed to the climate.

For many centuries up to our time abuna from Egypt was not only the primate of the Ethiopian Church, he was often as not the only bishop.[14] But when abuna Matthew died in 1926 the negus Haile Salassie, voicing popular "progressive" opinion, demanded the independence of his church from Egypt. Negotiations went on for three years and ended in a compromise: the patriarch of Alexandria, John XIX, appointed a Coptic monk, Cyril, as abuna, and at the same time ordained four Ethiopian bishops. These bishops had no dioceses but were as it were auxiliaries to abuna. Shortly after, Anba John ordained a fifth bishop in the person of the *itshage*. These innovations were taken to be a sign of the beginning of the end of Coptic authority in Ethiopia, a process which was hastened by the Italian conquest of the country. Abuna Cyril was sent to Rome and Cairo in 1936 to arrange for the abolition of the Egyptian connection, but his own attitude was suspect and he was refused readmission to Ethiopia. Only three other bishops were then living, and two of them opposed the Italian policy. Thereupon the viceroy, General Graziani, proclaimed the complete independence of the Ethiopian Church, and nominated the third bishop, Abba Abraham, who was blind, to be its first patriarch. At the same time a new *itshage* and three other bishops were appointed and consecrated, to whom several more were added later.

---

[14] From time to time overtures were made to the monophysite Syrians and Armenians by the Ethiopian kings to get bishops from them.

The Coptic patriarch, still John XIX, was naturally stupefied by such an exhibition of high-handedness. Negotiations for a settlement were opened with the Italian government, but nothing came of them, and eventually the patriarch John excommunicated Abba Abraham. The last-named died in 1939, and was succeeded by one of the bishops whom he had consecrated, Abba John.

After the Italians were driven from Ethiopia during World War II, Abuna Cyril (Qerillos) was restored to office, and the link with the Coptic patriarch was again joined. But it seems certain that the next abuna will be an Ethiopian, and that this church will become quite independent in principle as well as in actuality.

ORGANIZATION AND PRESENT STATE

Abuna and bishops. Abuna is metropolitan of Aksum, but his residence is with the royal court at Addis Ababa. He alone has the right to ordain (presumably the other bishops now help him), dispense from vows, consecrate *tabots,*[15] and exercise ordinary jurisdiction generally. He consecrates and crowns the king.

Lower clergy. These do not form a distinguished body – in fact, they are the most insufficient of any Christian priests in the world. In general they receive no training and are ordained in batches without examination or certificate of fitness, whence scandals of illiteracy, evil-living, simony, and invalid ordinations. Hardly any of them understand their liturgical language, Ge'ez, and some of them scarcely ever exercise sacerdotal functions; nor do they preach or otherwise instruct their flocks. They are married and form a large semi-hereditary priestly caste. A reform of the clergy is expected before long, and the first step will be the establishing of some sort of seminary. Numerous deacons are ordained as youths.

The *dabtaras* are lay clerks who are in charge of the music

[15] A box which must be on the altar of every dissident Ethiopian church; it contains the wooden altar-board (*tabhlitha*). There are national legends about the Queen of Sheba and the Ark of the Covenant concerning this piece of furniture, which is treated with great reverence.

of the services, teach in the schools (in theory schooling for all males over twelve has been compulsory since 1907), and supply a little of the education which the ordained clergy lack; the offices cannot be celebrated without their help. They look down on those in sacred orders.

Monasticism. What learning there is in the Ethiopian Church is found among the monks, and they enjoy a respect of which they are more worthy than the secular clergy, but there are so many of them and their life so loosely controlled (or not at all) that their standard is very uneven. Many are wanderers, some are hermits, and the rest live in community, but the common life is very sketchy. They are divided into, as it were, two "congregations" or observances, that of Ewostatewos, with its chief monastery at Dabra Bizan, near Adua, and that of Takla Haymanot, with its headquarters at Dabra Libanos. The last is situated in the mountainous Salaleh district of Shoa, where there are many monks, and the "abbot general" is the *itshage* referred to above. He ordinarily lives at Gondar and, being an Ethiopian, the head of so many monks, and exercising authority over so much property and so many churches, he has often been the rival of abuna, who has the disadvantage of being a foreigner. From time to time the itshage has definitely wielded more influence than abuna, administering the metropolitan see during a vacancy (which generally lasts a long time); he is now a bishop.

The monks follow versions of the "rule of St. Antony," very few of them are priests, and there have been periods in the past when their influence was stronger and better than it is at present. Their life when properly led is severe, but their intellectual interests and theological speculations are apt to be of an ingenuity that topples over into superstition.

There is a small number of hermitesses and a few convents of nuns near one or other of the monasteries; this arrangement has not been without abuse. The principal monasteries, besides those mentioned above, are Dabra Naquaquad on an island in Lake Haik, Lalibala (a great pilgrimage shrine), Dabra Tabor, Dabra Zait, and Addis Alam (*dabra* = mount).

The faithful. Figures given for the population of Ethiopia vary, but it seems to be around 8 million (including Eritrea). Of these, 4 million are estimated to be monophysite Christians (mostly in the regions of Shoa, Amhara, Gojjam, and the Tigre); Mohammedans and heathens are numerous, and there is a number of Jewish (by religion only) Falashas; Catholics number only about 50,000 all told, of both rites. As elsewhere in Africa, Islam gains ground in some districts at an alarming rate. The three principal dialects spoken are Tigre in Eritrea and the north, Tigrinya around Aksum, and Amharic, the official language, in the south.

It is not surprising that the Ethiopians, hemmed in by Islam and for centuries in only difficult contact with the oppressed Christians of Upper Egypt and not at all with any others, should still be the most backward of all Christian bodies. The general run of the people is excessively ignorant, and Judaic, pagan, and superstitious elements are mixed in popular belief and observance. Among some of the more educated a low morality is joined with a taste for remarkable theological speculations. In particular, concubinage and what amounts to polygamy are common and "trial marriages" were the custom in Ethiopia long before they became fashionable among peoples reputedly less "backward." There is a great outward show of devotion in the observance of severe fasts and of ceremonies, but use of the sacraments is rare. Great veneration for the angels is joined with an extensive demonology, and the numerous sacred springs and trees are the scene of observances which it is hard for a Christian to justify. But in spite of this dark picture, true religion is not dead: European missionaries have not failed to find good and lovable qualities in the Ethiopians, and promise for the future. Moreover, sight must not be lost of the fact that they have clung to Christianity (in however unsatisfactory a form) for centuries, when they could easily have succumbed to Islam or reverted to heathenism. The prospects of reunion among the Christians of Ethiopia have been referred to in Volume I, when speaking of the Catholics.

DOGMATIC DIVERGENCES

The Ethiopic Church undoubtedly professes Monophysism, but, as has been said, its theologians seem to have no very clear idea of what the Catholic doctrine about Christ's two natures is. There are at least three schools of belief about the hypostatic union and birth of our Lord, and the controversies are endless. They do not seem to have considered the procession of the Holy Ghost (*Filioque*).

It is as difficult to be precise on many other points of the Christian faith, since there is no official statement of doctrine. Like the Copts, they have some curious beliefs about the state of the dead before the last judgement, e.g., that the just enjoy a terrestrial paradise ("the bosom of Abraham") while the wicked are confined underground or on the sea; but they pray for them. They receive a number of uncanonical books (e.g., Enoch, the Apocalypse of Baruch, the "Shepherd" of Hermas) into the canon of Holy Scripture.

Again like the Copts, their baptismal rite is sufficient and doctrine on the point orthodox, but the sacrament is often administered so carelessly or fancifully that those who are reconciled with the Catholic Church are baptized conditionally. Moreover, owing to the custom of ordaining *en masse* it is extremely doubtful if Ethiopic orders are always valid (even if the ordinands were properly baptized).[16]

The prevalence of irregular sexual relations in Ethiopia has been referred to above, but it must be made clear that the unity and indissolubility of marriage are held in theory; it is taken for granted, however, that they are an ideal above the attainment of ordinary men and women and the abuses are tolerated without question, though a priest would not be expected to bless or recognize a polygamous union.

---

[16] Dr. Fortescue's point that, as long as they are ordained by the Coptic patriarch, the orders of *abuna* and other bishops are valid, unfortunately does not certainly hold good (see p. 209).

LITURGY AND CUSTOMS

The liturgical rites of the Ethiopians are in origin those of the Copts,[17] translated into Ge'ez (Cf., Catholic Ethiopian usage, Vol. I, pp. 148–151). These rites have been subjected to some rather surprising modifications and additions, particularly by way of ritual dancing.

Church buildings. Churches are very numerous, mostly built of mud and thatch and round in shape, divided by high partitions into three concentric circles with the altar in the middle (*Kedus Kedusan*, Holy of Holies); the second division (*Makdas*) is for singers and communicants, the third (*Kene Mahlet*) for the assembly. The polygonal and rectangular churches (which are usually the older) have a similar internal arrangement. The people often assist from outside the church. The Blessed Sacrament is not reserved but the *tabot* (see note, p. 217), whose blessing by abuna constitutes the consecration of the church, is on every altar, which has a flat crucifix and three or more candles. The holy images are all flat pictures.[18] Ethiopian churches are notably dark, dirty, and untidy.

Vestments. The sacrificial garments are a white or coloured "alb" (*kamis*); the Coptic *kidaris*, called *hebanie* or *ghelbab* (see p. 210), which bishops and monks wear over the head but others round the neck; a coloured girdle (*zenar*) worn under the single-piece stole; cuffs (*akmam*); and the full *kaba*, *felonion* or chasuble. Over the last named (sometimes sewn to it) is worn the *lanka*, a kind of embroidered tippet with scalloped edges and five longish pendants (alleged to symbolize the five wounds of Christ; it is worn by secular dignitaries as well). Bishops and abbots wear a handsome and picturesque triple crown, and carry a hand cross to bless with; on ceremonial

[17] This, and the bond with the Coptic patriarch, does not justify the newspaper practice of referring to Ethiopian clergy as "Coptic priests." You might as well call American Episcopalian ministers "English clergymen" because their services derive from the Church of England prayer book.

[18] Curiously enough, in one of the rock-hewn churches at Lalibala there are statues of St. Peter and St. John carved in the wall, to which great reverence is shown.

occasions grand umbrellas are carried over them. The ordinary dress of the clergy is a black or white gown and *kalemaukion* or a round cap. The T-shaped staff, used to rest on in church by many Eastern monks, is in Ethiopia a token of priestly office.

Altar-bread. This is a flat cake, four inches in diameter and three quarters of an inch thick, stamped with a pattern of squares. It should be baked before every celebration. This bread is leavened, but it is said that unleavened bread is used on Holy Thursday.

The *Eucharistic Liturgy* is celebrated only on Saturdays, Sundays, and feasts in the smaller churches, and the other offices – with their dancing, singing, and their music of drums, rattles, and bells – is the more popular service among many.

The words of institution (which apparently the Ethiopians admit to be the consecrating form) include the words, "Take, eat; *this bread* is my body . . ." and correspondingly, "*this chalice.*" There has been argument whether such a form is valid and, though it probably is, the words "bread" and "chalice" have been deleted in the Catholic edition of the Liturgy.

Like the Coptic, the Ethiopian Liturgy has numerous and remarkable testimonies to belief in the Real Presence, and it also has evidence of the regard in which St. Peter and his holy see were formerly held; not only is this found in the texts for the feast of SS. Peter and Paul but also in a special commemoration on August 13 in honour of Peter's profession of faith (Matt. 17:13–19). The martyrology for the day ends with the words, "Hail Peter, made leader of the apostles and of priests throughout the world!" Ethiopian devotion to our Lady is so enthusiastic as to become superstitious in some of its manifestations, which appear to divinize her.

The *Divine Office* has had its present form only since the fourteenth century. It consists principally of psalms sung by the *dabtaras,* the rhythm marked with rattles of bells and stamping of feet.

All dissident Ethiopian *liturgical books* are still in manuscript, except the "missal," which was printed in 1926.

Confirmation and *Anointing* are no longer in use, the first apparently through confusion with the anointings at baptism, which it immediately followed; the second has not been satisfactorily explained.

Penance. Confession takes the form of saying, "I have sinned. Absolve me," to which the priest replies, "May you be forgiven," or of a self-accusation of murder, adultery, secret theft, or breaking a fast; but as a rule the sacrament of penance is administered only to the dying.

Eucharist. Communion, very rarely received by the lay people, is administered in both kinds separately, the species of wine in a spoon; but since the wine is often an infusion of raisins, made without due care before each celebration, there is another doubt of validity here. As there is no reservation of the Eucharist, viaticum cannot usually be given to the dying.

Kalendar. According to Ethiopian chronology we are now (1947) in the year A.D. 1939, but their annual kalendar is similar to that of the Copts. Their new year's day is August 29 according to the Julian reckoning, September 11 according to the Gregorian. Easter is dated according to a system devised by an Egyptian monk named Ammon at the end of the fourth century. The saints' days are those of the Copts, but sometimes on different dates and with local saints added or substituted: they include Pontius Pilate (because he said he was "innocent of this man's blood!") and other unlikely people. Several feasts (e.g., our Lord's birthday, our Lady, St. Michael) occur every month.

Penitential seasons. There are forty fasting days in Lent, which include Sundays (a unique observance), and at many other times, including a modified form every Wednesday and Friday. Strict fasting includes abstinence from butter, eggs, and milk as well as meat, but there is no fasting at all during the fifty days of paschal-time.

A notable characteristic of the Ethiopians is their Jewish observances. The practice of circumcision and clitoridectomy has no religious significance, but they distinguish between clean and unclean meats, observe days of purification, and regard

Saturday as well as Sunday as holy. The *tabot* in the cathedral at Aksum is looked on as the original Ark of the Covenant, brought from Jerusalem by the Queen of Sheba or by the child she had by King Solomon, from which boy the rulers of Ethiopia claim descent – hence the title "Lion of the Tribe of Juda." But that descent is a common oriental boast.

BIBLIOGRAPHY

Fortescue, *The Lesser Eastern Churches* (London, 1913).
Coulbeaux, *Histoire politique et religieuse de l'Abyssinie,* 2 vols. (Paris, 1929).
Somigli, *Etiopia Francescana nei documenti dei secoli XVII e XVIII,* 2 vols. (Quarrachi, 1928).
*Walker, *The Abyssinians at Home* (London, 1930).
*O'Leary, *The Ethiopic Church* (London, 1936).
*Hyatt, *The Church of Abyssinia* (London, 1928).
*Jones & More, *Abyssinia* (Oxford, 1935).
*Mercer, *The Ethiopic Liturgy* (Milwaukee, 1915).
Anon. (tr. Matthew), *The Teaching of the Abyssinian Church* (Milwaukee, 1936).
Mathew, *Ethiopia* (London, 1947).

CHAPTER XI

THE MONOPHYSITE CHURCHES OF THE ANTIOCHENE RITE

1. THE SYRIAN JACOBITE CHURCH

THE position in the patriarchate of Antioch after the Council of Chalcedon was much the same as in that of Alexandria, except that even western Syria was never solidly monophysite like Egypt. Those that refused to accept the council's decrees were to a considerable extent moved by political, anti-imperial passions, and were egged on by dissident Egyptian monks. The patriarchal throne of Antioch, like that of Egypt, was bandied between orthodox Catholic and Monophysite occupants until the Emperor Justinian I imprisoned all bishops professing or suspect of Monophysism. The sect would then probably have died out in Syria had it not been for the action of the Empress Theodora, who favoured the heretics. At the request of the chief of the Ghassanid Arabs, Harath ibn-Jaballah, she procured the clandestine consecration of two monks in the year 543, one of whom, Jacob al-Baradai, spent the rest of his life secretly organizing the monophysites in Syria. He gave them a patriarch (called "of Antioch" but residing eventually in eastern Syria) and is said to have ordained twenty-seven bishops and over two thousand priests. From this time on there were two churches in Syria, that of the orthodox Catholics (Melkites) and that of the monophysites, commonly called the Jacobite Church, after its tireless organizer.

When the Roman emperors ceased to tolerate the monophysites they were welcomed in Persia, and their faith spread from the centres of Tur Abdai, Takrit, and Mar Mattai, always, of course, opposed strongly by the Nestorians. In 629 the bishop of Takrit became a metropolitan with suffragans under him, and this Jacobite primate in Persia later received the special title of *mafrian*, "fructifier." Those Jacobites who were still subjects of the Empire welcomed the Arab invasion in 636, and were alternately patronized and persecuted by their conquerors; very soon large numbers of them turned Mohammedan and these mass apostacies went on more or less steadily. Farther east their history under the Mongols was similar to that of the Nestorians, and the invasion of Timur Leng, in 1394, left very few Jacobites in Persia and eastern Syria, though they somewhat revived later.

Already in the seventh century they had scholars in liturgical science (e.g., James of Edessa, d. 708) and the Jacobite tradition of scholarship is long and honourable. In the twelfth and thirteen centuries, as in the West and in Ethiopia, there was a revival of religious and intellectual life. Its great ornament was Barhebraeus (Gregory Abdul-Faraj), who was as good as he was learned, a man of great wisdom and knowledge, who sincerely deplored the differences of Catholics, monophysites, and Nestorians, and was revered by them all; he died in 1286 and was buried at Mar Mattai. Another great scholar, just before Barhebraeus, was Dionysios bar-Salibi (d. 1171). At this time there are said to have been twenty Jacobite metropolitan sees with a hundred bishoprics in Syria and Asia Minor and eighteen more under the *mafrian* further east. For long the patriarchal residence was at Amida (Diarbekir, in Mesopotamia) or the monastery of Mar Barsauma, near Melitene, till the great patriarch and chronicler Michael I the Syrian (1166–1199) moved to Mardin, southeast of Diarbekir.

The Jacobites had fairly amiable relations with the Crusaders, and at the instance of Dominican and Franciscan friars there were several movements of patriarchs and bishops for union with Rome, notably in 1237 and 1247, but this promising phase was followed by a long period of internal disorder;

simony was rampant, and at one moment there were three or even four rival patriarchs. This state of affairs, with Mohammedan persecution added, did much further to weaken the Jacobites and to produce that state of vegetation which has scarcely been dispelled yet. After the Council of Florence the representatives of the metropolitan of Edessa signed an act of union at Rome in 1444, but it never came into operation.

In consequence of the encouraging attitude of the then Jacobite patriarch, Naamat-Allah, Pope Gregory XIII sent a legate to Aleppo in 1583, who paved the way for the establishment of the Capuchins and Jesuits there in 1626. Jacobites at once began to come into communion with the Holy See and in such numbers that by 1656 they were strong enough to elect a Catholic, Andrew Akijian (his name sounds Armenian) to the vacant see of Aleppo. Five years later he became patriarch. The dissidents resorted to violence, and when Andrew was succeeded by Peter, ex-Jacobite bishop of Jerusalem, they opposed a patriarch of their own. The present Catholics of the Syrian rite date from this time, but for a hundred years it looked as if they would be destroyed by persecution.

Before his death in 1783, the then Jacobite patriarch nominated as his successor the archbishop of Aleppo, Michael Jarweh. He had recently become a Catholic and, hastening to take possession of the patriarchal residence at Mardin, he gained the support of four bishops and sent to Rome for confirmation of what he had done. The anti-Catholic party meantime elected another patriarch, who succeeded in getting a *berat* of recognition from the Turkish government and so carried on the Jacobite patriarchal line.

Between 1820 and 1850 five more Jacobite bishops abjured their heresy and schism, and nearly all the faithful of Damascus and the southern Lebanon followed them. Outstanding among these bishops was Mar Matthew Nakar, of Mosul, who was a relentless persecutor of Catholics until his own reconciliation in 1832, when he was imprisoned and cruelly beaten by a Turkish magistrate at the instance of the Jacobite patriarch, ibn-Sayar. The other converted bishops were Antony Samhiri of Diarbekir, Issa Mahfuz of Jerusalem, James al-Haliani of Damascus, and another. Neither the patriarch nor any of his bishops replied to Pope Pius IX's invitation to the Vatican Council, but several more bishops were reconciled some years later. Two of them returned to schism: the patriarch, Ignatius Abdul-Massih, was deposed in 1905 and Gregory Sattuf, bishop of Homs, who had been a Catholic since 1896, apostatized when promised his place on the patriarchal throne;[1] Abdul-Massih himself became a Catholic in 1913, but reverted soon after. Their original abjuration of Jacobitism was chiefly due to quarrels and grievances – as, indeed, is too often the cause in these "submissions."

In 1913–1914 the Jacobite layfolk for the first time obtained a council to assist in ecclesiastical administration, but soon after they were devastated by the Turks during the war, together with their Armenian, Nestorian, and Catholic brethren; thousands of clergy and laity were massacred or deported, and more were swept away by famine.

A synod was held in Mosul at the end of 1930, whose legislation suggests that life is returning to the remnants of the once great Syrian Jacobite Church. It provides for the establishment of a seminary and schools, for revision and printing of the liturgical books,[2] that religious books must be censored, that the monastic rule shall be reformed, that monks shall not serve parishes, and other matters. In the following year the patriarch Mar Elias III Shakir visited Malabar to try and restore order (see p. 239), and there died. He was succeeded by Mar Severios Barsum, archbishop of Homs, a prelate of wide knowledge and experience (he was brought up in communion with the Holy See), as Ignatius Ephrem I.

---

[1] Fortescue says the appointment cost him £500 Turkish.

[2] The permission to have organs in church would seem to be a startling innovation; yet Barhebraeus wrote in the thirteenth century that organs could be allowed in church.

ORGANIZATION AND PRESENT STATE

Patriarch. The head of the Jacobites is "Patriarch of the God-protected City of Antioch and of All the Domain of the Apostolic Throne" (i.e., St. Peter's). He is elected by the other bishops (who must consult the faithful) and since the fourteenth century has always on election added the name of Ignatius to his own in memory of the great bishop of Antioch martyred at Rome *c.* 107. Before World War I he lived at Dair az-Zafaran, near Mardin, but as that is in Turkish territory he now lives at Homs. With the advice of a council he appoints, ordains, transfers, or deposes all bishops, and he consecrates the holy chrism for his church. He and his fellow bishops are bound to perpetual abstinence and, of course, to celibacy. His relations with the Jacobites of Malabar are referred to later (p. 237).

Mafrian. As we have seen, the mafrian was originally the primate of the Jacobites in Persia and elsewhere outside the Empire, and as such had wide powers. But since the fourteenth century the office has become titular only, and the title ("Mafrian and Katholikos of the East") is given to the metropolitan of Jerusalem or of Mosul who acts as vicar-general of the patriarch and governs his own see by a deputy. He very often becomes patriarch.

Bishops. The dioceses were much disorganized by World War I, and several of them were deserted. They are now Jerusalem, Mosul, Aleppo, Bairut, Gazireh, and Cairo, whose prelates have the title of metropolitan, as has the abbot (*rabban*) of Mar Matta, but no suffragans. Two metropolitans without dioceses form part of the patriarch's council. The bishops are drawn from the monks, and are subject to strict canons against nepotism.

Lower clergy. Hitherto the standard of the parish clergy has been low owing to the lack of training facilities, and their material condition is very bad; like so many others in the East, they have to supplement the offerings of their flocks by working at a trade or on the land. Many of them are ordained much too young, in spite of canons to the contrary. Deacons, who are numerous, may be married *after* ordination, but even the widow of a priest may not remarry. Formerly a priest was nearly always a native of the village he served.

The archdeacon (who is a priest) acts as vicar-general and the *periodeut* (visitor) conducts visitations of parishes. *Chorepiskopos* is a titular dignity.

Monasticism. The once numerous and flourishing Jacobite monasteries have long been reduced to a few struggling houses; now some of them are in a more precarious condition than ever. The chief monasteries are Dair az-Zafaran, Mar Markos (St. John Mark's) at Jerusalem, and Mar Matta, near Mosul, which together have hardly a score of monks. Biblical studies represented till recently all that was left (among the Jacobites) of the ancient Syrian tradition of scholarship, but now even these have practically been given up. The rule of the monks is "Antonian," and the life is very austere and penitential.

The faithful. The Jacobites usually call themselves simply "Syrians," but ecclesiastically like to add the epithet "Orthodox," to which they are in no sense entitled. They have now been reduced to about 90,000 souls and, though often distinguished as West Syrians on account of their Antiochene rite, mostly live in Irak; there are some 10,000 in Syria and the Lebanon, others in Palestine and Egypt, and a very few left in the southern Turkish provinces. There are a few thousand Syrian Jacobites in the United States of America, under an apostolic, i.e., patriarchal, delegate.

The Jacobite people, hard-working peasants, are much attached to their religion, fast rigorously, and are capable of greatly benefitting by the instruction and education that so few of their pastors are qualified to give. On the whole, they have resisted the blandishments of American Protestant missionaries and reacted violently against the protestantizing tendencies of Mar Gregory Sattuf (both before and after he was a Catholic). Towards reunion with the Catholic Church, on the contrary, they show a certain disposition, especially in Syria: for example, 4500 reconciliations took place in Aleppo, Homs, and Bairut alone within four years. It is often said that only the shortage of Catholic priests of the Syrian rite stands between the Jacobites and unity. It should be borne in mind that the Catholic Syrians, with their separated Jacobite brethren, having kept their native rites and Aramaic liturgical language, represent the original church of our Lord's own earthly home land in a rather special way.

DOGMATIC DIVERGENCES

The Jacobites were never under suspicion of the extremer form of Monophysism taught by Eutyches, and though they continue to repeat monophysite formulas they can neither explain nor defend them. They say that the Holy Ghost proceeds from the Father alone, but some of their theologians have written orthodoxly on this matter. They believe that eucharistic consecration takes place at the invocation of the Holy Ghost. They deny the existence of Purgatory but, as Dr. Fortescue observes, they "have a theory which comes to the same thing," and they pray for the dead; but they say that none of the just will be admitted to the presence of God before the day of judgment: in spite of this they pray to saints, and certainly no Jacobite would deny that our Lady is in heaven.

LITURGY AND CUSTOMS

In divine worship there are not very great differences between the usages of the Jacobite and Catholic Syrians (See Vol. I, pp. 158–163).

Jacobite church buildings are more generally in the traditional form. The Blessed Sacrament is reserved in a covered chalice, either standing on a gradine or in a wooden tabernacle. A curtain hangs from the front of the *ciborium* and is drawn across at parts of the Liturgy and when the altar is not in use. The gospel book lies on a lectern in the choir or just outside the screen. Women are separated from men in the nave, either in a gallery or a screened-off space. Seats are not usual and there are very few holy images (pictures).

Dress. Bishops and monks wear the *schema* (in Syriac *eskim*) at all times: this is a long strip of black material, hood-shaped at one end which goes over the head, the other end hanging down the back under the outer garment; it is covered with little white crosses. The episcopal turban or sacerdotal *kalemaukion* is worn over the schema.

Liturgical language. This is Syriac, with the "western" pronunciation and characters. Most of the Jacobites speak Arabic, but those around Tur Abdin and elsewhere have modern Aramaic dialects. The Scriptural lessons, Creed, Lord's Prayer, and certain other prayers of the Liturgy may be sung or read in either tongue, or in the Turkish or Kurdish vernacular.

The *Eucharistic Liturgy* is celebrated usually only on Sundays and feasts. Strictly speaking, the Jacobites never concelebrate, but on Holy Thursday and other great feasts several separate Liturgies are celebrated at the same time at several altars or on improvised altars, the senior alone celebrating aloud. There are 64 known Syrian *anaphoras,* but only a few are in use, of which the principal is "of St. James." A liturgy of the Presanctified exists but is not used by the dissidents.

Penance. This sacrament, and holy communion, are not in frequent use. The penitent kneels before the priest, who is seated at the door of the church, and accuses himself, often in general terms; absolution is preceded by several prayers and psalms.

Anointing is administered by one priest (instead of the proper seven), who first consecrates the oil. It is said to be sometimes given to persons who are certainly dead.

Kalendar. The Julian reckoning is still in use (except among the Jacobites in the U.S.A.) and the ecclesiastical year begins on the Sunday nearest to October 31.

Penitential seasons. During Lent (seven weeks) and the "fast of Nineveh"[3] a complete fast from food and drink lasts till noon, with abstinence from certain foods for the rest of the day, except on Saturdays and Sundays. Nearly all Wednesdays and Fridays are days of abstinence, as well as periods before SS. Peter and Paul, before the Assumption, before Holy Cross day, and before Christmas. The Mosaic forbiddance of certain foods is in force.

Jacobites make the sign of the cross from left to right, with three fingers or the middle one alone. Their ordinary reverence is a deep bow.

BIBLIOGRAPHY

Fortescue, *The Lesser Eastern Churches* (London, 1913).
Lammens, *La Syrie,* 2 vols. (Bairut, 1921).
*Parry, *Six Months in a Syrian Monastery* (London, 1895).
Labourt, *Le Christianisme dans l'Empire Perse* (Paris, 1904).

[3] A fortnight before Lent begins. The "fast of Nineveh" is an observance known in all Eastern churches except the Byzantine: it commemorates the penance of the Ninevites at the preaching of Jonas.

ear why they did not apply to the Nestorian katholikos, or
if they did, why he did not oblige. But a yet more surprising
thing happened: these Indian malcontents whom the Portuguese represented to be panting for the heresy of Nestori
turned to the Syrian Jacobite patriarch in Mesopotamia
representative hierarch of the opposite heresy, the hated
ophysism. In 1665 he sent his mafrian, Mar Gregory, to
bar to examine the situation but resolutely refused
Thomas Palakomatta a bishop. This situation lasted
dred years, the Jacobite patriarch sending ordai
from time to time to the Malabarese schismatics
be called Jacobites, though whether a professio
faith was required of them we do not know
tion being exercised so far as they were
of priests, all Thomases, of the Palakom
themselves the title of "metran").
It is usually taken for granted th
the Jacobite Liturgy and rites wher
visited Malabar, but Father Be
monk, in his sketch of the hi
ography) states positively th
continued to use the Chald
that the Antiochene (We
use till thirty years later
In 1700 some Jacob
olic Chaldean patri
who would reco
patriarch sent o
main in Malabar by
leader Thomas IV wrote
left the Catholic Church on a
wanted to come back – with him
more was heard of this. Then at last,
ite patriarch agreed to ordain Thomas V
been refused before probably because the
wanted to keep the Indians closely under their ju

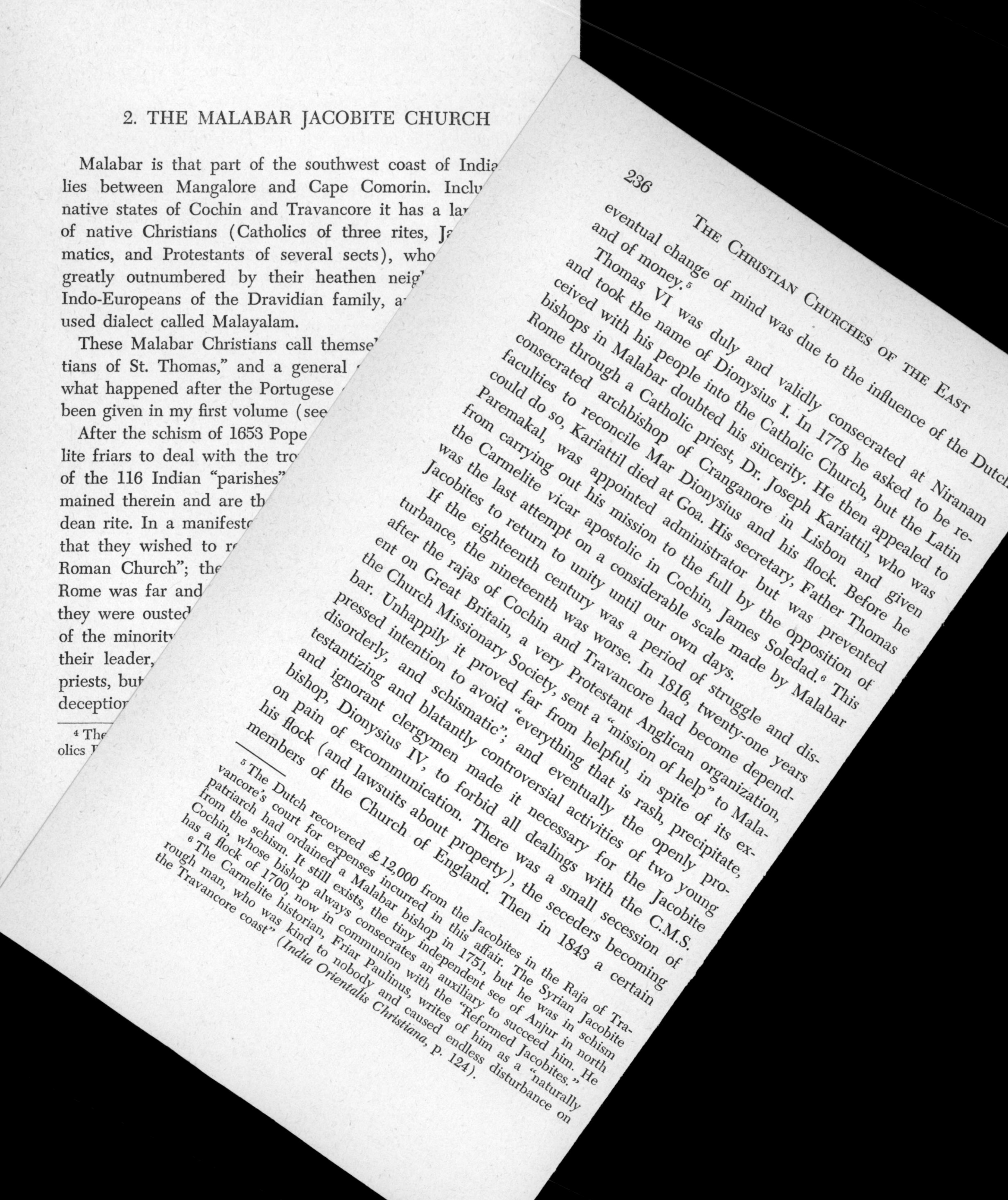

2. THE MALABAR JACOBITE CHURCH

Malabar is that part of the southwest coast of India
lies between Mangalore and Cape Comorin. Inclu
native states of Cochin and Travancore it has a lar
of native Christians (Catholics of three rites, Ja
matics, and Protestants of several sects), who
greatly outnumbered by their heathen neig
Indo-Europeans of the Dravidian family, a
used dialect called Malayalam.

These Malabar Christians call themse
tians of St. Thomas," and a general
what happened after the Portugese
been given in my first volume (see

After the schism of 1653 Pope
lite friars to deal with the tro
of the 116 Indian "parishes"
mained therein and are th
dean rite. In a manifesto
that they wished to r
Roman Church"; the
Rome was far and
they were ousted
of the minority
their leader,
priests, but
deception

[4] The
olics I

eventual change of mind was due to the influence of the Dutch and of money.[5]

Thomas VI was duly and validly consecrated at Niranam and took the name of Dionysius I. In 1778 he asked to be received with his people into the Catholic Church, but the Latin bishops in Malabar doubted his sincerity. He then appealed to Rome through a Catholic priest, Dr. Joseph Kariattil, who was consecrated archbishop of Cranganore in Lisbon and given faculties to reconcile Mar Dionysius and his flock. Before he could do so, Kariattil died at Goa. His secretary, Father Thomas Paremakal, was appointed administrator but was prevented from carrying out his mission to the full by the opposition of the Carmelite vicar apostolic in Cochin, James Soledad.[6] This was the last attempt on a considerable scale made by Malabar Jacobites to return to unity until our own days.

If the eighteenth century was a period of struggle and disturbance, the nineteenth was worse. In 1816, twenty-one years after the rajas of Cochin and Travancore had become dependent on Great Britain, a very Protestant Anglican organization, the Church Missionary Society, sent a "mission of help" to Malabar. Unhappily it proved far from helpful, in spite of its expressed intention to avoid "everything that is rash, precipitate, disorderly, and schismatic"; and eventually the openly protestantizing and blatantly controversial activities of two young and ignorant clergymen made it necessary for the Jacobite bishop, Dionysius IV, to forbid all dealings with the C.M.S. on pain of excommunication. There was a small secession of his flock (and lawsuits about property), the seceders becoming members of the Church of England. Then in 1843 a certain

[5] The Dutch recovered £12,000 from the Jacobites in the Raja of Travancore's court for expenses incurred in this affair. The Syrian Jacobite patriarch had ordained a Malabar bishop in 1751, but he was in schism from the schism. It still exists, the tiny independent see of Anjur in north Cochin, whose bishop always consecrates an auxiliary to succeed him. He has a flock of 1700, now in communion with the "Reformed Jacobites."

[6] The Carmelite historian, Friar Paulinus, writes of him as a "naturally rough man, who was kind to nobody and caused endless disturbance on the Travancore coast" (*India Orientalis Christiana*, p. 124).

Matthew, an ex-student of the C.M.S. college at Kottayam who had been excommunicated by Dionysius IV for heretical activity, went to Mardin and asked the Jacobite patriarch to ordain him bishop – and for some unfathomable reason the patriarch did. Then Matthew (now Mar Athanasius) returned to Malabar, gathered round him those Jacobites who wanted to "reform" their church from within, and tried to oust Dionysius IV. The resulting quarrels and litigation lasted for upwards of fifty years. In 1875 Mar Dionysius V invited the Jacobite patriarch, Ignatius Peter III, to come and help him. Mar Ignatius came, excommunicated Matthew's successor, Mar Thomas, and his followers, divided Malabar into dioceses and ordained six suffragan bishops for Dionysius. But it was not till the end of the century, when the Hindu courts finally decided against the reformers' claims to property, that they definitely broke away and formed a separate body.

They are commonly known as the "Reformed Syrian Christians," but call themselves the Mar Thomakkar, St. Thomas Christians, as if they were the only such in Malabar. Their tendency is Protestant: they still use the "orthodox" Jacobites' liturgy, purged of references to Dioscoros as a saint and of anathemas of Chalcedon and Pope St. Leo the Great, which is good; but also of prayers for the dead, invocation of saints, etc., which is not good.

Yet more trouble began in 1909 when a Jacobite patriarch of Antioch again visited Malabar, namely Abdullah (Gregory) Sattuf, who had been a Catholic bishop (see p. 228). All the Malabarese Jacobites were willing to recognize a very limited primacy of jurisdiction in the patriarch, but some of them denied him any administrative competence in their affairs. There was a fearful fuss and the patriarch excommunicated the Malabar metropolitan, then Dionysius VI, and set one Mar Cyril in his place. Dionysius appealed to the ex-patriarch of Antioch, Abdul-Massih, who came to Malabar, excommunicated Cyril, and nominated one of Dionysius's bishops, Mar Basil, to be supreme head for the Indian Jacobites with the title (new in India) of katholikos. More long lawsuits arose out of this strife, the courts of Travancore deciding in 1923 and again in 1928 against the patriarchal party. The split still continues, the unfortunate faithful being bandied about between the "patriarch's party" of those who want to depend on the patriarch of Antioch and the "katholikos's party" of those who want to be completely autonomous. The effect on the people's religion of these generations of squabbles and lawsuits can be imagined.

Neverthless, side by side with this deplorable state of affairs, there was a certain quickening of religious consciousness among some of the Malabar Jacobites; this became noticeable about 1868, when it was confidently expected that the metropolitan, Dionysius IV, would lead a large number of his people back to the Catholic Church, though this did not in fact happen. In 1919 Father Givergis (George) Panikerveettil, who had had a brilliant career as a professor in various Indian colleges and was an outstanding figure among Indian Christians, founded at a place he called Bethany a religious brotherhood, "of the Imitation of Christ," for missionary and educational work, followed by a similar institute for nuns (for whom there was no provision among the Jacobites). In 1925 Father Givergis was consecrated bishop, taking the name of Ivanios.

At a synod of Jacobite bishops of the anti-patriarchal party held in the same year to consider measures for the spiritual regeneration of their church, Mar Ivanios was commissioned "to open correspondence with the Church of Rome with a view to explore the avenues of ending schisms so far as Malabar was concerned." In response to his overture the Holy See replied that, if the bishops abjured their errors and schism, their Antiochene liturgy and customs would be maintained and, upon verification of the validity of their baptism and ordination, the bishops would be confirmed in their offices and jurisdiction. Of the five bishops concerned, only two, Mar Ivanios and his suffragan, Mar Theophilos, accepted the invitation. They were received into the visible communion of the Catholic Church in 1930, followed at once by two *rambans* (solitaries, who were also bishops designate) and other clergy, religious of the Imitation, and a thousand lay people (there have been many more since then including two more bishops).[7] To distinguish them from their fellows of the Chaldean and Latin rites in Malabar, they are called the Syro-Malankara Catholics.

The loss of two such capable and loved bishops as Mar Ivanios and Mar Theophilos, with so many clergy and lay people following them, alarmed the Jacobites, and early in 1931 the patriarch of Antioch, Mar Elias III Shakar, was sent for, and the viceroy of India, Lord Irwin, with two Anglican bishops, Dr. Gore and Dr. Westcott, were invited to give their advice and assistance. The patriarch raised the excommunication from Mar Dionysius but resolutely refused to recognize a katholikos in Malabar: he feared, and not without reason, that to do so would be the end of any jurisdiction of his see over Indian Jacobites. Then he yielded a little: he would perhaps recognize a katholikos under his own primacy, if the present titular, Basil III, would admit that his two predecessors were intruders. Negotiations went on for twelve months – and then the patriarch Elias died (his memory is greatly revered by both parties in Malabar). Just before his death Mar Ivanios had published an open letter to him, imploring him to return to Catholic unity and quoting passages from their common liturgy in support of the prerogatives of the see of Peter.

In 1937 some approach was made to the Russian emigrant Synod of Karlovtsy (see p. 83) with a view to examining the possibility of a union between the Malabar Jacobites and the Orthodox. To forward this end there was subsequently founded in Travancore the Fellowship of St. Thomas and St. Paul, whose president is an Indian bishop, and vice-president a Russian archimandrite; the Metropolitan Nestor of Manchuria is its patron.

[7] No litigation followed these events. Mar Ivanios and Mar Theophilos set the grand example of not going to law in order to try and retain their possessions; they were literally penniless and homeless till a generous and sympathetic Hindu came to the rescue with a small piece of land.

ORGANIZATION AND PRESENT STATE

It seems that the Malabar Jacobites are passing through a definitive process of being organized into two independent sects, called respectively the "Bava (patriarch's) party" and the "Orthodox (katholikos's) party." The Bava party has a metropolitan and three suffragans who claim jurisdiction over all the Jacobite dioceses in Malabar; "The Katholikos of the Indies,"[8] metropolitan of the opposite party, has likewise three suffragans, and they claim the same jurisdiction. The Bava party is strong in north Travancore and throughout Cochin.

Episcopate. The Jacobite sees established in Malabar in 1875 were Kottayam (the primatial see), Quilon, Thumpaman, Niranam, Kandanad, Cochin, and Angamaly; in 1909 the Southist see of Knanaya, which is not territorial, the Southists being scattered over several dioceses, was established. The bishops are in fact divided between the two parties as just explained, and other bishops are ordained as the exigencies of local politics are deemed to require.

The bishops must be monks, but as there are no Jacobite monasteries in Malabar they are chosen from among celibate priests, called *rambans,* who live as semi-solitaries.

Lower clergy. Lack of education has always been an affliction of the Indian Jacobite clergy but of late years this has been somewhat improved, largely owing to Anglican interest that is more enlightened than in the early days of the C.M.S. (Mar Ivanios, for example, was a master of arts of the University of Madras.) There is a seminary at Kottayam, and a number of clerical students go to various Protestant colleges — often with equivocal results.

Only married priests are appointed to the parochial cure of souls, and most clergy are in fact married (before ordination).[9]

---

[8] It is said that he is silly enough to call himself "Patriarch of Antioch" as well — though without claiming any jurisdiction over the Jacobites of Syria!

[9] The early C.M.S. missionaries were very busy inducing girls (for some of whom the British civil authority provided dowries) to marry widowed priests, contrary to the canons.

Priests are called *katanars* and deacons *shamashe;* the *prodott* (*periodeutes,* "visitor") is a minor prelate who acts as vicar-general, rural dean, etc. There are also *chorepiskopoi.*

The faithful. The Malabar Jacobites number some 363,000 souls (there are over a million Catholics of three rites, Chaldean, Antiochene, Latin), and seeing how much they have suffered by the formation of quasi-Protestant and Protestant sects[10] it is not surprising that they distinguish themselves by an epithet – unfortunately it is that confusing word *Orthodox* again.[11]

There are two social castes among all the Malabarese Syrians, called "Northists" and "Southists." The last named, a small minority, are supposed to be the descendants of some of the Syrians who, according to local traditions, came to Malabar with one Thomas Cana in the fourth (much later?) century. The Northists claim to be the superior race, and quarrels were frequent between the two castes, which do not intermarry. As among the Catholics, there is a special Jacobite bishop with personal jurisdiction over the Southists.

The Jacobites, like all the Malabarese, have a strong taste for education; since the coming of the British, schools of all grades have arisen and the people have made good use of them. Their religious temper is characterized by an addiction to elaborate exterior observances and long prayers, and they have a most unhappy appetite for litigation and quarreling among themselves, as their history shows; but there is a strong undercurrent of honest piety and good will.

DOGMATIC DIVERGENCES

The Monophysism of their brethren in Syria has little, if any, serious part in the consciousness of the Malabar Jacobite

[10] There are among others, the "Reformed," numbering some 144,000 with three bishops; 88,000 or so Anglican Syrians; and the sect of Anjur (see p. 236, note). Add the Mellusians, several other odd schisms from one body or another, and the results of a half dozen different Protestant missionary societies among the heathen (totalling some 240,000 souls), and one doesn't know whether to laugh or cry.

[11] St. Thomas Christians of all obediences often refer to themselves as *Nazranis.*

Church, and little stress is laid on those other principal points which are at issue between the Catholic Church and the dissident East. But their schism is quite definite: as we have seen, this first arose through errors, misunderstandings, and the difficulty for India of keeping in touch with Rome in the seventeenth century; it has been kept on through the force of human passion and the tendency of schism to disintegrate into subschisms unless it is speedily repaired. But the movement of Mar Ivanios, now metropolitan of Trivandrum, has opened a new era, of which the Malabar Jacobites at large have not been slow to see the significance. Hitherto reconciliation with the Catholic Church has meant the adoption of unfamiliar forms of worship and customs, either Chaldean or Western: that is no longer so, and the flow of secessions from the "Orthodox" to the "Reformed" that went on before 1930 is now being somewhat diverted to the plenary Christianity of Rome.

LITURGY AND CUSTOMS

The church buildings in Malabar are plain, aisleless rectangles, with the roof of choir and sanctuary sometimes higher than that of the nave. The larger and older churches have, especially on the western façade, a good deal of applied ornament and architectural features that are a curious mixture of Indian fashions with European influences. The altar stands in a raised sanctuary (with the curtain proper to the rite), within, but not behind, a screen painted and carved in a very florid way.

The liturgical rites of the Malabar Jacobites are practically those of the Syrian Jacobites (see p. 231, and Vol. I, pp. 158–163). The following points may be noticed.

All the audible parts of the *eucharistic liturgy,* except the words of institution, are said in the vernacular Malayalam. Holy Communion is received kneeling back on the heels in the Indian manner.

Absolution is given in a deprecatory form ("May God forgive . . . .") to clergy, in an indicative form ("I forgive . . . .") to

Courtesy, Fr. Eugene Hoade

CYRIL, ARMENIAN PATRIARCH OF JERUSALEM

Courtesy, Fr. Eugene Hoade

ARMENIAN CATHEDRAL OF ST. JAMES AT JERUSALEM

Courtesy, Fr. Eugene Hoade

EASTERN HIERARCHS AT JERUSALEM

Centre: The Orthodox Patriarch. Left to right: Coptic, Syrian, Armenian, Ethiopian

Courtesy, John Connolly

GREEK AND RUSSIAN CONCELEBRATION OF THE LITURGY, IN LONDON

Courtesy, La Bonne Presse

TOWARD REUNION: CATHOLIC ASSUMPTIONISTS AND ORTHODOX MONKS AT THE BULGARIAN MONASTERY OF RYLA

laity. Confession and Communion are not frequent – often only on Holy Thursday.

The rite of *holy anointing* is more simple for a lay person than for a priest.

Fasting is supposed to involve no food or drink before sunset, but in practice generally ends far earlier. There is a special fast for girls, of eight days before the feast of our Lady's birthday.

Bishops wear, on appropriate occasions, a rather exotic mitre, evolved from that of the West.

BIBLIOGRAPHY

Fortescue, *The Lesser Eastern Churches* (London, 1913).
Mackenzie, *Christianity in Travancore* (Trivandrum, 1901).
Panjikaran, *Christianity in Malabar* (Rome, 1926).
Bernard, *Brief . . . History of the St. Thomas Christians* (Trichinopoly, 1924).
Schurhammer, *The Malabar Church and Rome* (Trichinopoly, 1934).
*Rae, *The Syrian Church in India* (Edinburgh, 1892).
*Mingana in the *Bulletin of the John Rylands Library*, July, 1926 (Manchester).
†Cheryan, *The Malabar Syrians and the Church Missionary Society* (Kottayam, 1934).

CHAPTER XII

THE MONOPHYSITE CHURCHES

3. THE ARMENIAN CHURCH

THE scattered people whom we call Armenians were formerly localized in the country which is bounded, roughly, by the Caucasus and Taurus Mountains, the Black Sea, and the Caspian Sea: Greater Armenia was to the east of the river Euphrates and Lesser Armenia to the west, later covering Cilicia to the Mediterranean. The Armenians are an Indo-European people, who call themselves Haikh and their country Hayastan, on account of a mythical descent from Haik, great-great-grandson of Noe.[1] They have always been a very distinct people, with what we should now call a strong national sentiment, but their geographical situation was against their enjoying sovereignty for very long consecutive periods, and they have been controlled and exploited in turn by the Medes, Romans, Persians, Byzantines, Arabs, Mongols, Ottoman Turks, and Russians.

The definitive conversion of the Armenians to Christianity was the work of St. Gregory the Enlightener,[2] a Parthian, who was made bishop by the metropolitan of Caesarea in Cappadocia in 294. He baptized their king, Tiridates, and Armenia

[1] Haik is said to have been the son of Thogorma, son of Gomer, son of Japheth, son of Noe (Gen. 10:1–3). Gomer was a popular *radix*. He was made the ancestor of the Gauls (Josephus: *Antiquities,* i, vi, i) and so — in the eighteenth century! — of the Welsh (Evans, *Drych y Prif Oesoedd*).

[2] The non-Catholic Armenians are often distinguished as "Gregorians," they having evolved the theory that St. Gregory established a completely independent national church under his own rule; the blessed epithet "Orthodox" is also used sometimes nowadays.

had the distinction of being the first nation to embrace Christianity officially and as a body. In 374 the new church repudiated its canonical dependence on the church of Caesarea, and became an isolated body under its own primate (the *katholikos*); he was, and admitted that he was, subject to the universal pontifical authority of the Holy See — but that meant in practice much less than it does now.

During the first half of the fifth century St. Isaac (Sahak) the Great reformed the Armenian Church on Byzantine lines and, with St. Mesrop, translated the Bible and the Liturgy into their vernacular. Owing to war with their Persian overlords the Armenians took no part in the monophysite troubles which culminated in the Council of Chalcedon (451); but some fifty years later, moved largely by political motives, a national synod repudiated that council. The Armenian church thus cut itself off from the communion of the Catholic Church, and has ever since been reputed monophysite, though it is not, as has been already mentioned, in full and clear communion with the other monophysite churches.

For the next seven hundred years the story of Armenian Christianity was one of bloody persecution by Persians and Arabs from without and quarrels within. That the persecutions from which all Christians suffered in the middle east in those days was sometimes in a measure brought on themselves is made clear by the Armenian chronicler Haithon, who tells us how the Christian wife of the Mongol prince Hulagu in the thirteenth century, "had permission to destroy the Saracens' mosques and to forbid religious services in the name of Mohammed, and so enslaved the Saracens that they dared not show themselves." No wonder the Mohammedans retaliated as soon as they got the chance. The Armenians who had fled westward and formed the kingdom of Little Armenia welcomed and helped the Crusaders, and at the end of the twelfth century were reunited with the Catholic Church (there had been considerable negotiations with the Orthodox, too, e.g., at the council of Hromkla in 1179). A great worker in this cause was St. Nerses Lambronazi, archbishop of Tarsus, who in the year of his death (1198) assisted at the coronation of King Leo II of Little Armenia, who was crowned at Tarsus by a papal legate, Cardinal Conrad von Wittelsbach, with a crown sent by Pope Celestine III, and anointed by the katholikos, Gregory Apirat. Outside Cilicia the union was weak or non-existent, but the Western ritual and practices adopted from the Crusaders affected the whole Armenian Church and have persisted to this day. The union was maintained till the Saracens took Akka in 1291; in the following year the patriarchal cathedral and residence at Kalat ar-Rum were captured by the sultan of Egypt, who carried off the patriarch, Stephen IV. The union persisted in a weak and decayed form till the end of the kingdom of Little Armenia in 1375. After that, though Dominican friars were very active among the Armenians and individual katholikoi were in communion with Rome,[3] the church as a whole was in schism again. Individuals and groups of Armenian Catholics are met with throughout the Middle Ages and later, but they had no hierarchical organization till the eighteenth century.

Till the fifth century the seat of the katholikos of the Armenians was at Ashtishat on the Euphrates in southern Armenia; then for a long time he had no fixed residence, till about 1110 it was removed westward to Cilicia, being eventually fixed at Sis, northeast of Adana, in 1293. Meanwhile the bishop of Aghtamar, an island in Lake Van, had achieved some measure of independence and in 1113 received (or took) the title of katholikos, while from 1311 the bishop of the Armenians in Jerusalem called himself patriarch, though for centuries the dignity was purely nominal. In 1441 the supreme see was moved from Sis to Etshmiadzin (Valarshapat) near Mount Ararat in Armenia proper, which from its connection with St. Gregory the Enlightener is the oldest and greatest Armenian shrine; henceforward the katholikos of Sis had to take second place. Finally in 1461 the sultan Mohammed II (!) gave the bishop

[3] At both Etshmiadzin and Sis, e.g., Gregory IX Mussabegian of Sis in 1439.

of Constantinople the title of patriarch with civil and ecclesiastical jurisdiction over all the Armenians in the Ottoman empire.[4]

Armenia sent four representatives to the Council of Florence and a decree of reunion was published, but nothing of importance came of it — except the famous instruction *pro Armenis* on the sacraments, in the bull "*Exultate Deo.*" In the sixteenth century the katholikos of Etshmiadzin, Stephen V (1542–1564), visited Rome, and about 1640 a patriarch of Constantinople was reconciled by Father Clement Galano, a Theatine clerk regular; Jacob IV of Etshmiadzin made a profession of Catholic faith shortly before his death in 1680. In 1703 Nahapet I of Etshmiadzin wrote to Pope Clement XI declaring that "The Church of Rome is the mother of all churches, and we must obey her." But in the nearer east during the seventeenth century Jesuits and Capuchins fostered a really strong Romeward movement among the Armenians; of this the political interests of France took advantage, most unfortunately for the movement, for the dissidents could and did denounce it to the Turkish government as "European aggression," and thus got official backing for persecution.[5] The chief centres of the movement were at Constantinople and Aleppo, where in 1633 the katholikos of Sis, Khachador, and the local bishop submitted to the Holy See, as did the bishop of Mardin, Melkon Tasbasian, in Mesopotamia.[6] In these neighborhoods the Armenian Church was literally split into two parties, reunionists and dissidents: members of each could be found in the same families and worshipping side by side in the same churches, many of which were opened to Latin Catholic

[4] The word *katholikos* was first used of the Armenian primate, to designate the supreme bishop of a great church who yet was dependent in a measure on a patriarch (to say nothing of the Supreme Pontiff). But later the Armenians inverted the dignities, or rather the words, making "katholikos" mean "patriarch" and "patriarch" mean nothing in particular. But after 1441 "katholikos" meant not so much either when applied to Sis and Aghthamar.

[5] The political intrigues of a French ambassador to the Porte were directly responsible for the outbreak of persecution which culminated in the martyrdom of Gomidas Keumurgian (beatified in 1929).

[6] There were others. Two of them turned Mohammedan under persecution.

preachers.[7] Eventually, in 1742, a Catholic patriarchate was established at Kraim in the Lebanon, where the Armenian patriarch of Jerusalem, Sergius, and the bishop of Damascus, Stephen, went to live when they had to leave their sees on account of their adherence to Rome. The Armenian Catholics had become so numerous at Constantinople by the beginning of the nineteenth century that the word *Catholic* in that city popularly meant one of the Armenian rite and nothing else; and for some time now Constantinople had been in fact a more important ecclesiastical centre than Etshmiadzin itself. But it has been cursed with internal quarrels, largely due to the large part that the laity takes in strictly ecclesiastical affairs.

While dissidents were persecuting Catholics in the west Persians were persecuting dissidents in Armenia; and so the Armenians naturally supported Russia in her designs upon Persian and Turkish territory. But when the Russians occupied the greater part of Transcaucasia in 1829 the erastianism of imperial Russian politics was extended to the katholikate of Etshmiadzin which was completely submitted to the state. This and other vexations[8] caused trouble throughout the century and put an end to any hope of union between the Armenians and the Orthodox. As for the katholikate of Sis (Cilicia, Syria, Mesopotomania) it simply vegetated, with an occasional upheaval, under the Turks.

The period of the Vatican Council saw a schism of Catholics to the dissidents arising out of Pope Pius IX's bull "*Reversurus*." There were involved several bishops, a number of lower clergy and lay people, and all the Antonian monks, a congregation founded early in the eighteenth century in the Lebanon by Abraham Attar. Their abbot, Malachy Ormanian (d. 1918) eventually became dissident patriarch at Constantinople and

[7] Such a situation was by no means uncommon in those days. For example, among the Melkites and in Greece where, as is clear from their *relationes*, the Jesuit fathers regarded the Orthodox as being in purely material schism and treated them on almost the same footing as Catholics (see, e.g., *L'Unité de l'Eglise*, No. 80, p. 757 et seq.).

[8] Any non-Orthodox priest who dared to baptize a Mohammedan became liable to imprisonment.

wrote a history of his church that has been translated into English (see bibliography); it is rather bitter against Rome. The invitation of the Holy See to the Vatican Council was cordially received by the then patriarch at Constantinople, Paul, but, like all the Armenian hierarchs, he waited for a lead from the katholikos at Etshmiadzin. He, George IV Kerestegian, was disposed towards reunion but was subjected to pressure by the Russian government and did not reply directly to the invitation. The other bishops accordingly refused politely or were silent.

All through their history the Armenians have been children of oppression and persecution, never worse treated than by the Turks at the end of the nineteenth century and during World War I. In 1890 took place the first of the series of massacres by the Turks, which, carried on in 1893, 1895–1896, and 1909, decimated their nation and horrified the world. The war was the occasion of an intensification of massacre and deportation which came near to destroying the people and their church altogether. From 1915 onwards the greater part of the population of Turkish Armenia was expelled, and many more perished in their wanderings over the mountains. Tens of thousands of refugees fled to Syria, Irak, Egypt, Bulgaria, Greece, the United States; they can be found in groups in many other parts of Europe, Asia, and America. In 1914 the number of dissident Armenian Christians was reckoned at 3½ millions; today there can scarcely be 2½ millions.

In 1921 the Armenian republic in Transcaucasia, which includes Etshmiadzin, adopted the soviet regime and became part of the federated union of soviet socialist republics. The faithful there accordingly suffered under the bolshevist attempt to destroy all religion: many churches were pulled down or secularized, monasteries suppressed, part of the patriarchal buildings at Etshmiadzin made into a government office, the clergy persecuted. But on the whole it seems true that they suffered less than their Orthodox Georgian neighbours, and that godless propaganda has been less virulent. Candidates for the priesthood still resort to Etshmiadzin, and material help is received

gone for help in his works to Catholic rather than Anglican dignitaries. To the beautiful church and monastery of St. James at Jerusalem he added a school of theological studies and a large library, both staffed by well-trained and competent scholars, and reorganized the printing press.

Patriarchate of Constantinople. The Armenian patriarch of Constantinople is appointed by the "national assembly" (14 clergy, 52 laymen); he is assisted by an ecclesiastical council for religious affairs and a very troublesome lay council for temporal administration. This organization is no longer recognized by the Turkish government, and the see has lost practically all its former importance since most of the Armenians have been driven from Turkey. The patriarch has under his jurisdiction some 75,000 souls in the Turkish republic, 38,000 in Greece (with a bishop at Athens), 10,000 in Rumania with a bishop at Bucarest), 20,000 in Egypt (with a bishop at Cairo), and a few thousand in Cyprus. All the other former dioceses have disappeared.

Bulgaria. The Armenians of Bulgaria now number 25,000. They formerly were subject to Constantinople, but since 1927 have been autonomous under an archbishop with one suffragan bishop. This state of affairs was duly recognized by the katholikos of Etshmiadzin – much to the indignation of the patriarch of Constantinople. The first archbishop for Bulgaria, Stephen Hovaghimian, throughout his life had very good relations with delegates apostolic and other representatives of the Catholic Church.

Before the old organizations were destroyed there were a number of districts governed by abbots or vartapets with ordinary jurisdiction but without episcopal orders.

The lower clergy. Their national disasters reduced the means of training the Armenian clergy almost to nothing, but the past twelve years have seen the establishment of efficient seminaries at Antilyas and Jerusalem, each with a printing works and lay school attached. These are insufficient for requirements, and other aspirants to the priesthood have to be content with a brief period of instruction from an experienced priest who teaches the rudiments of Christian doctrine and how to carry out the rites. The present katholikos of Sis sends some of his students to the interritual college of the Jesuit fathers at Bairut. Unless a monk, no man can be ordained deacon unless he is married, and a widowed priest may marry again provided he ceases to exercise his sacerdotal office; but in some parts such remarriage now carries no restrictions. The only dignity open to a married priest (*terder*) is that of *archpriest*, who supervises a group of churches. It is still not unusual for a household to have its own recognized confessor who performs the other occasional offices of a parish priest for it (*taneretz* or *dzikhater*, "overseer of the home").

A peculiar and important rank in the Armenian hierarchy, conferred by a sort of ordination ceremony, is that of *vartapet*. He is a hieromonk or widowed priest of superior learning and ability, especially authorized to preach and teach. Vartapets are put in charge of responsible posts and the bishops are taken chiefly from among them. There are two classes, major and minor, of vartapet, and their token of office is the *gavazan*, a staff similar to the Byzantine pastoral staff.

Monasticism. Over twenty-five years ago Mgr. Ormanian wrote that, "The days of hermits and contemplative monks are gone forever; today the sole business of the monasteries is to prepare the celibate clergy for their priestly duties"; and in fact dissident Armenian monks are better described as celibate priests who discharge all the higher ecclesiastical duties and enjoy a considerable prestige over their married brethren. Formerly there were numerous communities of them living in monasteries; today there may be very small groups still at Etshmiadzin and elsewhere, and there is the Brotherhood of St. James at Jerusalem. This last has some thirty-five hieromonks and a score of unordained monks; there is also a small convent of nuns in Jerusalem.

The faithful. The Armenians have been likened to the Jews (and to the Welsh), that is, they are a subject people who have maintained their national solidarity under oppression and among foreigners and have suffered from the dislike of their neighbours,[11] not only on account of defects in the Armenian character but as well because of their superior intelligence and ability. Many of them are attached to their church almost solely as a national symbol; many others have been goaded into secular revolutionary activity by their sufferings at the hands of the Turks and Russians: there is a strong Armenian element among the leaders of bolshevism. Materially successful Armenians in the cities easily drift into indifference and infidelity. In the patriarchate of Constantinople the ambition of the laity to control ecclesiastical life has been the source of endless trouble and damage; this has been much less under Etshmiadzin, where Russia allows no lay interference except her own. In response to promises of the Soviet government, considerable bodies of Armenians from Syria have recently returned to their homeland within the U.S.S.R.

Mgr. Ormanian points out that the history of Armenia as a nation shows no trace of those brilliant qualities which his countrymen have displayed as individuals. "Those qualities," he goes on, "have always been neutralized in national affairs by the passions of the moment, by jealousies and by unbridled ambitions. . . . When encompassed on every side by the greatest dangers they did not brace themselves with prudence and moderation."

The scholarship of the early days of the Armenian Church, whose work is still of very great value, has been kept up only intermittently, chiefly by the Catholic Mekhitarist monks; when we consider the people's history nothing else can be expected.

DOGMATIC DIVERGENCES

That the Armenian Church has never in intention or fact officially professed the monophysite heresy has been maintained

[11] So long ago as the fourth century St. Gregory Nazianzen said, "I do not find the Armenians to be a noble people. They are very sly and vicious." The Greeks never did like the Armenians.

by a number of scholars, Catholic and non-Catholic, Armenian and foreign. And it is certainly true that the reference to the two natures of Christ in the catechism published at Etshmiadzin is a perfectly orthodox statement of right doctrine. It is also true that the dissidents sing the Trisagion in the Liturgy thus: "Holy God, holy strong One, holy deathless One, *who wast crucified for us,* have mercy on us." This form was invented by Peter the Fuller at Antioch towards the end of the fifth century, and was used as a monophysite symbol. But if the words are addressed to God the Son *alone* they are quite orthodox – and it is alleged that that is how the Armenians do use them.

For the rest, except that they reject all oecumenical councils after the third, the dogmas of the Armenians are much the same as those of the Orthodox. They have never formally rejected the procession of the Holy Ghost from the Father and the Son, and for the Real Presence they use a word which means "transubstantiation" exactly. They believe that our Lady was sinless but deny her immaculate conception; they say that the invocation of the Holy Ghost is necessary for the eucharistic consecration; and they deny a place and state of purgative suffering, yet pray for the dead.

Divorce with the right to remarry is canonically admitted (at any rate by some bishops) for adultery of a wife only in theory, but in practice to either party, and for other offences as well.

LITURGY AND CUSTOMS

The text and celebration of the Liturgy and the Divine Office and the administration of the sacraments are, with some divergences, the same among the dissident as among the Catholic Armenians. These have been set out in Vol. I, pp. 188–196. The following differences may be noticed:

Vestments. Armenian bishops have used the Western mitre and crozier since the time of the Crusades (they also wear a ring on the little finger). It is curious that the Latin ritual practices then borrowed (which the dissidents claim to be customs of immemorial antiquity) were retained when the schism re-opened, and in a few trifling matters Western influence continued to make itself felt; for example, the mitre worn by even dissident bishops is not the soft low cap of the twelfth century, but a towering curved affair copied from the worst Roman models of the eighteenth, and their crozier likewise is of the baroque pattern.

The ordinary dress of the clergy is a black, wide-sleeved gown and the *pakegh*, a low conical black cap; bishops, monks, and other celibates, wear over this a veil (*veghar*), which makes a pointed head-dress characteristic of the Armenians.

Altar-vessels and bread. The vessels are the same as in the Byzantine rite, without the "star" and spoon. The Armenians alone among all dissident Orientals use unleavened bread for the Eucharist (It is like a large Western host but thicker and not crisp) and, alone of any ancient Christian church, do not mix water with the wine.

Eucharistic Liturgy. This is generally celebrated only on Saturdays, Sundays, and great feasts. Organs are now allowed in church, but are still rare.

Penance. Only married priests may hear the confessions of lay people, which is done in the house or sacristy. The priest sits on the floor and the penitent kneels, confessing only the principal sins; absolution is generally deferred for a few days and immediately precedes communion.

Eucharist. Communion is given in both kinds, the Sacred Body being dipped in the Precious Blood and put into the mouth. It may be received by children of any age and is given, by touching the child's tongue with the intincted Host, to babies immediately after baptism and confirmation. The faithful are expected to go to confession and to communion at least at the Epiphany, Easter, the Assumption, the Transfiguration, and the Exaltation of the Cross, but the last two occasions are generally neglected.

Anointing. This sacrament has been disused altogether by the dissidents since the fourteenth century.

Orders. The Armenians are the only dissident Christians of the East who have four minor and three major, or sacred, orders as in the West; they also count the offices of vartapet, bishop, and patriarch or katholikos as separate orders rather than simply as ranks in the hierarchy. The katholikos or patriarch is consecrated by twelve bishops (when they can get them), with a rite paralleled nowhere else in Christendom.

Kalendar. Feasts during penitential times may only be celebrated on Saturdays and not at all in some others, e.g., Easter to Pentecost. The Julian kalendar is followed and there is a national reckoning of years from the eponymous ancestor Haik, who is put at 2492 B.C. The non-Catholic Armenians are the only Christians who still do not observe Christmas as a separate feast, celebrating our Lord's birthday as part of the Theophany (Epiphany), from January 5 to 13.

Penitential seasons. The periods of fasting and abstinence or of abstinence alone are numerous, totalling some 160 days in the year, and the devout observe them with great care. The strict fast lasts only till noon, but abstinence forbids all except vegetable foods (honey excepted).

All Armenians make the sign of the cross as in the West, and their proper reverence is a double genuflection, but that is being supplanted by a deep bow in the degree that European clothes are adopted. There is very little *cultus* of holy images among the dissident Armenians, except where they have come under strong Western or Orthodox influence.

In speaking of these lesser Nestorian and monophysite Eastern churches, expressions implying ignorance, superstition, and an easy morality must unhappily be often used. But it must be always remembered that they have all been for centuries subject to relentless persecution or isolation from the rest of Christendom or both: they are faithful remnants which throughout temptation and tyranny have at least clung to the name of Jesus Christ and to some idea of His Church on earth.

BIBLIOGRAPHY

Fortescue, *The Lesser Eastern Churches* (London, 1913).
*Lynch, *Armenia, Travels and Studies,* 2 vols. (London, 1901).
Tournebize, *Histoire politique et religieuse de l'Armenie* (Paris, 1910).
†Ormanian, *The Church of Armenia* (London, 1912).
†Seth, *Armenians in India* (Calcutta, 1937).

CHAPTER XIII

REUNION OF THE EAST

SUCH a book as this is quite inadequate to give a just idea of the complexity and depth of the Christian East. Its external complexity and variousness are made plain; but the profundity and richness of its spiritual life and thought through the ages, the delicate *nuances* and the cogency, or otherwise, of its religious ideas, are another matter: a matter beyond the ability of this writer to expound, and therefore beyond the scope of what he writes. Nevertheless the subject of this volume cannot be left without a reference to the possibilities and prospects of reunion between two out of the three great broad divisions of Christendom, the Catholics of the West and the Orthodox of the East.

The divisions among Christians are an outrage of that unity and brotherly love which our Lord desires among all who profess to follow Him. It ought not to be necessary to emphasize this, but there is a tendency among Catholics to slip into the way of regarding the division of Christendom into, roughly, Catholics, Orthodox, and Protestants as a normal state of affairs; from this it follows that we sometimes seem to regard non-Catholics as enemies to be kept at bay rather than as what they are, brethren to be reconciled.

Anyone who has read carefully the preceding pages, in which I have tried neither to extenuate nor to emphasize the shortcomings of the dissident Eastern Christians, will see quite clearly where the weakness of those churches lies: it is in separation from the divinely guided Centre of Unity and from spiritual and temporal communion with the huge body of faithful of all nations who form the visible Catholic Church. But the Christians of the West, as well as of the East, have suffered and tended to develop one-sidedly through being deprived, for nine hundred years, of each other's contribution to philosophy, theology, general culture, and Christian life, and the balance can never be redressed from one side only. "If a spirit of servile dependence and an excess of power in civil governments has driven the East into schism, the great fault of Westerners, individualism, has torn from us certain joyous elements of the Christian heritage which the East has kept. For example, whoever has had occasion to assist at an Eastern Liturgy, even if only in the little church of some Ukrainian country parish, and has been struck by the intimate participation and inspired collaboration of even the most simple peasants in the wonders of the liturgy, that perfect whole of teaching, prayer, and sacred action, he can begin to estimate the treasury of doctrine, living faith, and encouragement to religion of which Catholics in the West are deprived. . . . There is no essential and insurmountable antagonism between Eastern and Western Christianity. The things which keep us apart from one another are the same things which keep us respectively from the complete richness of life of the Church. The East has to reconsider the conception of the relations between the temporal and the spiritual power which have been imposed on her by princes; the West has to remedy the evils which have been brought about by individualism, an influence essentially at enmity with the Church. From the Catholic unity of East and West there would be reborn a well-ordered and stimulating variety of forms of religious life – for the Church includes them all within her unity, in spite of spiritual divergences in ways of thinking and living such as are conditioned by the race, genius, history, and civilization of various peoples" (Dr. Andrew de Ivanka, in *Irénikon,* t. IX, no. 5, 1932).

The problem is the more actual and urgent because so many of these Christians are within Russian soviet territory, where at any time the intensive campaign of godless teaching and persecution, whether open or camouflaged, may be resumed; where in any case and inescapably, whatever the ostensible good relations between church and state, there is explicit and avowed antagonism between the official ideas and aims of a highly-centralized state and the life and teaching of Jesus Christ. It is well to remember that of the hundreds of clergy and thousands of laity there who during the past twenty-five years have given their lives for Christ's name's sake, nearly all did so without the help of that strength and sense of solidarity which come from communion with the Apostolic See of Rome and the world-wide Catholic Church; and that when, at the command of Pius XI, the vernacular prayers after low Mass are offered for Russia, 99 per cent of those for whom we pray are not visibly members of that Catholic Church: the significance of this has not yet been sufficiently recognized. In the meantime, the present "understanding" between church and state in Russia serves to aggravate the differences among Christians. At the very time when, for example, many Catholics are better disposed towards their Orthodox brethren than ever before, high ecclesiastics in Russia make open and unprovoked attacks against the Catholic Church; and there is no doubt that they have been stirred to do so by the Soviet government, which uses latent hostility towards Rome among the higher Russian clergy in support of its own political, social, and ecclesiastical policies.

The dissident churches of the East are all churches that once were Catholic. At various dates they became definitively separated from the centre of unity either by schism or heresy: nevertheless, they all profess the Catholic faith, in a greater or less degree, almost in its entirety; they have maintained the precepts of Christian morality more or less as held by Catholics; they are governed by canon law with which that of Eastern Catholics is at least nominally identical; they worship God with liturgies and rites which they share with Eastern Catholics and which the Church recognizes as of equal authenticity and dignity with those of Rome; with one or two local and doubtful exceptions, their orders and sacraments are valid. As ecclesiastical bodies they have maintained an organic continuity with churches that were in communion with Rome and represent the authentic Catholic Christianity of the East of the first ten centuries, modified by the history of the subsequent nine hundred years during which they have been separated from, and in varying measures opposed to, the theological developments and religious life of the Western church.

It is therefore only to be expected that, in an epoch when Christianity is more seriously opposed than at any time since the Ten Persecutions, and unity accordingly more than ever imperatively necessary, all the popes from Pius IX onwards have been especially preoccupied with the problem of Eastern reunion: and not only from the point of view of the defence of Christianity but also from that of the perfecting of Christians. Schism, separation, is one of the most appalling of evils, whether for an individual or for society. It is true that the Church teaches that those inculpably separated from her visible communion may nevertheless belong to her in an invisible way; but obviously this alone is not the sort of inclusion in one fold under One Shepherd, the unity willed by our Lord, and that so many souls should not be visibly united to His Church cannot but be a matter of the very gravest concern to His Vicar on earth.

Among the last five popes Leo XIII stands out conspicuously for what he did on behalf of the East, both Catholic and dissident, and after him Benedict XV. But in the seventeen years of a most remarkable pontificate Pius XI eclipsed even the noble efforts of his two great predecessors. He took up the work with yet greater urgency, tenacity, and clearly defined purpose than those who went before him, and on a wider scale than they did. Labour for reunion of the East, he declared, was not to be just one of his works but his chief work, an undertaking that should characterize his pontificate. And in all that he did for those Orientals who are already Catholic he looked beyond them to the serried masses of their still separated brethren.

It is impossible even to mention here all the Pope's activities in this matter (much less the multifarious works to which they gave rise), so numerous were they and so wide their scope:

they extended from sending in 1922 a mission of relief (under the American Father Edmund Walsh, S.J.) for the starving people of Russia to addressing the whole world on the subject of Christian unity, from pontifical protest and diplomatic measures against bolshevist barbarism to establishing colleges in Rome for Russian and Rumanian seminarists. Three of these things may be selected for special mention, because they so clearly and consistently demonstrate the mind of the Holy See.

In 1924 the Pope addressed a letter to Dom Fidelis de Stotzingen, abbot primate of the Benedictines, in which, after pointing out the special aptitude of monks "for the apostolate of reconciliation with our separated brethren," he asked that one abbey in every Benedictine congregation should be specially concerned with Eastern affairs and that there should be sent to them "carefully chosen men who shall fit themselves for the work of reunion by special study of the languages, history, customs, mentality, and especially the theology and liturgy of the Eastern peoples."[1] Both by the fact of their being monks and by the large and conciliatory spirit of their institute the Benedictines are peculiarly fitted to appeal to religious people in the East, who have been so much influenced by monasticism. "They alone, among all other orders," said Leo XIII in 1893, "excite no mistrust among the Orientals"; Dom Cabrol, in his Life of Cardinal Pitra, tells of the respect and even reverence with which that Benedictine was received, as a simple monk, both by Russian monks and by the highest hierarchs of the Orthodox churches; and Metropolitan Szepticky in writing on the restoration of Slav monachism says, "What could be finer and more useful for the East than Benedictine abbeys of the Byzantine rite?" One result of Pius XI's appeal was the establishment of a special monastery at Amay, in Belgium, where both the Latin and Byzantine rites are in use and the monks devote themselves to the study of Eastern, particularly Russian, affairs. During its short history this monastery (now at Chevetogne) has been

[1] This has been done, so far as the United States is concerned, by the abbey of St. Procopius at Lisle, Ill.

the people at large must be prepared by the Holy Spirit so that they may desire what is defined, concluded, and proclaimed under the inspiration of that same Holy Spirit. Then only is authority's decision rooted and made fruitful in the hearts of the faithful."

It is precisely in, so to speak, the making ready of the ground for the people to be prepared by the Holy Spirit that the ordinary Christian has his part in this vital business of reunion. In some countries, Great Britain and Ireland, for example, where Orientals are few, Catholics can hardly go beyond the formation, by prayer, resolution, and study, of their own religious consciousness, laboriously learning a spirit of genuine charity towards all men, making themselves large-minded and well-informed.[2] Such interior spiritual dispositions, loved by the heart as well as approved by the mind, are absolutely necessary: without them all efforts towards reunion will only increase and aggravate disunity. But in North America, where there are so many dissident Orientals, there is opportunity to go further – and a grave responsibility not to give our separated brethren a false idea of the Church or a false idea of what Catholics are expected to be, to do, and to believe.

The fundamental difficulty which the Orthodox experience in relation to the Catholic Church is not so much doctrinal as in understanding the Christian value of certain characteristics of Catholicity. They do not see that our complete idea of the Church, especially with regard to her exterior authority and the infallibility of the Sovereign Pontiff, is a spiritual reality and has spiritual meaning for us – to them it smacks of sheer worldliness. Or again, their judgement that spiritual pride is inherent in Catholic religion, because, for example, we believe that God's almighty "doing" does not exclude real "doing" by man, that men can be co-operators with God for righteousness and salva-

---

[2] "So far from being an obstacle," says that distinguished scholar, the late Abbot Fernand Cabrol, "the exact knowledge of facts is, on the contrary, of the greatest assistance to true religion" (*The Mass of the Western Rites*, London, 1934, p. ix).

tion. Yet we too profoundly believe in man's "nothingness," in the absolute necessity of God's action in us by grace, in the need to cast self aside and to put on Christ. So, their chief problem being psychological, a matter of spiritual sensibility, it is not enough to give them "catechism explanations" or to hand them works of apologetic (which in any case need very careful and sensitive selection). We have to show them in a living way not only that Catholics are Christians but that they are Christians because Catholic: that certain specifically Catholic things are a necessary part of a vital spiritual order. And that can only be done by personal contact. Exchanges of thought, discussions (*disceptationes*), between Catholics and Orthodox, were recommended by Pope Pius XI (*Acta Apostolicae Sedis,* 1924, p. 491),[3] but it is quite clear that such things are out of the question until we have first cultivated the acquaintance of Orthodox people in the ordinary social relationships of life. Without some sort of social intercourse between Catholics and Orthodox, the present frozen divisions and bitter misunderstandings between these two great bodies of Christians will go on indefinitely, with increasing harm to mankind, and the primary facts that we should bear in mind and the fundamental principles that should govern our relations with Eastern dissidents have been admirably summarized by Dom Lambert Beauduin, O.S.B. (*Revue Catholique des Idées et des Faits,* October 23, 1925):

"The Orthodox find a profound opposition between the Catholic conception of Christianity and their own, an opposition based on a juridical conception and a mystical conception respectively of the Church. It seems to them that for Catholics the Church is above all a visible social organization on the lines of human societies, that it is a mighty international institution which monopolizes religious life in every sphere of activity. Many Catholics, they discover, look on the Church simply as a

[3] In *Eastern Churches Quarterly,* Vol. I, No. 4 (Ramsgate, 1936) Father M. J. Congar, O.P., gives an account of "retreats" under Catholic auspices that took place annually in France before the war; Catholics, Orthodox, and Protestants met together for mutual enlightenment.

Christ. Rome, as ever, shows us the way: in her official pronouncements and documents she now always refers to the separated Orientals simply as *dissidentes*, "dissidents."[4]

As the Easterns are apt to accuse us Westerners of "dry rationalism and profane worldliness," so are we prone to dismiss their religion as mere "yearning and sentiment" or "ceremonial superstition." We must look higher and deeper than that. "Men were made that they might love one another," wrote Cardinal Mercier. "Those who from a distance believe themselves to be antagonists often find unexpected sympathies on better acquaintance. This, of course, does not constitute unity, but it helps towards it. Men and groups of men who have lived for long estranged from one another in an atmosphere charged with animosities, planted in the depths of their consciousness by agelong tradition, will hardly be prepared to yield to arguments thrust upon them by their opponents, however closely reasoned they may be" (Pastoral letter on the "Malines Conversations," pp. 6–7. Malines, 1924). No more will any lasting good be achieved by any efforts which do not spring from a soil of patience and humility, a humility not only personal but also collective, such a humility as befits the followers of the God who stooped to become man, who was silent before His accusers. The acerbities of religious conflict – whether of the fifth or the sixteenth or the twentieth century – have no place here. "Defiance," "ringing challenges," calling names, imputing motives – these do not build up the kingdom of Christ.

Throughout the whole world, especially since the calamitous

---

[4] Mariu Theodorian-Carada tells us how, in 1878, the Orthodox metropolitan of Jassy in Rumania, Calinic Miclescu, was in Paris and was invited by the chapter of Notre Dame to be present in choir at solemn Mass in the cathedral; henceforward he was notably friendly to Catholics, and there is reason to believe that he was reconciled with the Church on his deathbed. A Latin priest in Palestine told me that it was his custom when he passed any non-Catholic priest in the street always to greet him with a gesture of respect. An Orthodox priest stopped him one day and said: "If all your fellow clergy behaved as you do, Palestine would have returned to Rome years ago." An exaggeration, no doubt, but it shows which way the wind blows. It is not for nothing that the French language has the same word for "manners" and "morals."

discord and immeasurable catastrophe of two great wars, an intense desire for the unity of Christendom has arisen, a desire springing from an acute consciousness of how our divisions flout the will of Christ that "all may be one." It is the business of Catholics to play a leading part in this movement – not to stand aside and watch the struggles of others. But their efforts will be wasted if they do not act in unison with the clearly expressed mind of the Supreme Pontiff: on the one hand, with love, gentleness, and well-informed understanding; on the other, without that particularism which seeks to make everyone conform to our Western pattern in things outside divine revelation. It is right and proper that we Westerners should value the rites and usages and traditions and glorious history of the Latin church above all others; they are our own, and they have formed western Europe and us. If we go further than that and think that they confer some theoretical and practical superiority, then in face of our brothers of the East let us at least remember the motto of our own chivalry, *Noblesse oblige.* But even that attitude, the faintest sense of superiority, is to be deplored: it is arrogant and has no basis in essential reality or the economy of the Catholic Church, and will make a thousand times more difficult that reunion of the Christian East which already seems almost beyond hope. "But," said Leo XIII, "let not this hope be considered utopian, for that were unworthy of Christians. The promise of our Lord must be fulfilled: 'there shall be One Fold and One Shepherd.' . . . Difficulties there are, but they shall in no wise discourage our apostolical zeal and charity. It is true that rebellion and estrangement have fostered a deep-rooted dissent in men's hearts: but shall that make us give up hope? Please God, never."

The cause of Eastern reunion put before us so persuasively and authoritatively by pope after pope is one that requires an infinitude of patient and loving work, on a big or the tiniest scale – and we must look for no appreciable result in our time. The separation has subsisted for nine hundred years: it cannot be mended in nine hundred days. Above all, Catholics must pray

Fliche & Martin, *Histoire de l'Eglise* in 24 vols. *Passim,* as published (Paris).
Fortescue, *The Greek Fathers* (London, 1908).
*Hasluck, *Christianity and Islam under the Sultans* (London, 1929).
Hughes, *A History of the Church.* Vols. I–III (London, 1934–1946).
*Hussey, *Church and Learning in the Byzantine Empire* (Oxford, 1937).
Janin, *Les Eglises orientales et les Rites orientaux.,* 3 ed. (Paris, 1935).
——— *The Separated Eastern Churches* (St. Louis, 1934).
*Kidd, *The Churches of Eastern Christendom* (London, 1927).
Lagier, *L'Orient Chrétien des Apotres jusqu'a Photius* (Paris, 1935).
Lubeck, *Die Christlichen Kirchen des Orients* (Kempten, 1911).
Roth, *Geschichte des Byzantinischen Reiches* (Leipzig, 1904).
*Runciman, *The Byzantine Civilization* (London, 1933).
Sesostris Sidaruss, *Les Patriarchats dans l'Empire ottoman* (Paris, 1907).
*Scott, *The Eastern Churches and the Papacy* (London, 1928).
Silbernagl, *Verfassung und gegenwärtiger Bestand sämtlicher Kirchen des Orients* (Regensburg, 1904).
Various hands, *The Pre-Nicene Church* (London, 1935).
†Vasilyev, *Histoire de l'Empire byzantine,* 2 vols. (Paris, 1932).
*Wigram, *The Separation of the Monophysites* (London, 1923).
†Popov, *A History of the Council of Florence* (London, 1861).

LITURGY AND ART

Attwater, *Prayers from the Eastern Liturgies* (London, 1931).
Bayet, *L'Art byzantin* (Paris, 1924).
Bréhier, *L'Art byzantin* (Paris, 1924).
*Brightman, *Liturgies Eastern and Western,* Vol. I (Oxford, 1896).
*Dalton, *Eastern Christian Art* (Oxford, 1925).
*Gluck, *Die Christliche Kunst des Ostens* (Berlin, 1923).
Hanssens, *Institutiones liturgicae de ritibus orientalibus* (Rome, 1930).
——— *De Missa rituum orientalium* (Rome, 1932).
Kalorz, *Myths and Realities in Eastern Europe* (London, 1946).
†Kondakov, *The Russian Ikon* (Oxford, 1927).

Nilles, *Kalendarium manuale utriusque Ecclesiae orientalis et occidentalis,* 2 vols. (Innsbruck, 1896–1897).
Rahmani, *Les Liturgies orientales et occidentales* (Bairut, 1929).
*Rice, *Byzantine Art* (Oxford, 1936).

REUNION

Bourgeois, *Reunion with the East* (C.T.S. of London).
Congar, *Divided Christendom* (London, 1939).
d'Herbigny, *East and West in the Unity of Christ* (C.T.S. of London).
Lialin, "Concerning the Eirenic Method" in *Eastern Churches Quarterly,* Vol. III, Nos. 6–8 (Ramsgate, 1939).
Lilienfeld, *Pour l'Union.* Documents and extensive bibliographies of reunion writings (Amay, 1927).
Tyciak, *et al., Der Christliche Osten: Geist und Gestalt* (Regensburg, 1939).

PERIODICALS

Echos d'Orient, quarterly (5 rue Bayard, Paris).
L'Unité de l'Eglise. Every two months (same address). Published from 1922 to 1937.
Irénikon. Every two months (Prieuré d'Amay, Chevetogne, Belgium).
Eastern Churches Quarterly (St. Augustine's Abbey, Ramsgate and 480 Lexington Ave., New York).
Russie et Chrétienté, quarterly (Centre "Istina," 39 Rue François-Gérard, Paris).
Der Christliche Orient (St. Augustine's College, Munich).
Orientalia Christiana. A valuable double series of articles and monographs, beginning in 1923, published by the Oriental Institute at Rome (7 piazza S. Maria Maggiore).
Stoudion. A most valuable periodical publication in 6 vols., ending in 1930 (12 via Vespasiana, Rome).
**The Christian East,* quarterly (S.P.C.K., London).
†*The Russian American Orthodox Messenger,* monthly (New York).
†*Sobornost,* quarterly (S.C.M. Press, London).

sacrament for the recipients. It comes in fact after the words of institution.

EXARCH (*Gk.*, ruler). The primate of an independent church, between a patriarch and an archbishop; but more usually now a priest or bishop with a special charge. Also a title of honour.

FILIOQUE (*Lat.*, and from the Son. *Gk.*, *kai ek tou Huiou*). The phrase added to the Nicene Creed in the West which Photius in 863 declared to be a "corruption of the Faith."

FIRMAN (*Persian*). An order or licence from the sultan of Turkey.

GE'EZ. Classical Ethiopic, the liturgical language of that rite.

GREAT CHURCH. The official name of the Orthodox Church of Constantinople, having reference to the Holy Wisdom church.

HAGIA (*Gk.*, holy things). The sacred elements after consecration.

HAIKAL (*Ar.*, temple). The sanctuary of a Coptic church.

HEGUMENOS (*Gk.*, leader). An abbot.

HESYCHASM (*Gk.*, *hesukhia*, quiet). (1) The state of a monk in the third grade of Eastern monasticism. (2) A theory of mysticism emanating from Mount Athos in the fourteenth century.

HIERARCH (*Gk.*, sacred ruler). Any high member of a hierarchy, but especially an archbishop or patriarch.

HIERODEACON. A monk who is a deacon.

HIEROMONK. A monk who is a priest.

ICONOCLASM (*Gk.*, image-breaking). The campaign against the veneration of holy images and the accompanying persecution, centered at Constantinople, from *c.* 726 till 787 and from 814 till 842.

IDIORRYTHMY (*Gk.*, one's own arrangements). A type of Orthodox monastery in which the monks live alone or in groups, partly supporting themselves.

JULIAN KALENDAR. Issued by Julius Caesar in 45 B.C., corrected under Pope Gregory XIII in 1582. The Julian reckoning is now 13 days behind the Gregorian.

KARSHUNI. Arabic written in Syriac characters.

KATHOLIKOS (*Gk.,* universal delegate). The title of the heads of the Nestorian, Armenian, and Georgian churches, now equivalent to patriarch.

KUMMUS. A Coptic abbot; also a title of honour for any priest of that rite.

LAURA (*Gk.,* alley). Formerly a monastery consisting of rows of separate cells or huts; now any sizeable monastery.

LITURGY, THE (*Gk., Leitourgia,* a public duty or work). The Eucharistic Sacrifice, i.e., "Mass."

MAFRIAN (*Syr.,* fructifier). Nowadays, the title of the vicar general of the Jacobite patriarch.

MALKA (*Syr.,* king). The eucharistic leaven in the Nestorian Chaldean rite.

MANDYAS (*Gk.*). (1) A short cloak, part of the monastic habit. (2) A sort of cope, worn by bishops.

MAR (*Syr.,* lord). Title given to saints and bishops in the Syriac rites; fem., *mart.*

MASNAPHTO (*Syr.*). A small hood worn by bishops of the Antiochene and Nestorian Chaldean rites.

MATRAN, METRAN. Title of the first hierarch after the Katholikos in the Nestorian Church; also used for metropolitans in the other Syrian churches.

MEGALOSKHEMOS (*Gk.,* great habiter). The highest grade of Eastern monk.

MELKITES (*Syr., Malok,* king). Name given to the Catholic and Orthodox Byzantines of Syria, Palestine, and Egypt.

MELLUSIANS. A Nestorian sect in Malabar, named after Mar Mellos and dating from 1874.

METANY (*Gk.,* penance). Great, a complete prostration; ordinary or little, a profound bow, taking the place of the Western genuflection.

METOKHION (*Gk.*). An estate or *cell* belonging to a monastery.

METROPOLITAN. In strict Byzantine usage, equivalent to a Western archbishop, but nowadays nearly all Orthodox bishops are called metropolitans.

MILLET (*Turkish, millah*). A subject "nation" of the sultan of Turkey.

MYRON (*Gk.,* sweet oil). The Holy Chrism, which may be blessed only by patriarchs or other primates.

MYSTERY (*Gk.,* something hidden). The ordinary word for a sacrament in the East.

VARTAPET. A rank in the Armenian hierarchy, below the episcopate.

VICAR PATRIARCHAL. A local representative appointed by a patriarch.

VLADYKA (*Sl.*, lord, master). The Slavonic form of address to a bishop.

XEROPHAGY (*Gk.*, dry food). The stricter form of Eastern fast.

ON VISITING ORTHODOX CHURCHES

THE conditions in which Catholics may visit the churches of the Orthodox and other dissidents is largely a matter of local custom, sometimes of definite local legislation, but a few general principles and facts may be usefully set out here.

There is nothing in principle against a Catholic visiting an Orthodox church out of friendly curiosity, interest, for information, or in some lawful official capacity, either in or out of service time, provided that there is no *communicatio in sacris*, that his presence is passive and not active, that there is no danger to his own faith and that no scandal is given to his neighbour.[1] In point of fact, there are certain dissident churches in the world which for extrinsic reasons the Holy See encourages Catholics to visit by the grant of plenary indulgences therefor; such are, for example, the Armenian church of St. James in Jerusalem (on the site of the apostle's martyrdom) and other non-Catholic churches in Palestine.

I have referred elsewhere to the recognized frequenting of dissident churches by Catholics in the Levant during the seventeenth and eighteenth centuries, and in that and other parts of the world mutual official visits of state are the regular thing. A representative of the Catholic Coptic bishop and others were present at the consecration of the Ethiopian abuna Cyril by the dissident Coptic patriarch at Cairo in 1925; all the Catholic rites were officially represented by clergy at the enthronement of the Orthodox patriarch of Alexandria, Meletios II, in 1926, and at the funeral of the Orthodox patriarch of Jerusalem, Damianos, in 1931 the apostolic delegate to Palestine, the Latin patriarch of Jerusalem, and the Franciscan guardian of Mount Zion were

[1] He need, of course, take no account of pharisaical scandal.